W9-DID-989

Kipling's Error III:
They Were Good Americans

The Partial Biography of
Lloyd Brooks Mitchell
and
The History of the B-17 Flying Fortress
Kipling's Error III

KIPLING'S ERROR III:
THEY WERE GOOD AMERICANS

BY BROOKS MITCHELL, PH.D.

FOREWORD BY
STANLEY I. HAND COL. USAF (RET)

21ST CENTURY PUBLISHERS

PREVIOUSLY BY BROOKS MITCHELL, PH.D.
Bet on Cowboys, Not Horses

Original Cover Art: Bryan Allison
Book Layout and Design: Seraph

Library of Congress Control Number: 2005903320

Mitchell, James Brooks, Ph.D.

Kipling's Error III: They Were Good Americans
By Brooks Mitchell, Ph.D.
p.cm
ISBN 0-9607298-6-0
1.*Kipling's Error III.* 2. Mitchell, Lloyd Brooks (1918-). 3. Military history.
4. B-17 Flying Fortress. I. Mitchell, James Brooks, Ph.D. II. Title

1234567890

21st Century Publishers, 1320 Curt Gowdy Drive Cheyenne, Wyoming, 82009,
307-638-2254
Copies may be ordered from publisher. Quantity discounts are available.

List of Acknowledgments

I wish to acknowledge the following people for their invaluable contributions to the completion of this book:

- **Roberta Satterfield** for her tireless efforts in transcribing the diaries;

- **Geoff Ward** for his contributions and allowing me to refer liberally to his book, "The Snetterton Falcons";

- **Kate Tarasenko** for her work in helping me sequence and organize the material so that it would flow in a logical fashion;

- **Van Neie**, the son of Captain Reuben Neie, for allowing me to use his father's diary;

- **Mrs. Florence (Lakey) Huebing** for allowing me to use the diary of tailgunner Leo Lakey;

- **Mr. Richard Haseltine** for entrusting me with the original copy of his diary and artwork, without which this book would be much less significant;

- **Amanda Mitchell** for conducting the original oral interview of my father;

- **Joe Jones**, the brilliant artist and creator of the painting, "Day in the Clouds";

- **Bryan Allison** for outstanding work in designing the book cover;

- **Rick Maturi** for valuable assistance in organizing the final project and publication;

- **Steven Antosiak** for supplying me with the diary of Joe Kotlarz.

CONTENTS

VIII

INTRODUCTION
By James Brooks Mitchell

My father, Lloyd Brooks Mitchell, is my hero. I have been blessed in this life to know many people of character and accomplishment, but none stands above my father. This book is my effort to record the heroism and quiet dignity of this great man.

Lt. Lloyd Mitchell is directly descended from James Davis, a patriot who served with George Washington in the American Revolution. James Davis was rewarded for his service to the American cause with one hundred eighty acres in Big Bottom, Tennessee. Lt. Mitchell was born and spent his early years nearby in Sparta, Tennessee. He, like his ancestors, became a warrior and served his country when duty called. Lt. Mitchell served in World War II as a navigator on a B-17 Flying Fortress in the early and most dangerous times. He and his nine crewmates survived and were all awarded the Air Force's Distinguished Flying Cross.

I've authored many publications, mostly based on business subjects as part of my responsibility as a professor at the University of Wyoming. As a writer, I sometimes struggle at the beginning of a project. I might approach it with a few false starts, but when I get a strong foothold in the particular subject, the writing usually flows.

As a biographer, however, the subject is my father, and I have struggled for years with committing pen to paper for his story. I have delayed writing and compiling this book, especially regarding the part of his life when he served in the Air Force during World War II, for a very long time.

In part, this is because the term "biography" somehow signals a life completed, and that is not the case. Also, as my father's eldest child and first son, I have struggled with my own objectivity. The older I get, the more profoundly I understand my father's accomplishments, and this has been difficult to write about. It has often brought me to tears to think of his dignified comportment as a man, his dutiful steadfastness as a father,

Kipling's Error Crew: Back row l-r Leo Lakey, Steve Malinowski, Joe White, Lowell Nelson, Dick Haseltine, Joe Kotlarz; Front row l-r Lloyd Mitchell, Manual Mendolson, Ole Asper, Ruben Neie and, reflecting on his deeds as an Air Force navigator who flew twenty-five bombing missions, his quiet heroism.

But I always knew that I had to tell my father's story. If I didn't do it, who would?

As any writer will tell you, writing is actually half writing and half preparation, in order to do justice to the task at hand. "Preparation," as a literary term, is also sometimes known as "procrastination." And I rationalized my delinquency in several ways.

I spent a lot of time going over books about the 8th Air Force and the 96th Bombardment Group, of which my father was a crewmember. I was surprised to learn how much is written about the 8th Air Force in general, and the Flying Fortresses – the B-17s – in particular. Judging by the volume of books available on the history of WWII aviation, there is clearly great interest in the subject. I can only hope that this book is worthy of that interest.

My discovery of this interest fueled the anxiety about my growing writer's block. I knew that history buffs and historians alike would read this book about my father, Lloyd Mitchell, his crewmates, and their collective experiences of "The Good War." I also knew

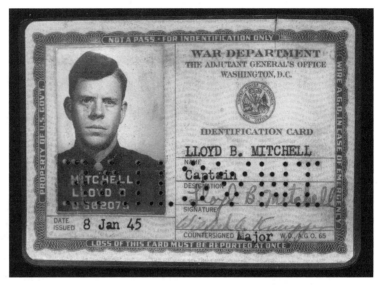

**Lloyd B. Mitchell
War Department
Identification Card**

that Dad's wartime diary and post-war memoirs revealed a deeply personal perspective seldom found in factual and objective recollections. I began to feel that I would be guilty of a monumental slight of history, decency, and respect if I did not tell the story of my father.

I decided I must formally interview my father, although I didn't think I could ever summon the courage to do it. I was also certain that Dad wouldn't want to do it.

As is the case with many veterans, the war was my father's very private experience. He never talked about it much when I was growing up, and I didn't think he would have much to say now. Besides, I knew that I would not be able to talk with my father at such an intimate level without a trembling voice and a face covered in tears. Who could blame me for wanting to wait for just the "right time"?

Three events changed my belief that my father would not want to talk about his war experiences. First, he sent me his wartime diary – not a copy, mind you, but the original.

Then my brother, Mark, sent me two cassette tape recordings of our father talking about his life and war experiences. These recollections were the result of Mark's daughter, Amanda, completing a high school assignment of recording the oral history of a relative. Thank God Amanda chose her grandfather. Now the evidence was clear: Dad wanted to talk.

The final event was that Dad sent me a copy of the diary of one of his crewmates, Sgt. Leo Lakey. While Dad's own entries are personal and reflective, Sgt. Lakey's are detailed and technical. Eventually, I also obtained a copy of the diary of their pilot, Lt. Ruben Neie (affectionately nicknamed "Rube"), and of Sgt. Dick Haseltine and Sgt. Joseph Kotlarz. I had five sets of recollections from the same crew.

After compiling all these elements, it was much easier to sit down with Dad. My fears of trespassing into his long-hidden and private memories fell away, and I was able to gather the stories that revealed a colorful, wide-angle picture of his early life.

"KIPLING'S ERROR"

"Oh, East is East, and West is West, and never the twain shall meet..."

This is the opening line of Rudyard Kipling's epic poem, "The Battle of East and West." For the ten young men who formed the 413th Squadron of the 96th Bombardment Group of the 8th Air Force, however, Kipling's declaration was in error. They soon discovered that half of their newly formed squad hailed from points east of the Mississippi and half from the west.

Kipling's Error became the fitting moniker of their B-17 bomber, a World War II "Flying Fortress." There would be a second and a third incarnation of the ship, ultimately ferrying the boys of the 413th through twenty-five dangerous but successful missions – alive, if not intact – by September 23, 1943, earning each man of the original crew the Distinguished Flying Cross with four oak leaf clusters.

The name *Kipling's Error* refers to three different airplanes. *Kipling's Error III* was the fourth plane flown by my father and his crewmates. The first plane was *Ophelia Bumps*, which flew into trees while still in the states and never made it to the European Theater. Miraculously, the crew survived and was assigned another plane, which was named *Kipling's Error*. It, and *Kipling's Error II*, were so badly damaged in combat that they were permanently grounded and made "hangar queens" for spare parts. The crew finished its missions in the fourth plane, *Kipling's Error III*. After my father and his crewmates finished their twenty-five missions, the great *Kipling's Error III* was shot down on her 55th raid with her replacement crew in a final, fatal mission over the Baltic Sea on April 11, 1944. All were killed in action.

The original crew of *Kipling's Error* comprised the following personnel: co-pilot Lt. Olie Asper from Oregon; bombardier Lt. Manuel Mendolson of Pennsylvania; engineer Sgt. Lowell Nelson from Minnesota; assistant engineer Sgt. Ed White of New Mexico; gunner Sgt. Steve Malinowski of Ohio; tail-gunner Sgt. Joe Kotlarz of Nebraska; radio operator Sgt. Dick Haseltine of Maine (the artist who designed the nose art for the plane); gunner Sgt. Leo Lakey of Illinois; Lt. Ruben Neie, their pilot from Texas; and navigator Lt. Lloyd Mitchell of Oklahoma.

The diaries of the last five men named in this group – Kotlarz, Haseltine, Lakey, Neie, and Mitchell – are the foundation of this book. There may be more diaries in existence, but I couldn't locate the decedents of White, Mendolson or Malinowski. I did contact the widow of Ole Asper, but she was not aware of a diary.

The 8th Air Force was created in Britain in June of 1942 under Gen. Ira Eaker. It conducted its first raid in August of that year, a small-scale assault on France's Rouen railroad center. By September, the 8th Air Force was expanded to incorporate U.S. forces. Their fighting roles were distinct. The U.S. conducted daytime precision bombing missions, while the R.A.F. conducted nighttime saturation bombing. While the crew of *Kipling's Error* could not retire from active combat until they had flown twenty-five bombing missions, in all of 1942, the entire U.S. fleet flew a total of only twenty-seven missions.

The original design of the B-17 made it vulnerable to frontal attacks. An improved nose-turret design, along with the development of other technology (both planes and flight suits), as well as advanced warfare strategy (such as tighter flying formations), combined quickly in the early months of 1943 to help turn the tables in the air war. Eventually, the Allied Forces overcame German air superiority, but not without crushing defeats and the incalculable loss of human lives.

While many Air Corps men claimed to have flying in their blood, others, including Lloyd Mitchell, were primarily motivated by duty, inevitability, and ambition. Many, like my father, came from hardscrabble, poverty-ridden lives. The Great Depression was behind them, but just over their shoulders. Infantry pay was as low as the risk to one's safety was high. Those who were able to get accepted to flight training school did so. Officers' commissions came quickly and, with them, substantial raises in pay.

After the crew of *Kipling's Error* formed in the summer of 1942, they shipped out to several locales for training, including Washington State, Idaho, South Dakota, and Texas. In addition to classroom training, they logged as much airtime as they could, and invariably worked in some recreational flying by buzzing each other's stomping grounds when they were in the area. Training took its toll in unexpected ways. Several of the men were grounded with infirmities ranging from toothaches to earaches because of the effects of being airborne at extreme altitudes and temperatures to which they hadn't adapted.

By April of 1943, the men started their incremental flight toward England, where they would eventually make their home base for conducting most of their bombing missions. On the way, they would lose their first plane, *Ophelia Bumps*, to an unfortunate landing effort involving the co-pilot, who was manning the main controls for their beloved pilot, "Rube" (beleaguered by an ear infection, but determined to ship out anyway), and some trees that interfered with an engine and a wing or two. The men managed to muster a confounded laugh about an incident that posed a genuine threat to their survival.

As I've said, my father was the navigator of the crew. He had earned his pilot's license before obtaining his driver's license, and he took to navigation quickly. The crew's first transatlantic flight had them bound for Prestwick, Scotland, and it was this journey that truly tested my father's mettle as well as his skill. His re-telling of this flight may be the first time he ever revealed just how diligent and determined a navigator he was. Because of adverse weather conditions, he relied solely on celestial navigation to land the plane safely. To this day, my father can read any star in the sky. Some of my first childhood memories are of my father describing the constellations to me at night. I have seen him do the same with many of his grandchildren.

By May, the men were preparing for their first missions and witnessing their first casualties. Dogfights were rarer than catching flak while flying in formation, especially if they were Tail-End Charlie, even with reliable P-47 fighter escorts and Spitfires draw-

HISTORY

Activated in Salt Lake City during 1942, the 96th Bombardment Group (H), started its crew training in Boise, Idaho during August of that year before moving to other training bases in the United States at Walla Walla, Rapid City, Pocatello, and Pyote, Texas. Moving on to Salina, Kansas, the 96th deployed overseas for combat in England with thirty aircraft, thirty-five crews and as many staff and maintenance personnel that could be carried in the B-17s. The Air Echelon arrived at Grafton Underwood, Northants, by the end of April 1943 and the Ground Echelon, having crossed the Atlantic on the Queen Elizabeth, were sent to Andrews Field, Great Saling, Essex.

The 96th was not supposed to fly combat until the Ground Echelon arrived; however the weather improved and approximately ten days after they had arrived the crews started flying combat missions with limited ground support. After a disastrous first mission, that was aborted, the 96th went on to fly a long, distinguished and often bloody service that was to last until May 1945.

The Air Echelon moved to Andrews Field on 27 May 1943 and flew from there until 7 June 1943 when the whole group moved to its permanent base at Snetterton Heath, Norfolk.

Distinguishing itself during many 8th Air Force battles it led the Third Air Division on many occasions. It was awarded two Presidential citations: one for leading the Third Air Division on the first *Shuttle Mission* to North Africa, having flown on after bombing German aircraft factories at Regensburg. The second citation for leading the 45th Combat Wing to Poznan, Poland in spite of heavy enemy opposition and atrocious weather conditions. The 96th also led the Third Air Division on the infamous second *Schweinfurt Mission* .... rated by historians as one of the greatest air battles of World War Two. Again in the lead it took part in the first *Shuttle Mission* to Russia, where, after bombing Ruhland, Germany, it flew on to Poltava where after landing it was attacked by the Luftwaffe in a night bombing operation; losing sixteen of the twenty one aircraft dispatched to German bombs.

During two years of combat, the 96th had many claims to fame among aircraft and personnel; but there stands three unenviable records of which the group would rather be without.

(1) *The second highest number of aircraft missing in action by any group in the 8th Air Force — 189 aircraft.*

(2) *The highest losses by any Bomb Group in the Third Air Division.*

(3) *The highest losses sustained by any Bomb Group in the 8th Air Force over a three month period — sixty-five aircraft lost between March and May 1944.*

AIRCRAFT MISSING IN ACTION — 189

OTHER AIRCRAFT LOSSES — 50

MISSIONS FLOWN — 321

TOTAL BOMB TONNAGE DROPPED — 19,277

AIRCREW KILLED — 938

ing and returning fire. If the crew got the order to ditch, it was better to be captured uninjured as a P.O.W. than to get strafed while parachuting to the ground. Either option was preferable to dumping in the freezing North Sea, where recovery was always difficult, and survival was generally no more than an hour.

The 1943 CBO, or "combined bomber offensive," of the USAF and RAF, had the aircrews on continuous standby for missions, with barely enough time to sleep before rolling out again. Their targets were military and industrial alike. They dropped bombs that destroyed electricity-producing dams, submarine pens, airfields, supply depots, ball bearing and synthetic rubber plants, and repair yards.

The average survival rate of airmen never climbed much above sixty percent. The men of *Kipling's Error* not only overcame the odds, but they were also beholden to some unseen benefactor, as evidenced by a couple of providential incidents. One of them occurred in Germany in mid-August in a pivotal battle covered in the *Saturday Evening Post*. Had it not been for malfunctioning cockpit equipment and a dose of luck, that story would have been much abbreviated.

Whether it was luck, skill, divine intervention, or a combination of all three, those factors forged to create another opportunity for the men of *Kipling's Error* to continue to fight.

They undoubtedly found more truth in the poem's later lines:

> *"There is neither East nor West, Border, nor Breed, nor Birth,*
> *When two strong men stand face to face, though they come*
> *from the ends of the earth!"*

While writing and assembling this book, I had to confront my father's history. Some of it was very painful. Even today, I get tears when I think of the abject and brutal poverty my beloved grandparents and my father and his brothers endured. It is beyond comprehension to me. If God would grant me one wish, I would give them every dime I have been blessed to accumulate in this life.

But their spirits were not broken. My father and his three brothers, John, Charles, and Don, all helped each other, financially and morally, until the four of them earned college degrees. The Mitchell family valued education, and they shared a desire to be strong, contributing members of American society. All of my father's children, myself, Martha, Sarah, David, and Mark have earned college degrees and have lived successful and productive lives.

I was also pained by the hours I spent gazing into the photograph of the *Kipling's Error* crew. They are all gone, except for my father and Sgt. Haseltine. I wish I had become interested in this story at a younger age; I could have met these men. I have spent several days trying to contact their families to learn as much as I could about them. I had no success in the cases of White, Nelson, Malinowski, and Mendolson. Perhaps some reader of this book will give me a clue, and I can share this history with the families of my father's crewmates.

I began to know some of the crew and in a strange way, I felt I was invading their privacy. I wanted to discover they were a "band of brothers," forever bonded together by an intense wartime experience. After all, what could be more intense than twenty-five missions in which you would either all live or die? Every man on *Kipling's Error* controlled the life of every other man. But that was not the case. Other than occasional reunions, my father only stayed in touch with Rube. In reality, these ten men were from widely divergent backgrounds. At least three of the crew (Lakey, Malinowski, and Kotlarz) were Polish Catholics, and Mendolson was Jewish. Both of these backgrounds would have been very foreign to my father. After the twenty-five missions, each went his own way with the knowledge each had done his duty, and the crew had survived against overwhelming odds.

I was, and am, deeply moved by one poignant entry in my father's diary. He made the entry after seeing the bloodied and battered remains of some friends removed from a crippled plane. The entry was simply stated, "God rest the souls of these American flyers." And then, there was the basis for the title of this book: an entry made on May 31, 1943, my father's reflection on the loss of three crews. "May God's blessings be with Stevenson, Holcombe, McMath, and their crews. They were good Americans." This book is a testament to their bravery, sacrifice, and heroism.

A hero, the dictionary says, is a person "noted for feats of courage and nobility of purpose, especially one who has risked his life… A person who is endowed with great courage and strength, celebrated for his bold exploits, and favored by the gods." Surely all of the men and women who struggled and fought with us and for us during World War II are heroes.

For the men of *Kipling's Error*, their "feats of courage" were their twenty-five missions. All of the men of *Kipling's Error* have observed, in one way or another, that if a man ever claimed that he wasn't afraid in times of battle, he was either a fool or a liar. Someone once said, "Courage is what we get after we accomplish the deed we dread" – not at all convenient, but invariably true.

Their "nobility of purpose" was dictated to them; they found themselves in head-to-head opposition with an enemy. Failure at the larger objective – winning the war – was not an option.

They were "celebrated for their bold exploits," but that was something that my father and his nine brothers-in-arms often shunned; they repeatedly said that they were just doing their duty to their country and to each other. In fact, as is documented time after time in their diaries – whether they were being lectured by a visiting general, marching in parade for a newsreel crew, or flying formation for Eleanor Roosevelt – these boys couldn't wait to dispense with all the pomp and circumstance and get back to work.

And that they were "favored by the gods," well…they lived to tell the tale, raise families, and lead productive lives. That is being "favored," indeed.

My father and the rest of his crew were men put upon by their times – men who summoned their inner resources because they had no other choice. They did what they had to do, without the leisure of pausing to contemplate their fear or their glory. Between missions, they played as hard as they worked. They appreciated the beauty of foreign lands and foreign landmarks. They complained little. They remarked on their random good luck – whether it was the chance of drinking hot cocoa, or sleeping on a cot instead of the ground, or the miracle of dodging a piece of shrapnel by mere degrees.

They mourned. They prayed. They celebrated. They survived.

They carried their pragmatism into their lives back home, leaving it to the movies to romanticize their combat experiences. Their memoirs suggest that the men of *Kipling's Error* – indeed, many men of their generation – weren't given to expressions of intense emotion, despite the extreme conditions they endured. How does one inure one's self to the highs and lows of training: laughing with a crewmate one day, cleaning his remains off a plane and shipping his personal effects home to his loved ones the next?

And yet, much can be inferred from what these men left unsaid, as well as what they eventually revealed. This they did mainly by how they lived their lives after the war. They concentrated on raising families, pursuing college degrees, and earning a living wherever their new jobs took them.

They were undeniably human. They were also unquestionably heroic.

This book is the story of the crew of *Kipling's Error III*, in honor of what they did. It is a story of heroes for future generations. And it is my personal tribute to one of those heroes — my father, Capt. Lloyd Brooks Mitchell.

— *James Brooks Mitchell*

Captain Mitchell
Direct Descendent of Revolutionary War Veteran, James Davis

James Davis (1762-1831)
Served with George Washington in Captain Nathanial Lamb's
2nd Virginia Regiment

Ephraim Davis (1783-1843)

James Davis (1831-1917)
Tennessee Volunteers, Confederate Army

Mahalia Janetta (Nettie) Davis (1858-1925)
Married John F. Mitchell

James Walter Mitchell (1886-1976)
Married Celina Zella Gamble (1885-1974)

John William – Lloyd Brooks – Charles – Donald Emery
Married Mable Grace Apple, 5/2/1942 Died, 1992
Married, Nancy Hufschmid 1993

James Brooks	Martha Susan	Sarah Ellen	David Clark	Mark Hall
Mollie Rae	Jennifer Jeanne	James Silas	Michael Clark	Amanda Faye
Marcy Jill	Emily Jill	Mary Ellen	Emily Grace	James Welch
Tyler Brooks		Sally Jane		Amelia Grace
Kate Crompton		Laura Susan		Zachary Lloyd

FOREWORD

What a sincere honor and pleasure it is for me to write the foreword for *Kipling's Error III: They Were Good Americans.*

As the Commanding Officer of the 413th Bombardment Squadron, 96th Bombardment Group, Kipling's Error III assigned unit, I am very familiar with what they and their fellow B-17 crews went through during their days flying combat missions over Germany and occupied Europe. But before we talk combat, let's briefly discuss the early days.

The 96th Group, consisting of the 337th, 338th, 339th and 413th Bomb Squadrons, was formed at Gowen Field, Boise, Idaho in July, 1942. In September, the group was sent to Walla Walla, Washington for a month of training. Then in October, to Rapid City, South Dakota for more training and then in November to Pocatello, Idaho. In January, 1943, the group was transferred to Pyote Air Base in Pyote, Texas. At all these bases, the primary mission was to train and to be ready for combat; someplace. We really didn't care where, just to get out of those surroundings would be a plus. To give an idea of how desperate we were, in late November we were told we were going to Guadalcanal and we all cheered! When we finally got word in late February, 1943 that we were going to England, I don't remember that we cheered, but we were relieved. The crews were all well-trained as they could be, all the workings of the Group and Squadrons were in good order (we hoped) and the task ahead of getting to England was undertaken.

I want to make one comment about those days in Walla Walla, Rapid City and Pocatello, which none of us will ever forget – that was the twenty-four-hour clock. Second Air Force had us on a schedule where you would work eight hours, RR the next eight hours, then sleep or rest for eight hours. Our flight ended at midnight, you had eight hours of RR before you could go to bed. The mess halls were serving breakfast all day and all night! Now we might be going to a combat zone, but we could at least go to bed after flying if we wanted to!

What happened going to England? A lot happened, but we made it without accident or incident or loss of limb. When that occurred, I know I had nine B-17 crews who were as capable as any. Nobody backed down, nobody turned around, nobody quit. There was a task to be done and they were going to do that task come hell or high water, and they did regardless of the sacrifice!

I know this is supposed to be a forward about Kipling's Error III, Rube Neie's Crew, which was one of the best. But the other eight crews in the 413th fit into that "one of the best" category, too. At the time covered in the Kipling's Error III book, I was twenty-five-years old. At the time I am writing these words, I am eighty-seven, and God willing, I will never forget the names of the aircraft commanders and their crewmembers who went to England in 1943. I proudly list the names of these outstanding Americans: Lt. Walt Flagg; Capt. Jack Ford; Lt. Dick Jerger; Capt. Howard McClatchy; Lt. Hugh Moore; Lt. Rube Neie; Lt. Eldridge Shelton; Lt. Charles Tanner and Lt. Ralph Ward.

When the above crews flew their first combat mission in May, 1943, no bomber crew in the 8th Air Force ever successfully completed the twenty-five mission requirement and the first bomber raid in the 8th took place in August, 1942 and the attitude seemed to be, "no bomber crew ever will." But the attitude of despair never permeated our crews. On the fourth mission of Kipling's Error III to Emden, German fighters shot them up badly, putting a big hole in the right wing and created encumbrances. As Sgt. Dick Haseltine, radio operator, puts it, "We never felt fear of that sort before. Much of it was due to being half-frozen, hindered by oxygen masks, radio headsets, mikes, parachutes, bomb doors stuck, the sight of ships going down close to us, but we know for sure now, if ever Kipling's Error III knows fear, it will be a fighting type of fear to the last man! All guns blazing continually. As a crew, we are tops and feel that we've been through a good lesson in the school of education." Amen, Amen, all guns blazing – as a crew we are tops! And they were!

All of the above crews, except one, successfully completed twenty-five combat missions over Germany and occupied Europe. This was a feat unmatched by any B-17 bomber squadron in the 8th Air Force that flew combat missions in the 1943 time period, when the only fighter escort we had was German.

I could go on and on about how grateful I am to have had the honor to be associated with such an outstanding group of Americans as you are. When our country was at one of its darkest hours, you answered the call to come to its defense, and more than made it possible for the sun to break through the clouds. Always be proud and thankful to God you had the opportunity to defend your country, its way of life and its freedom. And I thank every one of you for making the 413th Bombardment Squadron one of the very finest ever. After many of you departed England, General LeMay selected the 413th to be equipped with radar to lead other groups when that group was leading the 3rd Air Division on a mission. Quite an honor.

Lastly, the crew of Kipling's Error III was tops. When the crew had around thirteen missions, I called Rube in and told him we were going to groom him for lead crew. He said in so many words, "Please, hell no. I want to stay in the Tail End Charlie position, where I can go anywhere in the formation to get away from fighters and at the same time not disrupt our formation. Please no!" So we complied with his request.

God Bless you, each and every one,

Stanley I. Hand
Col. USAF (Ret.)

GROWING UP AND THE PRE-WAR YEARS

The following are excerpts from tape-recorded interviews with Lloyd Brooks Mitchell by his granddaughter, Amanda Mitchell, and his son, James Brooks Mitchell. They describe the early years of Lloyd's life, including his family's ancestry. (Some of the content has been slightly expanded or compressed strictly for purposes of clarity.)

My dad always told me we were of Scotch-Irish descent, and I don't know when the Mitchells came into east Tennessee, but that's as far back as I can go back on the Mitchell side. My grandfather was John Franklin. My dad was James Walter and is buried in Rogers, Arkansas. My grandfather is buried in Cummingsville Cemetery, along with a lot of other Mitchells. And that would be in Van Buren County, Tennessee. My mother was from White County. My dad grew up on a farm in Van Buren County, and then he and Mom both taught school for, I don't know how long, two or three more years. I've got a picture of Dad in his class.

But then, in the middle twenties, about 1925, they moved to Akron, Ohio. Things weren't going well on the farm for them, and there were jobs in the North. So they moved to Akron, Ohio. Dad worked in the Miller Rubber Company there for a period of about four years, and the work was too hard for him. Dad was a small man, and in that type of work, you had to do a lot of lifting. So in 1927, he picked up and moved his family to southwest Oklahoma to Harmon County. Really, the earliest memories I have are of Akron, Ohio.

MOTHER'S FAMILY: THE GAMBLES

My mother's name was Gamble. Her name was Lina Zella Gamble, and she was one of sixteen children. Two of them died at an early age, and the other fourteen were raised to be grown. And, of course, my grandfather, William Solomon Gamble, was a farmer there in White County, close to Sparta. I don't know much about my great-granddad on that side, except that his name was Andrew Jackson Gamble. My great grandmother's name was Mary Paul. (And I'm sorry, but I just don't know one thing about the Pauls; I wish I did.)

DAD'S FAMILY: THE MITCHELLS

On the Mitchell side, my great-grandmother was Davis. She was the second wife of my grandfather, John Franklin. John Franklin's first wife was a Cummins. She wasn't really my grandmother. And then he married Nettie Davis. But after my grandfather's first wife died, not too long afterward (they had had the four children), he rode up on his horse one day to the Davis house and asked for Nettie – her name was really Jeannetta – and said, "Nettie, I've got four kids and I can't raise them by myself. Will you come help me raise them?"

So Nettie agreed, and then they had four children. They had James Walter (my father), Herbert, Ephraim and Bessie – now, that's the four that I remember.

Absolem Davis was an uncle of my dad's, and Absolem was a little "touched," I think. He lived kind of like a hermit, in a cave. They called it Ab's Cave, and they still call it Ab's Cave, the last time I was in Tennessee. Well, some of Ab's friends and relatives decided that it just wasn't right that Ab lived in that cave, so they forcibly removed him. And he did not like the civilized life, and it wasn't long until Ab decided to go back to his cave. And as far as I know, he lived his life out in that cave.

There is a genealogy of the Davis family that is quite interesting. There are some really interesting pictures, and it traces the Davis family back to James Davis, who was a veteran of the Revolutionary War. James Davis came out of Virginia or Tennessee. Boyd Austin, a distant cousin of mine, wrote out the genealogy. There is also a book called "A History of Van Buren County," which has some history about the Mitchells in it.

OHIO TO TEXAS

We moved in 1927 to Harmon County. One reason Dad selected Harmon County was that one of his half-sisters, Aunt Sally, and her husband lived there. I suppose they wrote and told Dad what a great county it was to live in. If they did, they really did deceive somebody! It wasn't all that swift! The rainfall was pitiful, and we landed there just before the Depression. So, it didn't prove out to be too good for our family.

I have kind of a faint memory of the move we made from Ohio. We had a "Baby Overland," and we averaged a hundred miles a day with that thing. It was about fourteen hundred miles from Akron to Harmon County, and it took us fourteen days. Had lots of flats. Those days, you didn't have spare tires. You had to pull that old thing off and put a cold patch on it, and keep it jacked up and hope it didn't go out on you too soon. We had lots of flat tires.

Another memory I have was that my kid brother, Don – he was about three years old – and we were having car trouble, and the two of us (I don't remember if I was one of the two involved or not) went across the road and found something interesting and hollered, "Come over and see this!" And Don dashed across the road and a car hit him smack on. We thought he was dead. We thought we lost him. Took him to the hospital and it turned out okay. He was stunned, but he wasn't bad off.

Then when we moved to Harmon County, we started renting farms. Dad didn't have enough money to buy a farm, and so we started renting farms. That wasn't too good, because when the land was good, people would farm it and they wouldn't rent it out. Generally, the rented land was the poorest-type land. So we didn't farm too many good tracts.

LIFE ON THE FARM FOR A KID

Recalling some of the life on the farm for a kid, I was nine-years-old. The kids started working early in those days. I started doing a man's work at the age of nine. We would get up early and milk the cows, slop the hogs, feed the horses, and then have breakfast. Then you would harness the horses and take them out to the field or you would grab a hoe.

We did lots of hoeing. We didn't have all of the modern means of farming they have now, where they would spray for weeds and all of that. You'd take a gooseneck hoe and go out there and chop the weeds out of the cotton. Or, if it was your turn – and we really kept close tabs on whose turn it was — we would get to ride a Go Devil. Hitch a team up to the Go Devil. Now, Go Devil is kind of a slide-type sled, and it's got two blades that stick out at an angle from the sled. When you planted your cotton, you would plant it on a ridge or plant it in a furrow, and have your cotton row in a furrow, and your two blades would cut through and cut the weeds off of the ridge. At the back of the sled, you would have some discs which you regulate, and the discs would throw dirt into the cotton, not cover the cotton up. It would throw dirt into the cotton and kind of get rid of some of the weeds that way. We would always like to do that rather than hoe, because you got to ride the sled. A team of horses pulled the sled.

We had a cultivator too. When the cotton got up a little bigger, why, you had a one-row cultivator. If you were fortunate, it covered two rows, but generally ours was just a one-row cultivator. It had some kind of blades on it which would go down the ridges and cut the weeds out. Generally, you would plant your cotton in May, and then two or three weeks later start working it. We would have to get out there and hoe. The weather was hot – oh, it was hot! Sometimes, it'd get up to 105, 106 degrees, and this was sand! We farmed in sand country, and that sand got – man, it must have been 115, 120 degrees. We'd reach out with our hoe, and dig a hole – dig a hole three or four inches deep for it to get a little cooler, and then we'd jump to that hole and stand there and hoe for a little while, and dig another hole. We'd look up in the sky for clouds. Boy, if we saw a thunderhead, we'd really hope it'd come our way so it would give us a little bit of shade. And that went on for several months – two or three months.

Then, as soon as you – you'd call it "layin' by" – got your crops laid by, you could go to school. Back then, we had school in July and August. And you think that wasn't hot. The little school we went to was the OM School. You'd have the windows open, but, man – man, that schoolroom was hot! We'd sometimes have three and four grades together and the teacher would teach three or four grades. Of course, it wouldn't be all that many kids.

That was life on the farm for a kid. We had moved from rented farm to rented farm. We would not stay maybe two or three years on one, then move to another. I went to the OM School when I started in the third grade. One year we moved out on the plains of Texas. I was in the fifth grade then. I got to study Texas history then, and I found Texas history very interesting. But then we came back to the OM community and I finished grade school in OM. Then I went to Arnett, which was five or six miles from there, and I finished high school. Now, a big part of the time, mainly while we were going to OM, we had to walk two and a half miles to school. That wasn't too bad, except in July and August. And then in January and February, it was so cold. I can still remember some of those cold 'northers' coming down, and walking home in them. But we didn't think we were being unduly punished – that's just the way of life. Then, about the time I started high school, I would bus. We would have to walk a mile up to the bus line, and the bus would pick us up. That was a lot better.

THE DUST BOWL

We were right in the middle of the big Dust Bowl. Now, the main part of the Dust Bowl started up in the Oklahoma and Texas Panhandle, and that was where the dust got all picked up and then carried onto the south and east. Those big dust storms would come in. You would see them rolling in and, oftentimes, we didn't know whether they were storm clouds or whether they were just a dust cloud. We would stand at the edge of the cellar or hole – just a kind of a hole dug out of the ground, with a wooden door, that we would use for a tornado shelter – to see whether it was a dust storm or not. And that was terrible. When those things hit, your visibility was limited. You could not see hardly, and it just covered everything in dust, and the house and everywhere else was just covered with dust. People would take handkerchiefs and wet them and tie them over their mouths and noses to breathe through. That was bad news. Most of the time were drought years when we were there. Of course, the rainfall in Harmon County is low anyhow. I think it's something like twenty inches annual and, oftentimes, we didn't get the average, and the years were bad.

COTTON FARMING

Cotton was the cash crop. When the Depression hit in 1929, and Wall Street failed in '29, the price dropped out of cotton. Cotton dropped down to five cents a pound of lint, and that was awfully low. When we gathered cotton in the fall, we would "fill bolls," we called it. We didn't pick cotton too much in Harmon County; it was mostly boll-pulling. We would have to get two thousand bolls to make five hundred pounds of lint, and Dad would get twenty-five dollars for the bale. When they would gin it, they would get to keep the seed. The gin would keep the seed for the cost of ginning.

And so, he'd make twenty-five dollars. Of course, he didn't get to keep all of that. I remember I would go to the bank with him in the spring, and he wouldn't have enough money to buy the seed with – oftentimes, we wouldn't have any grocery money – and he would go into the bank and look at one of those cold-eyed bankers and plead for enough money to buy seed and buy a little groceries. And then, come fall, he would pay it back with interest, and he didn't have anything left. I still – and I hate to admit it – but I still have kind of an aversion to banks because that was one of my earliest memories, looking at those old, cold-eyed bankers and pleading for money.

Of course, we lived on the farm, and the farms were old, maybe a quarter to a half-mile apart. And kids didn't have many things to do. No shows – no, that was impossible. It was nine miles to Hollis, and all the way we would have to go in the wagon or walk. Sometimes, when we got bigger, we would hitchhike. If you got to go to a show, that was a big, big happening. Of course, shows only cost ten cents then. Getting a haircut – I remember that. Boy, I got up to fifteen or sixteen, and I was ashamed of my mother's haircuts, but it took a quarter to get a haircut, and a quarter was a lot of money in those days. But every once in a while, I'd manage to save a quarter and get a haircut, and that was a big deal.

We generally had to work six days a week. Once in a while, Dad would let us off on Saturday afternoon, but that, too, was a big happening if you could get off on a Saturday afternoon. When we could, one of our favorite pastimes was chasing rabbits. Each family would have a greyhound or two, and the boys would brag on who had the fastest greyhound, and we would go out hunting rabbits. This was all around the time I was nine until about eighteen.

Once in a while, after we got bigger, somebody would have a party. I was a teenager, sixteen or seventeen. Started kind of looking crossways at a girl, you know, and we'd go to a "snap party." They called it snap. I can't remember too much about the game of snap, except a boy and a girl would be off over there holding hands, and another couple would come and they would chase each other around, and they would tag each other, and then the one who got tagged would have to go out and find another partner, or something like that. It was a very complicated game. And, oh – at one of those parties, they might have had a little band. Somebody with a fiddle and a guitar and a banjo might have played some popular songs then. Of course, I thought the band was pretty neat, but I am sure with today's standards, they would not rate very high!

School Days

Ah, thinking about school days… They would pick up in the summer after the crops were laid by, and then they would turn out come about October, as I remember. Cotton would get ready to pull, and so then they'd dismiss for cotton-pullin' for about a month, and then they would pick back up in school. Like I say, kind of primitive. I always loved school, though. I just always did like school. I was good – particularly good – in spelling. I loved spelling. Each year we'd have a county contest, and there was a whole lot of small rural schools in Harmon County, and I would represent my grade from OM in spelling, and I won first place – County First Place – several times. I liked to spell.

I liked arithmetic, but there was a kid in there that was a little better at arithmetic than me, and his name was Lloyd Mills. See, my name – I wasn't called "Lloyd" then. I was Brooks. Well, Lloyd and I would always contest each other to see who got to go to the County, and once or twice, I beat Lloyd. That was a real happening when I could beat Lloyd out and get to represent OM in the arithmetic match. Lloyd was a good friend. He and I went through all of grade school and all of high school together. He was a good buddy.

Mostly, school for me was a good experience. I loved to read. I remember, in Ohio, the first two grades, we studied phonics, and I would go around reading words on groceries and everything else. I loved to read and, as I said before, I loved spelling and arithmetic and history.

When I graduated from OM, I went to Arnett, which is a rural high school in Harmon County a few miles northwest of Hollis. I went all four years to Arnett and, again, I liked school real well. But there were some experiences that I remember that weren't too good. Going to high school, it was kind of a tradition that all of the boys would play hooky on April Fool's Day. We would get on the bus and have it made up beforehand where we were going to get off of the bus, some place between home and school. And we would play games all day and have fun. We knew when we got back that we were going to get a whippin' and the principal would call us in – this was even in high school – the principal would call us in, and we'd get a pretty sound whippin'.

I remember one time – and what caused me to do this, I'll never know, because it was a stupid thing to do. At a basketball game, after the game was over, I lit a firecracker inside the gym. Man – I caught down the line for that one! But mostly high school was a good experience.

One reason I think I liked school was I wasn't a very good athlete. I liked to play base-ball and I generally made the baseball team, but I wasn't good at it. And I lived too far away to play basketball. They'd practice after school hours. I lived so far away that if I stayed, I'd have to walk home, which would have been several miles. So I didn't try out for basketball. But to compensate for my lack of athletic ability, I liked to beat every-body in grades. So we'd have tests, and I'd generally hold my own on the tests, and I got to be salutatorian – number two spot. I should have made number one. I didn't. That was fun. There were only eleven of us in our graduating class!

MARBLES FOR KEEPS

When we lived in Ohio – I must have been seven or eight years old – and I had enough money and I went and bought a sack of marbles. They were such shiny, pretty marbles, and I was so proud of them, and I started home with my marbles. Well, there were a couple of neighborhood kids there, and they saw my marbles, and they conned me into playing marbles with them for keeps. That was a dumb thing to do, but I didn't know it. And, sure enough, they won all my marbles, and I went home just bawlin' my eyes out. I was so unhappy. John, my older brother, asked me what happened, and I told him. He said, "Come on. Go with me. Show me those kids." So I went back with John and showed him the kids. John talked them into playing marbles, and he got my marbles back, plus all of their marbles, because John was a good shooter.

EXTRA MONEY

In the spring when we were working Dad's crops, Dad couldn't afford to pay us any-thing for chopping and cultivating and plowing, so we would work real hard to get his crops laid by so we could go out and find a neighbor that needed some help. I remem-ber hiring out to one of the neighbor-farmers there, and he had a lot of Johnson grass in his cotton. And believe you me, Johnson grass is a real tough grass to get rid of. So he gave us ten cents an hour, but he wouldn't let you work by yourself. He insisted that he did the work with you because what he was afraid of was that you'd be taking too much time at the end of the row sharpening your hoe. We kept a rattail file, and we'd kind of sharpen our hoes at the end of the row, and he might give you three or four minutes to sharpen your hoe. He wanted you going right back down that row. And so, you'd work ten hours and you'd make a dollar, and that was hard work, but we didn't care. The idea of making a dollar was wonderful.

In the fall, we would hustle around and get Dad's cotton out so we could throw a sack on our shoulder and go out and fill bolls for one of the neighbors and make a little money that way. I remember one day that I was determined I was going to pull six hundred pounds of bolls. I was twelve years old. We found a neighbor that needed some help. It was after the frost and the leaves were off of the cotton, and it was what we called "bumble bee cotton." It only grew to about twelve or fourteen inches high, but it had lots of bolls on each stalk. So we would go through and we'd strip it. Instead of picking a boll off at a time, you'd just lop your hands onto the plant and come up the plant, and strip it and throw it into your sack, and grab the next plant. I worked from sun 'til sun and I got 603 pounds. I was so proud of myself and I got two dollars that day for pulling six hundred pounds. They were paying us thirty-three cents a hundred. But I was tickled! Oh, man – I felt rich when I went home that night!

Pulling bolls, our fingers got hurt. I had these canvas gloves on, but they would kind of wear out at the fingertips, and then those harsh burrs at the end of the cotton boll would kind of scratch and cut your fingers. Another bad part of the thing was your back would get so tired from stooping over that you'd have to get down on your knees. If you were wealthy enough, you'd have leather kneepads – now, that was a real luxury. Most of the time, we just had kneepads that our mother made out of quilted material and straps, and the old goat-heads would stick through those and get in your knees. And the sand burrs – they were mean, too. So, quite often, you would have sand burrs and goat-heads stuck in your knees.

Housing and Water

As for housing, it was tragic – the housing we lived in. People who owned tenant farms wouldn't spend a dime on the old cotton shacks. And they were just that – cotton shacks. Absolutely no insulation. No electricity. No running water. The flies in the summertime was just awful, just terrible! Most of the time, the water situation wasn't good. For several years, we lived up on the Salt Fork River, and I remember we had a well, just a dug well, and that thing would tend to go dry in the summertime. I remember Dad would lower us down into it. It was a deep well. It probably was 35, 40 feet deep. We would have a pulley and one of us kids would get on the bucket and ride that bucket down to the bottom of the well and dig the sand. It was all sand. And we'd try to deepen the well, and we would dig sand out and put it in the bucket, and they would pull us up. It was a wonder we had not been killed, because that blamed well was nothing but sand, and it could have caved in. But none of us was killed, luckily.

Our neighbor had a spring, and when the well went dry, we had to hitch the team up and put barrels in the wagon, and we'd go to his spring and load up the water and take it back. That was quite a chore, getting drinking water. You would have to get stock water also, because they had to have water.

That was when we lived out of Hollis. We lived in what was known as "Gyp County." It was a gypsum area, and that water… well, you couldn't bear to drink it. It was not fit for human consumption. Even the stock would have a hard time, in the hot summer weather, of drinking it. We had a cistern in our place, and we would catch roof water off the roof to fill the cistern up, and when it didn't rain, we would have to have water brought out from town in a tank truck for that cistern. But it didn't serve too good, and oftentimes you'd have birds roosting on it and bird waste would get in the water. It was a wonder we hadn't died from typhoid.

Food

We did not have a great variety of food. We raised gardens, but in that dry country, raising food wasn't too easy. Your droughts would hit hard and your gardens would dry up, but we would manage to raise peas and beans, and sometimes we had corn, if you could get it raised before the drought hit. As for meat, we raised hogs and we would butcher the hogs in the fall, and I always looked forward to that. We had a smoke-house. We would butcher the hogs and we would hang up the hams and the shoulders in the smokehouse, and Mother would go out and slice off some meat then. But come spring, why, that meat would get rancid and go sour on you, so you couldn't eat it. We very seldom had beef. We had a few cows, but Dad would keep all of the calves to sell for a little bit of cash money, and you couldn't afford to have beef. Come spring, we'd have fried chicken. Oh, a lot of fried chicken! So, in the spring, you'd have chicken and a lot of biscuits. Mother always made "tea cakes," she called them – they were little sugar cookies. And she always made a lot of chocolate pies.

But taking food to school was kind of a sad deal. We didn't have lunch buckets; we had an old lard can, a gallon-size lard can, and you'd drive nail holes in the lid and you would carry biscuits and bacon, and that would get sweaty and soggy. Come noon, it wouldn't be too good. I remember once, in a rare occasion, we had what we called "light bread" – what you call white bread, and sometimes we would call it "bought'n bread" – and, boy, if you had a light bread-and-lettuce sandwich, I drooled all the way to noon thinking about that. Hmm, hmm. But it was a rare occasion.

Government Programs and the CCC Camps

The government programs in those days – and there were a lot of them when President Roosevelt came into power in 1932, which was the heart of the Depression – a number of the government programs started to alleviate not only the farmers, but all of the people of the country. It was the time of the New Deal. I remember that, for some reason or another, Dad couldn't get into the WPA programs, because I don't remember really any income coming from the WPA – the Works Progress Administration.

The program that directly impacted our family was the CCC – the Civilian Conservation Corps. My older brother, John, graduated from high school in 1934 and then he went to a CCC camp out of Lawton, in the Wichita Mountains. There they built dams; they built bathhouses; they built trails; they built picnic tables, picnic areas and things like that. A lot of the work that the CCC did is still evident. For instance, John spent about three years in the CCC, and he came to Oklahoma City and went to Hill's Business College.

Then I went into the CCC directly out of high school. I graduated in '37, and then sometime in the fall of '37, I went to the CCC camp at Lugert. Lugert is twenty, thirty miles north of Atlus, and it's the present location of the Quartz Mountain State Park. There we did the same type of work: bath houses, picnic areas, picnic grounds, trails, dams and things like that. We made a dollar a day and we had to send twenty-five dollars a month home to our folks, and we got to keep five dollars a month. And that really did help Mom and Dad, to get twenty-five dollars a month coming in. That was really a big, big help to them.

I was fortunate enough to be the assistant camp engineer. The good part was, I liked to work. The camp engineer was a real nice guy to work for, and I drug the chain and held the rod for him. But the best part was, I had a building of my own to live in. I slept in the Camp Engineering Building and kind of watched over the equipment. But I hated those barracks. When I first got there, we lived in barracks, and there must have been forty, fifty guys to a barracks, and there was absolutely no privacy. The noise was terrible, and the guys were not all the best type of guys. So that really did please me to get to sleep in the Engineering Building.

The camp had an education program. There were education classes at night, and I took several of those. One thing I remember that really did help me out was that another guy and I went in together and bought an old Standard typewriter, and we also bought an instructional booklet, and we taught ourselves how to type. In my life, that has come in really handy. In addition to doing that, later at Cameron Junior College, I took a typing class and learned further, and I've used that skill for the rest of my life.

In addition to being the assistant camp engineer, I ran the water pump for a while. We were located on Lake Lugert and the water pump was down on the lake, and I'd go down and start to pump the tank full of water. The water tank sat up on top of a small mountain, and I'd pump it up until I saw the water running out of the tank, and then I'd set it off and I'd have the rest of the day to read. I really did get to do a lot of reading in those days.

By and large, the camp was a good experience. You met some kinds of rough characters there, but you had to learn how to deal with that. And I got to go home. It wasn't too far. It was about sixty miles from home, and I'd get to go home once in a while. I had to hitchhike home, but I didn't mind that.

MR. ENGLISH AND CAMERON JUNIOR COLLEGE

At the CCC, when I started out, I was kind of what was called a "pick-and-shovel" man. That's one of your lowest categories. And then I graduated into an assistant camp engineer. That's a high-sounding title, but all it meant was I drug the rod and the chains for the camp engineer. I have a very good memory about that. One day, the weather was bad, and we were sitting in the Engineering Building, and the camp engineer's name was English. He was an awful nice man. He said to me, "Mitchell, did you ever think about going to college?"

And I said, "Mr. English, there's nothing in the world I'd rather do, but I don't have any money. My folks don't have any money, and I don't know how on earth I could go to college."

And his reply was, "Well, I'll tell you what." He said, "I've got a good friend at Lawton at Cameron Junior College. He is a chemist from Oklahoma. His name is Clarence Breedlove, and I'll write Clarence to see if he could possibly find a job for you. What do you think about that?"

I said, "I'll do it! I don't know whether I can make it or not, but I'll surely try!" So, I got a letter back from Dean Breedlove. He offered me a nine-dollar-a-month job. Now, that was half room and board. Room and board cost eighteen dollars a month, and in January of 1939, I went to Cameron. I remember that first morning, a norther blew up. It was cold! And I had twenty-five dollars. Dad and Mom had managed, over a year and a half, to save twenty-five dollars. I had twenty-five dollars in my pocket. I had to walk down to Hollis, which is about two miles on Highway 62, stick my thumb in the air, and hitchhike a ride to Lawton, which is about one hundred miles east of there.

So, I started to Cameron in January of 1939. Made it. I don't know how, but I made it. When I was just at rock bottom – I mean rock bottom – John somehow or other would find five or ten dollars for me. He was working up here in the city and doing everything under the sun to make a buck while he went to Hill's Business College. He could always find – when it came down to rock level – a little bit of money for me.

I started there at Cameron in January of '39 and, after that semester, I went two more years – on into '40 and I graduated with the Class of '41. Those two and a half years, looking back on it, were perhaps some of the best times I ever had in my life. I loved school.

Starting in mid-semester, I took some sophomore classes, and I was scared to death. Man, I had been out of high school all of two, two and a half years, and I thought I was so rusty and so out of the habit, I wouldn't be able to make it. But, sure enough, I made straight A's! I made A's in everything I took that semester and, after that, I slowed down. I said, "Aw, this is a bunch of baloney," and so I started to have a good time. Well, I still made A's and B's, but I never did try to make straight A's.

I was taking agriculture courses then. I started out taking agriculture and majored in that because, you know, in those days and time, I thought everybody in the whole world farmed, and I thought that was the only occupation there was. But after I'd gone there about a year, I changed my major to chemistry because Dean Breedlove was teaching chemistry, and he was a good chem teacher. So I started taking all of the chemistry that I could, and all of the math that I could. Chemistry came easy to me – I loved chemistry. Math came awfully hard. I don't know – maybe it was because I didn't have a background in math in high school. I struggled in math. I remember particularly that I was taking a course in calculus, and that just about kicked me. I had a little buddy whose name was "Muscles." Now, Muscles must have weighed about 125 pounds. He had asthma. But he was a fun-loving kid and he had a head on his shoulders. He was a whiz at math, and Muscles pulled me through calculus.

I had an opportunity to learn to fly at Cameron. The government established what they called a CPT – Civilian Pilot Training Program. I am sure the people in charge of the government could see World War II coming on, and they wanted to train and get as many kids interested as they could in flying. So I enrolled in that program, and for forty dollars – a total of forty dollars – you could get your private pilot's license. And, incidentally, up until this time, I did not have a driver's license. So I got my pilot's license before I did my driver's license.

College Jobs

How did I make that other nine dollars for room and board? Well, that was the tough part of going to college. I would go to Lawton and, at that time, Lawton was a couple of miles from Cameron. I remember hitting the bowling alleys and I'd set pins. I remember I got a nickel a line. You didn't have the automatic pin setters then, and I remember having to be very careful because with those pins coming through, you could really break your leg if it hit you. You'd set them, and then you'd run and hide somewhere until the people bowled.

And then I got a job at the Fairmont Creamery. That was kind of heavy work sometimes. The cream cans, full of cream, might weigh seventy-five or eighty pounds. You'd have to sling them up on a truck and load the truck out to wherever they took the cream.

I remember one Christmas, I picked turkey feathers. They killed turkeys there and after they killed the turkey, they put it up on a chain, and the chain would go round and round, and you'd have people lined up picking feathers. Well, I got a job of picking tail feathers. Now, if you've ever tried to pull a tail feather out of a turkey, you know it's a tough job. Well, I did that, and I think I got fifteen cents an hour for that. I did that for a few days, and then, come to find out, I couldn't put a tie on. My thumb and my index finger were so sore, I couldn't button my shirt. Eventually, I lost the nails on my thumb and index finger because I had bruised them picking those blamed turkey feathers.

MABLE

I met Mable there at Cameron. I met Mable in the fall of 1939, and it wasn't too long after that I met her again in church. Mable, she was a dedicated Christian.

Mable had come down to Cameron from Bixby, where she grew up. So, we started dating, but there wasn't too much to do. Didn't have any money. Oftentimes, all I had, maybe, was a dime or fifteen cents, and we'd go buy a Coke and get two straws and share a Coke together.

One incident, I remember, was that my roommate, Clark Haws – he had a battery-powered radio, and that was something! And once in a while I'd have a date with Mable, and we would listen to The Lucky Strike Hit Parade, and we'd walk around campus listening to it. That would be our outing – that, and sharing a Coke. Sometimes I'd buy a package of Dentyne gum, and we'd share that.

I remember Mable telling me how she picked me out. Shortly after I started school at Cameron, I went to the church at Sixth and Arlington, the Church of Christ. Mable had a friend. Her friend's name was Velverde. Now, Velverde was tall. Velverde must have been about six-foot tall, and Mable was probably five-foot-four or five-foot-five, something like that. Me and another guy placed membership – you know, you go up front and tell them that you wanted to be a member of that church. So we placed membership. So Mable and Velverde, they are sitting back there, watching the proceedings, and Mable said, "I'll get the tall one and you get that other guy," which was me! Ha-ha! Well, it turned out just the opposite. Somehow or another, Mable and I got acquainted and started going together, and then Velverde and this other fellow, they married also. So both girls found husbands that night.

Mable was a lot of fun. We'd go off on church parties together. Go up to Wichita Mountains on hayrides, and things like that. I remember telling her one night we was up there, and we was kind of all to ourselves, and I told her where a pretty lake was. We started up to that lake, and it was quite a little bit farther, and she got suspicious of me, and I remember she said, "There is no lake up here! Let's go home!" She turned around, and we went back. She was afraid I was taking her to a nonexistent point. I wasn't. Really! There was a lake up there!

And so, we got along fine 'til, I don't know – must have been the fall of '40 or something – and she got mad at me. It was something I said. I popped off and said something I shouldn't have said. I don't even remember now what it was, but she got awful mad at me and, boy, I mean, she was mad! She dropped me like a hot rock. She wouldn't date me anymore. Wouldn't even speak to me.

Well, I flubbed around for a while. I was pretty unhappy about that because I thought a lot of Mable. And then she went up to Stillwater to school, and I eventually went to OU. It must have been sometime in the fall of '41 that I remember writing her and apologizing, and telling her I was sorry she got mad, and wanting to know if we couldn't date again.

So she agreed. She decided, "Well, I guess he's okay." So we were sweethearts again. I remember I went to see her then, her and her sister, Elizabeth, who lives in Tulsa. There's a bridge across the Arkansas there, close to downtown Tulsa. I don't remember what the name of the bridge is. I remember the night. It was a light rain – not a heavy rain – and we were walking across the bridge in the rain, and I asked her if she wanted to get married. She said yeah, she thought that would be all right. So, sometime in the fall there of '41, why, we decided we'd become engaged. We were going to make a two-some; we were going to make a go of it.

GRADUATION FROM CAMERON

I graduated in the spring of 1941 from Cameron. I went two and a half years there, and I started casting around, trying to find another school to go to. Well, I checked with Panhandle A&M up in Goodwill. I checked with OSU at Stillwater. I checked with OU in Norman. My dad knew a state representative, Mr. Crow, of Harmon County, so Mr. Crow got me a job at Norman.

A MEAN INCIDENT

The job at Norman meant room and board and laundry. I would be locked up with a hundred insane people from ten at night until two in the morning – that was quite a job.

I tried to study at night, but it was kind of hard to study. I'd get those guys to bed and tried to keep them in bed. There were about a hundred of them, and it was pretty difficult.

I remember one incident, and it was kind of a mean incident. One guy there came up to me and said, "Hey! I am going to kill you!"

I said, "Hey, look – I'm your buddy. I'm your friend. I've never done anything to you, and I don't intend to do anything to you." I tried to talk him out of it.

Well, about midnight one night, I was sitting there, trying to study. He slipped up behind me and grabbed me and tried to choke me. He was trying to choke me to death. Well, I was pretty strong then, and I managed to get a hold of him and take him to the floor, and I beat his head against the concrete floor until I knocked him unconscious. And I thought, "Well, that's the end of my job. I am going to be fired."

The superintendent called me in a day or two. He had heard about it. He asked me what had happened. I told him. I said, "Man, I didn't really want to hurt the guy, but he was trying to kill me, and I couldn't do anything else but." So he didn't fire me.

AT THE DOORSTEP OF THE WAR

EYE EXAMINATION

I came up in November for my Air Corps exams. I went to the Will Rogers Airfield, and there was a whole bunch of guys taking the exams at that time. I remember I did real good, and the doctor examining my eyes said to me, "Son, it's about noontime. You did so good on the rest of your exam, physical and all, and you are just not quite up to standard here on your eyes. But you've flunked your eye test. It looks like one of your eyes is checking out 20-30." And you are supposed to have 20-20 in both. He said, "Let's break for lunch and we'll come back and re-test you. I'll give you another chance at it, and maybe you can pass it."

I thought, "Okay." So, as we walked out of that room at lunchtime, I glanced up and I saw the number of the room. I ate lunch hurriedly – I gulped my lunch – then snuck back into that room, memorized that 20-20 line, and I could still tell you what it is: R, D, A, P, E, O, R, F, D, Z, N, B. So I passed the test.

NO EXEMPTION

I went to OU for one semester and I was taking chemistry. Come Christmastime, school was let out for Christmas vacation, and then it was going to take back up again in two or three weeks. In November of that year, I had come up to Oklahoma City to take my Air Corps examinations. I had tried to get the draft board chairman in Harmon County to give me an exemption. I had written to him and explained to him how I had three years in, and I was a chem major, and that would help the war effort, and all that sort of stuff. He didn't give me an exemption. I kind of blamed him then. But looking back, I can't blame him.

So, I thought, "Well, I sure don't want Infantry!" Inasmuch as I had a private pilot's license and knew how to fly the little, light planes, I came up to the city and thought I passed all of my exams. I went to see the dean there.

You can't imagine what a difficult time it was then in the fall of '41. This was before Pearl Harbor, but we could see World War II coming on. We could see there was nothing else but. So we were all in an uproar: "Shall we stay in school? Shall we go into the military? What shall we do?" I was twenty-three then.

Well, I went to the dean and I said, "Look, I passed my Air Corps exams. I would like to go home at Christmas and, if at all possible, I would like to spend a little time with my parents before I have to go into the military."

And he said, "I'll tell you what I'll do." He handed me a form and said, "You take this around to each of your instructors, and you get them to put down the grade that you have at Christmastime, and that will be your grade for the semester."

I said, "Okay." I was taking a rough course. I was taking calculus; I was taking physics, I was taking German. I was taking about four courses. I had passing grades, so the instructors wrote it down.

CALLED UP, AND MORE TESTS

In February of 1942, I was called. They called me. I had passed all of my exams, and they called me and said, you know, "Come. We've got a place for you." I went down to Houston, Texas, to Ellington Field.

Lo and behold, I got a notice from OU that I had received four incompletes! That rocked me! I thought, "Those dirty so-and-sos. They promised me I would pass with the grades I had at Christmastime." And they didn't follow through. That was my experience at OU! I still think that's part of why I don't like OU. They never gave me credit for those courses.

Then I was called back in for another eye test. I had been up to see Mable – she and I had got back together again – and when I came back down, I thought, "What?! I've already passed that blamed thing!" That caught me by surprise. I remember we had a long line, a long snaky line of men coming up and reading the eye chart. They had a partition there, and I started listening, and I thought, "Oh! That's not my line! That's a different chart!" My heart was sinking, and three or four people before I got up to read the chart, they changed charts again. Yeah! They put my chart on! So I whipped through that dude!

GETTING MARRIED AND NAVIGATION SCHOOL

Then I went into the Air Force. I went to Ellington for a little while, and then up to San Antonio.

Mable and I were married in May of 1942 while I was in navigation school at Kelly Field. I remember her coming down all by herself on the bus. Had a tin suitcase. Came down to get married. By ourselves. We got married in the Church of Christ there. She had a couple of friends there, a man and his wife, whom she had known in Tulsa, and they came to the wedding. I also had a best friend there, Clark Haws, who was my college roommate. Clark was at another base there. He was my best man.

So Mable and I got married on May 2, 1942. We wasn't supposed to. In those days, an air cadet was not supposed to be married. You were single when you went in. I remember one time I was out at the air base, and it came over the loudspeaker: "Lloyd Mitchell! Your wife wants you to call her!" Somehow or another, I don't know, I had to call. I'd been off on a flight or something, and that announcement scared me to death. I thought, "Your wife wants you to call her!" I thought they were going to kick me out, but nothing was said – ha-ha!

That was a good time there. It was hard work – navigation school – learning how to navigate, and how to, you know, tell a pilot where to go, what heading to take, and all of that. Two or three times I thought I was going to wash out. But Mable kept saying, "Nah – you're going to make it! That's what you say all the time – that you're going to bust out, but you've never busted out of anything yet, and you are not going to bust out of this!" Well, sure enough, I didn't bust out.

Mable had a place to live there in San Antonio. I was only making seventy-five dollars a month, and she worked at Joske's. I think there still is a Joske's in San Antonio. She worked at Joske's to help us make enough money to live on. I got to see her maybe once a week.

I remember one time trying to get a pass. It wasn't my time to take leave or get out, so I borrowed somebody else's. I've forgotten how we did it. Maybe we changed pass numbers or something. I borrowed one of my buddy's passes. They had photo identification on them. Going to the gate that night, I kind of hung my head so the guard couldn't see me. And I handed him my pass – my buddy's pass.

Then the guard said, "Hey, look at me." Then he said, "This is not you! You're Lloyd Mitchell!"

I said, "Yeah. How'd you know?" It was because he was a school buddy of mine! We had gone to school together. So, he let me pass. He said, "Here are the hours I am on the guard gate. You can come through any time you want to!" So, man, I had it made from then on!

Then I graduated from navigation school on July 4, 1942, and that was a great day, getting my second lieutenant's commission, because that meant a lot more money. It seems to me that I remember that we got something like $250 or $300 a month after graduating. That was a good salary. I went out to the bank, the Sam Houston Bank in San Antonio. They would loan money to fresh second lieutenants because they figured we were pretty good risks. I remember buying the officer suit. I got my uniform at Hart, Shaffner and Marx – they made the uniforms. Oh, it was pretty. I bought big trousers, and the blouse was kind of a drab olive-green. I bought bars – second lieutenant's bars – and I was so proud!

After that, I went to a base in Florida for a while. Mable didn't go with me because I didn't know how long I was going to be there.

SATURDAY, JULY 11, 1942—ELEVEN

State Men in Service

Congratulating Lieut. Lloyd B. Mitchell of Hollis, who gradu-ated Saturday from the Kelly field navigation school, where he received navigator's "wings" and a second lieutenant commission, is his brother, Yeoman Second Class John W. Mitchell, formerly of Hollis and now stationed in Washington, D. C. Also on hand for the graduation was Mrs. Lloyd B. Mitchell, shown in picture. Lieutenant Mitchell, who will be assigned to active duty with the army air forces, is now capable of directing the flight of giant bombers to any point in the world. He is the son of Mr. and Mrs. James W. Mitchell, Route 1, Hollis.

State Men in Service

Last Will and Testament

LAST WILL AND TESTAMENT

ALL of my estate I devise and bequeath to _MABLE GRACE MITCHELL_ (wife, ~~husband/daughter~~) for ~~his~~/her own use and benefit forever, and I here-by appoint _MABLE GRACE MITCHELL_____, my execu~~tor~~/trix without bond, with full power to sell, mortgage, lease, or in any way dispose of the whole or any part of my estate.

Dated ___July 27th___,194_2_.

Lloyd Brooks Mitchell
Signed in the presence of 3 witnesses.

Rt 1 Hollis Oklahoma
Residence.

Subscribed, sealed, published, and declared by _LLOYD BROOKS MITCHELL_, testator above named, as and for his/~~her~~ last will and testament in the pre-sence of each of us, who at his/~~her~~ request and in his/~~her~~ presence, in the presence of each other, at the same time, have hereunto subscribed our names as witnesses this _____27th_____ day of ___July____, 194_2_ at _____
Hendricks Field, Florida .
Place

Signature and addresses of 3 witnesses.
Name _Mae R. Fleming_
Address _Sebring, Fla._

Name _Leona M. O'Connell_
Address _Sebring, Florida_

Name _____
Address _B. Bayfill, Calif._

KIPLING'S ERROR CREW DIARIES

The following is a compilation of memoirs and combat diaries of five of the original ten crew members of Kipling's Error, the men of the 413th Squadron of the 96th Bombardment Group, 8th Air Force.

The diarists include: Lt. Lloyd Brooks Mitchell, navigator; Sgt. Richard (Dick) S. Haseltine, radio operator; gunner Sgt. Leo Lakey, gunner (whose diary was provided by his widow, Florence Lakey); tail-gunner Sgt. Joseph F. Kotlarz; and pilot Lt. Ruben ("Rube") Neie.

The diaries and memoirs are reproduced here in their entirety, with some minor edits for clarity. Some entries do not include exact locations or dates, but all are presented together in chronological order of events, until the crew split up. I was able to locate five diaries. It is quite possible that more are in existence and will someday surface and further add to the intense experience shared by these 10 men.

Included in this section are excerpts of interviews with Lloyd Mitchell, as conducted by his granddaughter, Amanda Mitchell, and his son, James Brooks Mitchell.

Also included are two excerpts from the book Snetterton Falcons II, the 96th Bombardment Group in World War II, edited by Robert Doherty and Geoffrey D. Ward, which describe two major battles involving the crew of Kipling's Error, as well as the personal account of one of those battles written by one of the Fortresses' co-pilots, Bernie Lay, as published in the Saturday Evening Post.

✤ After Florida, I went to Boise, Idaho, and that was where the 96th Bomb Group was formed. They brought in pilots, navigators, bombardiers, gunners, radio men and engineers and we all formed crews. After forming air crews, you stayed with your crew – throughout all your training, then when you went overseas, and when you fought combat – all with your crew.

I really had a good crew. This would have been the fall of 1942. Rube Neie was the pilot – he was from north Texas, from Cranfills Gap. Olie Asper was the co-pilot, from Oregon. Manuel Mendolson was a Jewish guy from Philadelphia. And then there was myself. That made up the four officers of the combat crew. Then we had six other guys: Lowell Nelson, who was the engineer; Ed White was the assistant engineer; and Leo Lakey, Joe Kotlarz and Steve Malinowsky were the gunners, and Dick Haseltine was the radio man. That makes up the ten.

We trained in several places: Walla Walla, Washington; Pocatello, Idaho; Rapid City, South Dakota; and Pyote, Texas. Do you know where Pyote is? It's at the end of the world – ha-ha! It didn't bother me too much. Some of the old boys were not used to the wind and the sand and the dirt – that's what you had in Pyote. And that wind and dirt would just blow – I thought it was natural, because that's what I was used to. But those guys from the East Coast – they complained bitterly. Their fate had landed them in Pyote!
— **_Lt. Lloyd Mitchell, navigator_**

My first ride in a bomber was as a passenger. As I remember it, it was a big roar – a few sinking feelings – as we'd suddenly drop or rise. But not bad at all. I decided radio operator was going to be all right. Gradually, we broke into operating. The hardest part was in learning to take to code, in spite of the terrific static.

Gradually, we were assembled into crews, and me and my pilot, Lt. Neie, a Texan, and proud of it; the tail-gunner, Joe Kotlarz; a Pole, Steve Malinowski, gunner, and our "praying" engineer. He prayed every time he was alone – either that, or read his Bible. Laughed at by the boys. I took my hat off to him and wished there were more like him.
— **_Sgt. Dick Haseltine, radio operator_**

DECEMBER 31, 1942

The ground seems to be getting softer instead of harder. We watch the temperature like hawks. But it doesn't seem to get any colder. Maybe a prayer would help.

Mrs. Stewart and her maid really are taking good care of their stranded U.S. flyers. We have a nice room with a bath all to ourselves. She even brought us a razor, toothbrush and toilet articles. But she forgot a very necessary item – a shaving brush.
— **_Lt. Ruben Neie, pilot_**

Note: My father explained that the incident above happened when they were taking a plane from Pocatello, Idaho, to Wright-Patterson field in Dayton, Ohio. They had to land in a cornfield because of engine trouble.
— **_Brooks Mitchell_**

JANUARY 1, 1943

New Year's dinner with Mrs. Stewart, and in the same old coveralls we ate Christmas dinner. But, let me tell you – the food was so good, I forgot about my clothes.

The flood is now 52 inches and is in my plane. The inbound engines will have to be changed because the water is up to them. All the instruments we took out of the plane are in safe hands, but the 200 yards of hip-deep, ice-cold water we had to wade through last night at 4 o'clock in the morning didn't help a thing. But we had to please the damn major from Patterson Field.

Attempted to load the damned plane on a river barge, but could not get a large enough barge. So, we just anchored her down, and when the water finally went down, we washed her out nice and clean with a power water pump on a riverboat. The river silt was two to four inches thick all through the B-17.

The flood is still up on January 7, when two U.S. flyers got word to return to Patterson Field, because the boys were fixing to move to my home state of Texas. Boy, we didn't lose a minute! I rowed across the Ohio River in a 12-foot boat to pick up our personal flying equipment, while

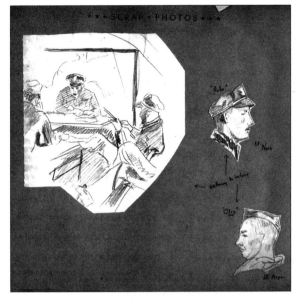

Sketches of Crew Members by Dick Haseltine

Asper packed out things we had on the Ohio side of Mrs. Stewart's house. We had quite a bit there because my pal, Lt. Shelton, sent our clothes and December mail, so we would have some clothes and word from home, even though we didn't get to enjoy the clothes but one day before we got word to return on the next train. I really owe Lt. Shelton – of Plainview, Texas – something, because our Christmas presents were also included on January sixth.

The last week we stayed with Mrs. Stewart, she provided us with civilian clothes. Boy, what a fit! But we really appreciated them.

A ride 17 miles in a pickup to a nearby train we loaded, and, ten hours later, we arrived at Patterson Field. It was late at night, but I just had to wake Shelton and let him see two happy boys on their return and, I must say, he was plenty happy to have me back to fight with again. But, as I went to bed, I could not sleep for thinking about the ass-chewing I was scheduled for in the morning when I reported to Col. Gilkie and Maj. Kasten.

Just as I thought, Maj. Kasten welcomed me home with really raking me over. Lt. Asper and I just stood at attention listening to him and Col. Gilkie. But we were very well-rehearsed on our answers, and they never crossed us up once. They tried their best to make it 'pilot error,' but we stuck together, and the cause remained the same (see report I wrote up for Records, which is in my mother's scrapbook). We finally were dismissed, and we left to gather our things to get started for our new field – Pyote, Texas. But you

can't realize how long we carried teeth-prints on our bottoms, and how much kidding we got from the boys as the "West Virginia Kids."
— *Lt. Ruben Neie, pilot*

JANUARY 9, 1943

✠ Finally on our way to Pyote. We were all delayed a day because we had our orders to report to Pocatello, Idaho – the field we came from. But our 96th Bomb Group was in Pyote. So, we finally got a telegram to report to Pyote. Lt. Shelton and I both kind of wanted to go back to Pocatello to see Genne and Pat, but I chose to go see my folks for a couple of days. We loaded an airliner to Dallas, Texas. Arriving at Oliver's, my brother at N.A.A., just a few minutes after he got to bed. He is a metalsmith with N.A.A. We woke him up and he took Lt. Shelton, my co-pilot Lt. Asper, and myself for a few days on the farm.
— *Lt. Ruben Neie, pilot*

JANUARY 14, 1943

✠ Lt. Neie returned from Dayton, Ohio, where he's been for the past couple of months, and we flew together – our whole crew. Sure seemed good! We, in a formation of five ships, buzzed the countryside. We zoomed down on one farmhouse, just as the old farmer was coming out of the barn with a pail of milk. He saw us coming, dropped his bucket, and scooted back into the barn. When we last saw him, he was still shaking his fist at us. Then we buzzed a herd of sheep, and they all started running around a pool of water – half one way, and half the other way – and came together – bang! It sure looked silly! During that drill, we smacked into the tops of about four apple trees and ran into a flock of birds. When we landed, we found the ball turret glass broken, and kindling piled up inside. They asked us, who gave us permission to plow with a B-17? More fun!
— *Sgt. Dick Haseltine, radio operator*

JANUARY 19, 1943

✠ Finally arrived in Cranfills Gap, and while we stayed to show off my hometown to the boys, I phone home to catch Mother and Dad before they were off for Sunday school. They had no idea that I was in any part of the country, but Mother never fails to recognize my voice.

For the last 50 miles, I have been having Shelton and Asper call my attention every time I say a cuss word, which the army really gives you as a bad habit, and what do you know? At Arthur and Hayden's house, I stopped, because Uncle Awalt and Hayden were in the road. The first question: "Did you get a Jap for me yet?" Being disappointed because we were still in the States, a quick reply: "Shit, no!" Boy, I was so embarrassed that I couldn't even apologize. (Did so by letter a month later.)

Mother and Dad did not go to Sunday school. I missed seeing Marvin because he had been in the Navy since December 9, 1942.

We didn't do much running around while at home, even though we did have Olive's car with a C-book. We spent most of our time visiting my kinfolk. One morning, we were squirrel hunting, but Shelton got sick and we had to come home. Uncle Oscar went with us, but he broke his gun and came home without telling us. So, we thought he had shot himself or something. But after looking for him for some time, we found him at home. Shelton was pretty sick to his stomach all that night.

The next day, we went to Hamilton to try to rent three Cubs and take Dad for a good ride. But the officers in charge would not let us fly any of his light planes. We were "qualified for B-17, four-engine Fortresses." That night, we three and Winnie Blume went to Waco, Texas. Shelton and Winnie went to a show, while Asper and I fixed a flat and made for some beer joints. The result was I thought the railroad was the highway, and I missed an opossum three feet from the end of my pistol three times.

Three days at home, and our time was up. What time? The three days was the same as AWOL. On January 13th, we left home and reported to our new field at Pyote, Texas, which is in almost the worst spot in Texas. That really gave the boys something to talk about. It was so dry and sandy there that rattlesnakes had a hard time making a living. However, the world's largest steaks were served at the Cactus Inn. Lt. Mendolson and I paid $4 for one steak which we split, and it took us about two hours to eat it! It was the largest, thickest and most tender steak either of us had ever seen or eaten.

Since I left the 96th at Pocatello on detached service for over a month, and had collected $180 per diem, the boys thought I had my gravy train. So, when I reported for duty at Pyote, I find my crew had been made Instructor Crew to train a bunch of new crews who had just joined us. This did not please any of us for several reasons. I knew if I were to instruct, we could not fly over my home, which was only 300 miles by air, because students are restricted to a 50-mile radius. But luck was with us, for we checked the new crews out within a week, and that put us back on combat status, which meant we could go anywhere we wanted, so long as we could get back in time.

So, then we flew over my house twice every week, and dropped a note inside a .50 caliber shell tied on a small parachute made from a rag and some string. We even buzzed at night with our landing lights shining in bedroom windows. One morning, we attacked home and Mrs. Sellers. Thought she was being bombed. Chuck Broyles got in his car and showed us a landing field in his oats patch. People had trouble smiling that morning, especially Uncle Oscar. Uncle Herman was run off his smokehouse, and his cows and mules almost tore the lot down. His goat left the place. I think Grandparents were scared we would hit a tree. Pedro Jones swears that we put our Fortress under his Hi-line. Merry Jones and Irwin were also afraid. But no one will ever know what a thrill it was to buzz the places I knew so well – every foot of the country. Arthur's house left his lot and Cranfills Gap was almost sucked up.

One day, a five-ship formation chased deer and coyotes all over West Texas. We also got Gail and Lamesa, Texas several times. I was a little afraid of Lamesa, but I knew the sheriff of Gail, and he told me to come back. In fact, he found me with a .45 pistol, which I had been looking for for a long time. He, Sid Reeder, is a swell Joe.

We also included Lt. Lloyd Mitchell, navigator's – my navigator's – house at Hollis, Oklahoma, in our extensive buzzing of towns in Texas and Oklahoma. I imagine we have enemies all over the two states. But to hell with them! We deserve a little fun!

I spent one of my 48-hour passes with Miss Jenny Smart of Lamesa, Texas. She's a very nice girl, but I cannot see any future in her. So, I guess I should really drop her off my life. But after going with a girl for three years, a fellow kind of gets attached to her, especially when they are good girls.

— *Lt. Ruben Neie, pilot*

JANUARY 20, 1943

Flew this afternoon with our crew. We went down to Lt. Neie's and buzzed his home. A pretty place. I didn't think Texas had any pretty places. On the way down, I drew a picture of a bomber on a cloth, and we made a parachute out of it with a .50 caliber bullet for a weight. Zoomed down and dropped it out of the tail into his front yard. We went down so close to the ground that I could wink at the neighbor's girl who was standing on the porch watching us. Visited all of his relatives in the same way and came home.

— *Sgt. Dick Haseltine, radio operator*

JANUARY 20, 1943

Parade on ramp today – wonderful things, these parades. Put on a nice clean uniform, step out into the wide open spaces, and, five minutes later, your eyes are full of dust, your pockets are full of dust, your clothes are full of dust… Ah! Texas! …Made an appointment with the dentist. Woe is me. Played football in the nice warm sunshine. Soaked in a lot of that Texas sun.

— *Sgt. Dick Haseltine, radio operator*

JANUARY 23, 1943

Marched in inspection parade today. Had to go out as a small platoon representing the 413th to be inspected by Col. Old. New regulation out that a member of each squad's combat crew has to guard his ship 24 hours. My time today – went on at noon to about sunset this evening. A second Louie came down and set up a camera and started taking pictures of the sunset across the ramp. I asked him if he had a permission pass, and he replied, "I'm Maj. Sot's photographer." I replied, "Have you a permit to take pictures here?" "No." So I asked him to go to the S-2 Office and get one. He got sore, and I picked his stuff up and went off to the ramp. Should have taken his plates, but I found out later that he was okay – still needed a permit, though. On four hours, off four hours. Not too bad. Received a letter from Sue Colligan of Portales, New Mexico, a girl who wrote to Marguite for a long time. It would be nice if we could meet.

— *Sgt. Dick Haseltine, radio operator*

FEBRUARY 25, 1943

✠ Almost everyone was getting a ten-day furlough, but by the time they came to Lt. Shelton and myself, there was only time left for one of us to go. So, we matched half-dollars in front of our C.O., Maj. S.J. Hand, and I won. But, as usual, my luck was against me. The day I was to leave, all leaves were canceled. Boy, were we mad! And, to top it off, if we wouldn't have had to fly a show formation for Mrs. Franklin D. Roosevelt, we would have gone home. But since it was for her, 19th Group, and for a newsreel, we just had to be flying the 27-ship formation, and when we landed is when we heard the bad news.

Listening in Lecture by Dick Haseltine

Lt. Mendolson had taken off the night before, and when we caught him by telegram to return, he was in Louisiana with a paid round-trip ticket to Pittsburgh. Boy, was he a handful to get along with. 24 hour passes, which came once every week, usually found my crew in Midland or Odessa hotels.

The Ace of Clubs of Odessa did not like Lt. Mendolson's and my presence one night. We had had a few beers, and when two MPs and Maj. Provasal and Maj. Manksel asked Lt. Mendolson and me to leave, we decided that we would stay a few minutes longer. But they got very eager to show their authority. While I was dancing, they jumped Lt. Mendolson again. He got sore and told the Major off. So, naturally, the Major charged him with sassing an officer, hitting an officer and being drunk. They had the books against him, and the next thing I knew, I was being dragged into a car, just to find my bombardier in the car in the hands of the Military Police. Naturally, our next stop was Odessa County Jail. It was time I began to talk, so I egged myself out of being locked up, but poor Mendolson woke up the next

Crew Killing Time in Pyote by Dick Haseltine

morning behind bars. Failing to keep him out, I decided to try to get him out. It was the least thing I could do, lying in a nice bed in the hotel just across the street from the jail. I took up the phone, called the jail, and asked for the marshal, giving him a big line that the lieutenant was on my crew and it was absolutely necessary for him to be released at once, for military reasons. Ten minutes passed, and Lt. Mendolson was in the room where he should have slept with me. We had a big laugh, but were worried when our commanding officer got word of it. By this time, we were expecting a six-day delay in the route to our next base, and we knew the worst that could happen to us for punishment was to cancel this leave.

About two weeks passed, and we heard nothing about our trouble at the Ace of Clubs. But, in the meantime, we B Flight had a good fight with C Flight one night. It was a friendly fight, but it turned out pretty rough. The two barracks were only 15 yards apart, and the fight started by throwing rocks against each other's building, but one of our shots went wild and hit "Pale Cat" – Lt. Miller – in a rather vital spot. Boy, then the fight really started. I saw a rock coming right toward Lt. Mendolson and I hollered for him to duck. He did, but he ran right into it. Boy, it really knocked the hell out of him. Now we had a manhunt on each side and the fight quieted down, until, all at once, Capt. McClatchy came over with a fire extinguisher and soaked our beds. He caught us off guard. All I could see was a tin bucket beside my bed. I picked it up and threw it at Mc. It hit him on the hand, cutting his hand. He retreated to his room. Lt. Mendolson followed him to see if he was hurt. Finding his finger cut, Mendolson persuaded him to come over to get some iodine on the cut. I saw him coming and, by that time, I had a fire extinguisher ready for him. The minute they stepped into my door, I let Mc have it. Before he could turn around, he was soaked. He ran back and got his extinguisher again. There we stood, pumping water into each other's faces. We both pumped until we gave out. The fight ended because of exhaustion. We were both soaked. Bed was a good place for the next eight hours.

The next 24 hours, I was airdrome officer. Just 30 planes landed in the meanwhile. It was my job to get them all transportation and, one time, two colonels came in and one refused to ride in my car, so he walked. The night before, Lt. McCall flew into the ground – undocked his plane – but none were killed. It is also the job of the A.O. to take care of all crack-ups. I had none.

'Notice for Lt. Neie to report to Col. Old immediately.' My first thought was, 'What have I done now?' But a good guess was it was the Odessa deal catching up with us. Just as soon as I could get my Class A uniform on, I struggled in as reported: "Lt. Neie reports as ordered." Yes – I was right. He knew the whole story, which was pushed by the C.O. of Midland Bombardier School, who demanded a court martial of both Lt. Mendolson and myself. Col. Old had me in a real sweat; however, he did say my good record was helping me out this time. I pleaded guilty and acknowledged the story he had against Lt. Mendolson. After chewing on me for a good hour, he dismissed me to go get Mendolson and return. He did, and I can still see Lt. Mendolson stand at strict attention for an hour, with sweat dropping from the end of each finger, saying, "Yes, sir," "No, sir," and "No excuse, sir" – the only three answers in the Army. Then, my turn came. The whole story was gone over again with both of us, and, finally, Lt. Mendolson and I were released until the next day. Knowing we were up for court martial, we did some worry-worry. But I did have a feeling I would be let off light. Next day, here we go. Same thing, all over again, but since we were scheduled for combat duty soon, Col. Old was good enough to let us both off with just a confinement-to-post until we left Pyote. Lucky we were, because only for one more week, while the other boys went to town each night, we stayed home, but we did drink enough beer and eat crackers and cheese. Our friends saw to it that we had a good supply.

At last, a six-day delay en route to our new post in Walker, Kansas, came on March 1, 1943. We had to call it a furlough because it was the first official time I had been home on leave. Being only 400 miles to Dallas by rail, I reported to Oliver, as usual, for his car to go the 100 miles I live from Dallas. He happened to be off duty, so he took me home, and we spent some time at home together, missing Marvin badly. But he was doing his part in the U.S. Navy.

"Ophelia Bumps" Artwork by Dick Haseltine

We spent our time fishing and hunting and visiting relatives. No girls left around our county. We didn't do much gallivanting. Almost every night, someone came to see us, and I can say I enjoyed seeing my old friends again, especially those I had scared so on my buzzing trips in my Fortress a few days before I got the chance to come home. Oliver had to go back to work before my six days were up. So I said goodbye to him. I enjoyed a couple of more days with Dad and Mother, and finally I had to leave again. They knew it was the last time they would see me before I came back from the war. But as I said goodbye at the train in Meridian, Texas, not a tear did I see, and, let me tell you, I really appreciated that. They helped me in every day in my war duties by being so brave at the end. My train pulled out, we waved, and my next stop was in Fort Worth, a short layover, and then I was on my way to Walker, Kansas.

— *Lt. Ruben Neie, pilot*

MARCH 6, 1943

✠ Arrived in Salina, Kansas and met up with four of the boys and, from there, we made a bus to Walker. The snow was about three inches deep, and no one came to meet us as was arranged. We had to walk about three miles across pastures and fields at two o'clock in the morning. Dark as hell, and, naturally, we had no warning when fences popped up in front of us.

Walker was supposed to be our last base in the U.S., so we caught lots of ground school and lectures. Here we also were assigned our finest ship as our own. It was a Vaga, but a very nice one, 12580. Ophelia Bumps was her name. So, after it was turned over to me, we spent most of our time cleaning and modifying her for combat duty. These are the things we had to do to it: put on 30 hours of flying time; swing Lt. Mitchell's and my compasses; check Lt. Mendolson's bomb-right hand-jacks; check P-143, T/Sgt. Haseltine's radio; check S/Sgt. White's top turret, as well as all guns; remove flammable, unnecessary equipment, and load the ship for a flight across the ocean. We also drew six .30 caliber rifles, four .45 automatic pistols, and one .45 submachine gun. With these, my own .45 pistol, and the 13 .50 calibers, on Ophelia Bumps my crew has 25 guns to take care of and use.

Russell, Kansas was our best place to go on pass. The Log Cabin was a pretty good honky tonk, and the Russell women were actually beautiful, especially Miss Winnie Hon and Miss Rozellie Mai (325 Maple). I would marry either one after I get back to the States, but I expect they will have something to say about it. Anyway, they were both nice and pretty. But, as usual, just as soon as you meet a girl – like that – the 96th always moves. This time to Salina, Kansas for our final touching up before we take off for England. Having a bad cold when we left Walker, I was really sick when we landed at Salina. So I reported to the hospital and that night, I broke out with the measles. Why couldn't I have had them while I was a kid! For four days and nights, I had a temperature of 104 degrees. I was a plenty sick boy, let me tell you! I stayed there for ten days, and then I got out too soon. But most of the boys had gone, and my crew was getting just as anxious to catch up with the fellows as I was.

— *Lt. Ruben Neie, pilot*

MARCH 6, 1943

✠ One incident I remember and, looking back on it, it was a sad incident. We were in Salina, Kansas, and that was the last air base in the U.S. before we went overseas. We were training there and hadn't been too long, and wasn't expected to stay too long. But whenever we got our shipping orders, we weren't allowed to talk on the telephone or tell anybody we were shipping out, or anything like that. I remember Mable had a room there, and had two or three false alarms, and she thought we were gone, and two or three days later, I'd show up. And then, finally, sure enough, we left for overseas. She told me later, "I stayed a whole week looking for you to come back, and you didn't come back. So I went home." And I thought about that. That was kind of sad. She was staying around, waiting on me to come back, and I didn't show up. It was hard. War was hard on the wives. It was as hard on the wives as it was on the men.

— *Lt. Lloyd Mitchell, navigator*

MARCH 10, 1943

✠ Left Salina in early evening for Walker in trucks. 'Twas cold, so we wore our zoot suits. People looked at us oddly. We sang to take up time – sang everything until we finished, and we were singing hymns. I like to hear the boys sing. It helps take the surface away and reveal what's really inside them. Quite a comfortable ride than we thought it would be. Arrived in Walker about midnight.

— *Sgt. Dick Haseltine, radio operator*

MARCH 25, 1943

✠ Flew from 1230 to 1545 today. Went down to Oklahoma to Tulsa and buzzed Lt. Mitchell's wife's house. Passed through some beautiful cloud formations. Had some trouble with a tooth that has been filled – seems that the change in pressure affects

Dead Reckoning Case of Lt. Mitchell

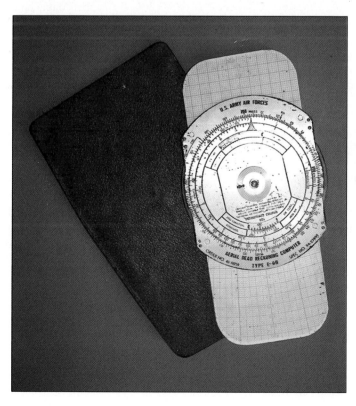

Aerial Dead Reckoning Computer used to navigate across the Atlantic as described on *pages 46-48*

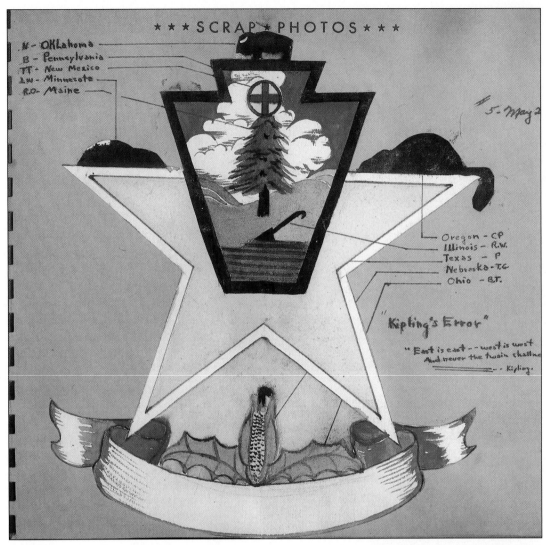

*** ★ SCRAP ★ PHOTOS ★ ***

N - OKLahoma
B - Pennsylvania
TT - New Mexico
LW - Minnesota
R.O - Maine

#5 - May 2

Oregon - CP
Illinois - R.W.
Texas - P
Nebraska - T.G
Ohio - B.T.

"Kipling's Error"

"East is east -- west is west
And never the twain shallne
- Kipling.

***Kipling's Error* Nose Art by Dick Haseltine**
(See page 56)

teeth so that they expand and contract. Mine suddenly grabbed hold and felt like a dentist was drilling a nerve – thought I'd pass out before we finally landed. Went to the dentist and he tapped, etc., and I felt nothing, so he referred to pull it.
— *Sgt. Dick Haseltine, radio operator*

MARCH 25, 1943

✠ Went out to the ship. Supposed to go up at 1:30 to get 35 hours before we start our cross-country. Went up on a local flight. The ship is in perfect condition. Flying time: 3:15. Sent Bernice a letter. Did not receive a letter from her today, nor yesterday.
— *Sgt. Joseph Kotlarz, gunner*

413th Bomb Group Patch

Went to town nearly every night and stumbled onto a small USO in a Presbyterian church. So I spent nearly every night there. Guess I'd always liked small things. We've named 5806 Ophelia Bumps, and I have a picture of a fat girl on the side of the nose. Lt. Neie is in the hospital with measles, so we are being held up here indefinitely!
— *Sgt. Dick Haseltine, radio operator*

MARCH 26, 1943

✠ Went out on a flight through Oklahoma. Sure had a lot of fun buzzing. Flying time: 4:35. Have to guard our own plane. Went on guard till 6:30 a.m.
— *Sgt. Joseph Kotlarz, gunner*

**96th Bomb
Group Patch**

MARCH 28, 1943

✠ Bernice may come in Salina by six o'clock tonight. Went to 8:30 mass here on the base. Also to confession. Did not to go communion on account of fasting.

Went on a flight for five hours via Kansas City and Topeka. Lt. Shelton our pilot. Flying time: 5.

Went down to the Union Bus Depot and met my Bernice. She sure looked nice. Went to the USO with her and we had a good time.

— *Sgt. Joseph Kotlarz, gunner*

MARCH 29, 1943

✠ Had a meeting today. Also had my teeth taken care of and had one filling put in on a molar. Checked in my helmet for one with earphones. Lt. Neie in the hospital on account of measles.

Met Bernice and had a perfect time with her, shopping and just messing around. Took her to supper, got her a Defense Bond ($100) in her name, and mother one ($100) with myself as co-owner. Sure had a nice time with my Bernice. Don't have time to get married on account of being on alert to move.

— *Sgt. Joseph Kotlarz, gunner*

MARCH 30, 1943

✠ Had a meeting this a.m. Bought a couple of towels, shoes, etc., at the PM. Called up Bernice, as she was supposed to leave on the 10:45 a.m. bus for Omaha. Just loafing around now. Bought a couple of pins and a wristband for Ma, Valeria and Cecelia. Called up home and talked with Ma, Shi, Valeria and Cecelia. Tom was not home.

— *Sgt. Joseph Kotlarz, gunner*

MARCH 31, 1943

✠ Came late at the combat crew meeting. Went out to the plane and checked, and put in life rafts. Loafing around, as usual. Went to mass now at the base. Sent Bernice a letter.

— *Sgt. Joseph Kotlarz, gunner*

APRIL 1, 1943

✠ Packing our ship for Gulf Hop. Our ship named Ophelia Bumps, with Ophelia a buxom-type girl, posed with a bomb in her right arm, ready to heave.

— *Sgt. Joseph Kotlarz, gunner*

APRIL 2, 1943

✠ Meeting at 8:00 a.m. Supposed to fire carbine on range; told to wait at end of meeting to get instructions for Gulf hop.

Gulf hop canceled on account of change of plans, and meeting at 1:00 p.m. Received letter from Stanley and Bernice. Told we are to leave as soon as possible for POE.

Tying everything down and getting set for leaving. We may wait for Lt. Neie or go with one of Staff Officers and meet Lt. Neie later.

Got a carbine issued to me. Sure nice. Better than the rifles we had to turn in at Walker.
— *Sgt. Joseph Kotlarz, gunner*

April 2, 1943

✠ Were all ready to take a hop to Louisiana out over the Gulf to Florida when we were called into operations, and Col. Old made the announcement we all wanted to hear: "This is it." We went to get ready to leave immediately, but as our pilot was in the hospital, we were to wait. And our destination was Maine!!!!
— *Sgt. Dick Haseltine, radio operator*

April 3, 1943

✠ Checking up on our entire plane. Cleaning tail-guns and getting equipment shortage.

> **Addresses:**
> Pvt. Stanley W. Kotlarz
> Class Number 64
> Co. H. 3rd Platoon, 1st PTR
>
> Francis J. Kotlarz, Sea 1/C
> U.S.S. Colorado, Box 6B
> c/o Fleet Postmaster
> San Francisco, California

Plane all gassed and serviced with oxygen. Ready to leave at any time. Lt. Neie still in the hospital.

Called Bernice up and she will come in tomorrow, with Ma, maybe.
— *Sgt. Joseph Kotlarz, gunner*

April 4, 1943

✠ Went to 8:30 mass at the base. Met Bernice at the Union Bus Depot. Ma didn't come because Valeria was sick.
— *Sgt. Joseph Kotlarz, gunner*

April 5, 1943

✠ Sure had a nice time with Bernice last night.

A new crew came up and almost took our ship, Ophelia Bumps. Lt. Neie out of the hospital, so we are getting ready to leave, and one reason the new crew didn't get our ship.

Went downtown to see my Bernice. Had a lovely time saying goodbye. We both were rather upset by it. Gave her $75 for a Defense Bond in my name, with Ma as beneficiary.

Left at 5:15 for the East Coast. Unable to land at Syracuse, NY on account of bad weather. This was 10:55 Central War Time.
— *Sgt. Joseph Kotlarz, gunner*

✠ We were in our barracks today waiting for word to move, when in walks a lieutenant and his crew and informs us that he and his crew are taking Ophelia on. We were dazed for a minute – all of our work gone to waste. I had a sentiment for her. So, we woke up and hurried around and got Lt. Neie out of the hospital – he practically forced his way out. We quickly packed. Got a jeep driver (nice-looking girl) and went into town to pick up some laundry, telegraph Jinny, and allow Joe and Lt. Mitchell to say goodbye to Bernice (Joe's girl) and Lt. Mitchell's wife. Finally got everything straightened out and left Salina behind at 1700 with our nose pointed at Syracuse, New York. It was a nice flight until we passed over Lake Erie where we ran into some snow. The nearer we got to Syracuse, the worse the storm got. At 2400, we circled Syracuse in the snow and radioed in for landing instructions. They replied that we were to proceed to Middleton, PA to land where visibility was better.
— *Sgt. Dick Haseltine, radio operator*

✠ So the day I got out, we flew to Middletown, Pennsylvania. When my crew knew I was out of the hospital, they immediately loaded the ship, we packed and we were off to the races. I was as weak as a kitten, so I let Lt. Asper be pilot and I was co-pilot. My engineers, T/Sgt. Nelson and S/Sgt. White, flew about half of the 1,200-mile trip, which took us nine hours to make. We were supposed to land in Syracuse, New York, but when we got there, the field was closed in. So we were directed by radio to proceed to Middletown, Pennsylvania.

By the time we reached Middletown, it was 1:30 in the morning, and then it took us about 30 minutes to locate the field. As we were on our final approach, our ship hit three trees that were 12 inches in diameter. It knocked our right engine, wing and flag all to hell. The ship was almost uncontrollable, but Asper and I finally got her straight again. Asper and I changed seats and I made a higher approach and landed okay. The wing and Number 4 engine had pieces of wood in them. No one was hurt, but part of the crew was scared to death. S/Sgt. White went back to the radio room, and when someone asked him what was wrong, all he could say was, "Give me a cigarette." Our landing lights out and we did not know about the trees, and that is the only reason we hit them. I was sick by this time (again), and the cold night air was not doing me any good. We were put up for the remainder of the night. The flight clogged my ears, and the four days we were stranded, I was pretty sick, but I had too much work to do to report to the hospital.
— *Lt. Ruben Neie, pilot*

APRIL 5, 1943

✠ We went to Presque Isle, Maine, for our jumping-off spot. We were flying our B-17. The night we left Salina, we were headed toward Presque Isle and ran into some real bad weather. We were supposed to go to one base that night, but it was socked in with clouds and weather. So, while we were in the air flying, they radioed us to go to another base – said we couldn't get into where we wanted to go. So, we had to go to Harrisburg, Pennsylvania, the alternate base, and I remember Rube calling down, telling me to give him a heading for Harrisburg. We had a little hard time finding it. The weather wasn't too good. Harrisburg was built right on the banks of the Susquehanna River, and right in the valley of the Susquehanna. Rube had been sick. He had been in the hospital very recently. He wasn't feeling too good at all, so he let Olie, the co-pilot, do the landing. We were coming into the air base there at Harrisburg, and there were big, high towers on the right. It looked like generating towers. Olie was a little nervous about them, and he was watching the towers to be sure he missed them. Well, he forgot to watch the runway, and there were some trees right on the edge of the runway – I could see Old Olie coming into those trees, and that thing was wobbling. I was sitting in that nose, watching everything. Olie come in and he sawed off a bunch of trees with the plane and, I remember, hearing those wings crack through the trees – I thought, 'Man, we are gone this time!'

"Ophelia Bumps" End by Dick Haseltine

The old plane squabbled and lurched, and kind of buckled, and then Rube grabbed the throttle and kicked all four forward throttles, and the plane managed to pick up flying speed again – the engines on the right were crippled, but they were still functioning – and we went around and come back around and landed.

Old Rube was a good pilot. I mean, he never lost his cool. I never saw him lose his cool. He was the type of guy who didn't push the panic button. You know, that's the way flying is. The kind of flying we were doing, everything could be roses one time, and the next minute, you just end up in a terrible predicament. But Rube could always think. He could always think.

But that was the first one we lost right there. There were logs stuck in the two right engines, and the right wing was torn. So we lost a plane there. We had to pick up a new plane. They sent a new plane in for us. They had to get a whole new wing and two new engines for that one. That was a very close call.

— *Lt. Lloyd Mitchell, navigator*

APRIL 6, 1943

✠ Landed at Middleton, Pennsylvania after crashing on the first approach. Entire right wing wrecked. Engines not harmed – not even an oil leak. Lucky no one was hurt, but it looked bad.

Woke up and told to report to Lt. Neie at the hangar. Arrived at Middleton at 2:30 a.m. Told Ophelia would not be ready for ten days.

Middleton is sort of an old town. Towns on the East Coast are so close together, it seems to me you can step from one to the other.

Flying time: 9:30 hours. Being as we are on per diem pay, we (the crew) moved into Harrisburg, PA on account of bad living conditions on the base. Dick, Nelson, Leo and myself got a room together at the William Penn Hotel. Steve and White got a room on the next floor.

— Sgt. Joseph Kotlarz, gunner

✠ We would have liked to settle there, but orders are orders, so off we went toward Pennsylvania. We were out of the snow by the time we reached Middleton, but it was really dark – pitch black. We flew for nearly an hour looking for a field, which was poorly lit. Our bombardier and assistant engineer were all in the radio room with me, as we finally sat silent, as usual. No guess as to whether landing would be good or not – everything seemed so dark during our approach – especially at night – no engine idling, and our subdued minds started thinking of a bed and sleep when, suddenly, engines roared and – whammo – we struck something. Full-throttle up and she was flying like a duck. Nelson came back and Eddie went up front. I had blown in the back as we let down, and Lt. Neie seen the trees at the end of the runway and had buzzed one of them. Lt. Neie put her in for a second try, and it was a rough but safe landing.

I don't think any one of us wasn't scared. I know, as we came in for a second try, everyone had his fingers crossed and breathed a little prayer.

We taxied up to a hangar, clambered out and looked her over. Number 4 engine was smashed – picked up a big hunk of wood out of it, and there was a huge hole between Number 3 and Number 4 engines. The skin under the wing was ripped and the edge was badly torn. It was a wonder (hats off to Lt. Neie) that we walked away from that landing, and I think maybe it was so because my little sister back home prayed every night that no harm come to "Dickie and his crew." Checked out bedding and slept.

— Sgt. Dick Haseltine, radio operator

✠ The next morning – early – we unloaded the ship and turned it over to the depot for repair. Estimated time for repair was ten days. But on the fourth day, we received another ship from Salina, Kansas, which we traded our old one for. So, we loaded her up and were almost ready to continue en route, but since Lt. Mendolson lived close, he was at home in Pittsburgh. He only got to stay one night and we called him back, since we had a new ship. Lt. Mitchell had a brother in Washington who he was going to see, but did not get time.

— Lt. Ruben Neie, pilot

APRIL 7, 1943

✤ Went out messing around and had a fairly good time last night. Woke up feeling fine and dandy. Went out looking over the town. Saw the state capital. Visited St. Patrick's Cathedral. Saw coal being dredged from the Susquehanna River. Saw a bridge designed by Ralph Madejski.

Called out to Middleton Air Depot to inspect new plane replacing Ophelia, and went to Harrisburg to look at new plane, serial number 42-4072.

Went with Dick and Leo and visited the National Catholic USO. Danced and went swimming.
— *Sgt. Joseph Kotlarz, gunner*

APRIL 8, 1943

✤ Had a perfect time last night. Woke up and got ready to go to base and pack up in the new plane.

Middleton Air Base has small runways with trees and hills on both sides. One reason we crashed in trees here was on account of no landing lights. On the trip from Middleton to new camp, saw New York, Boston, and quite a few large towns.

Left Middleton Air Base for Mitchell Field, New York. Saw a portion of New York and a heavy cruiser, and some destroyers in New York Harbor. Also, a blimp arrived from Mitchell Field, New York. Flying time: 5 hours. Left Mitchell Field.
— *Sgt. Joseph Kotlarz, gunner*

✤ We went up to Presque Isle, Maine and spent a little while there. Then we had to ferry the planes across the North Atlantic.
— *Lt. Lloyd Mitchell, navigator*

✤ On the fourth night, we were ready to go to Presque Isle, Maine. We stopped at Mitchell Field, New York for gas, and continued on to Presque Isle the same night. Maine was covered with snow and ice. T/Sgt. R.S. Haseltine, my radio man, lived in Dexter, Maine, so we gave his home and girlfriend a goodnight buzzing. We arrived safely at Presque Isle about one o'clock in the morning. We were supposed to be there only a short time, but several things happened that kept us there about two weeks – namely, engine trouble, hospital for myself and Asper, and bad weather.
— *Lt. Ruben Neie, pilot*

APRIL 9, 1943

✤ Arrived last night at Presque Isle, Maine at 10:00 p.m. Woke up and looked over the camp. A lot of snow here and plenty of natural camouflage – pine and birch trees plentiful. Sent Bernice a letter. First Lt. Clark Gable on the field here. Who did I meet here but Walt Maryanski, with whom I was drafted. Didn't do very much of anything. Dick Haseltine, our radio operator, got a break and went home.

First time I saw a PBT Catalina flying boat. To me, it looks like one of the Wright Brothers'.

Went out with Walt Maryanski and drank beer at the PX. Walt still a private.
— *Sgt. Joseph Kotlarz, gunner*

✠ My ears giving me hell again. I reported to the hospital for another seven days, and Lt. Asper was having a little trouble which required a drug that kept him grounded for ten days.
— *Lt. Ruben Neie, pilot*

April 10, 1943

✠ Woke up feeling bad after drinking beer last night. Snowing here now. Lt. Neie ordered to the hospital on account of ear infection. Lt. Asper ordered to hospital. Our ship grounded on account of not complying to T.O. Order.

Still snowing here, and hard, too. Went to confession. Now in the base chapel. Will go to early mass tomorrow.
— *Sgt. Joseph Kotlarz, gunner*

April 11, 1943

✠ Went to 7:30 a.m. mass and communion and offered it up for my honey. Ate breakfast at the PX. Saw Clark Gable this a.m. Went out and drew carbine ammunition.

Supposed to start on a 50-hour inspection on our plane. Plane has 73 hours on it and has never had an inspection pulled. Started on our 50-hour inspection.

Worked on our 50-hour inspection and did not even write to my Bernice.
— *Sgt. Joseph Kotlarz, gunner*

April 12, 1943

✠ Snow and sleet here. Woke up late on account of working till 3:00 a.m. on plane. Sent my Bernice and the family a letter.

Sure a lot of transports on this field, mostly C-47s and C-54s. C-54s are the biggest ships I've seen. C-47s are two-motored transports. C-54s are four-motored transports, with a dual-wheel landing gear (tricycle).
— *Sgt. Joseph Kotlarz, gunner*

APRIL 13, 1943

✠ Snow and sleet here again. Sent Bernice a gold compact and an Air Corps emblem bracelet and a gold cross. Sent Ma an Air Corps locket and chain, and cross and a medal. Sent an airmail letter home and one to Bernice.

> **Addresses:**
> Ancel A. Love, Jr.
> 402 East Main
> Ardmore, Oklahoma
>
> T/Sgt. Joseph R. Beljan
> 13959 Tudler Avenue
> Detroit, Michigan DA-5802

— *Sgt. Joseph Kotlarz, gunner*

APRIL 14, 1943

✠ Woke up early this morning. Snow and sleet here again. Sure a lot of different pilots around here. Royal Air Force, Air Transport Command, and Royal Canadian Air Force represented here. Sent Bernice a letter. Went out to the plane and checked. Sure cold here, and getting colder. More colonels and lieutenant colonels here than ever.

— *Sgt. Joseph Kotlarz, gunner*

APRIL 15, 1943

✠ Nice weather here this a.m. A perfect spring morning. Most of the bunch scheduled to leave this noon. Sent Bernice a letter. Borrowed $20 from Lt. Neie. Our oxygen system checked and found okay.

Most of the gang from the 96th left today, with the exception of a ship from each squadron. Ours was the only one out of the 413th due to Lt. Asper being grounded.

— *Sgt. Joseph Kotlarz, gunner*

APRIL 16, 1943

✠ Today is the day I am supposed to call home (7:00 p.m.). Bernice is supposed to be there. Worked and refueled the ship. Cold here today. Checking upper turret and installing radio ammunition box. Most of the regular permanent parties here have combination coats (Mackinaws) and parkas, on account of the cold and snow.

Called up "long distance" to home. Took 40 minutes for call. Cecelia and Valeria home. Bernice not there ($4.80).

— *Sgt. Joseph Kotlarz, gunner*

APRIL 17, 1943

✠ Snowing here again this morning. Presque Isle is a regular sort of imitation of a Western town. Very few paved streets here. Most of the people here have bad teeth due to shortage of calcium and iron in water. First thing you notice on the people are the bad teeth. Went downtown to Presque Isle. Bowled a few games and went to the show at the USO. Had a swell time tonight.

— *Sgt. Joseph Kotlarz, gunner*

✠ Lt. Asper and I both finally got well, and then the weather got bad, so all we could do was to take advantage of it and spent some time in Canada. And so, we did stay several days just loafing around. We had dates with Canadians who couldn't even say 'yes' and 'no' in English. They spoke French, but we got along fine. I wish I could describe the dates my ball-turret man, S/Sgt. Malinowski, had in Canada. They were really beauties! Oh, yes! Take our guess.

When I found out we would be here for some time, I gave S/Sgt. Haseltine a chance to go home, since he lived about 100 miles away and had not had a chance to go home the 18 months he had been in the Army. His people really think lots of me for giving him the chance. However, the other boys got a bit peed off, because they had to pull a 100-hour inspection on our plane, and Haseltine was at home having a good time. But I am glad he got to go. By the way, he got engaged on the trip to a very pretty girl. When he left, I told him to stay until I called him to return. So he got about 12 days' leave.

Capt. Clark Gable was living in the room next to mine while at Presque Isle. He is rather old-looking and pretty gray-headed. Someone tipped us off that you could not buy bourbon in England, so we purchased a case to take along.

— *Lt. Ruben Neie, pilot*

APRIL 18, 1943

✠ Went to confession and communion this morning, and had breakfast with Dick, Lowell and Leo. Supposed to leave today, but on account of bad weather between here and Gander, Newfoundland, we're stuck for another day. A B-26 Martin outfit came into our barracks last night.

Left for town with Leo. Went to concert with Leo and Dick, and met three girls from the Teachers Normal School. USO Anniversary Program here, and we sure had a good time. Went out to dinner with Leo and the two girls. Later, went out bowling and really had a swell time.

— *Sgt. Joseph Kotlarz, gunner*

APRIL 19, 1943

✠ Twenty-percent additional for foreign service. Lt. Neie called up and told us (crew) to be ready to take off. Went to hangar number four for briefing. Packing ship and getting ready. Entire crew goes to Finance and collected per diem $27, except Eddie and Steve, who are AWOL. Starting today, a 20% increase in pay for foreign service.

Getting all set to take off and the prodigals arrive, Eddie and Steve. Lt. Neie takes them over to collect per diem. At approximately 2:00 p.m., left for Gander, Newfoundland.

Froze coming here; no heater. Arrived in Gander at 5:05 p.m., averaging over 200 mph (tail winds). Difference in time here: one and one-half hours. Newfoundland sure nice and full with heavy, dense timber all over.
— *Sgt. Joseph Kotlarz, gunner*

APRIL 19, 1943

Today I first saw foreign land. Left Presque Isle, Maine at 1800 BCT. Arrived Gander, Newfoundland at 2100. Bad ears, and immediately in the hospital.
— *Lt. Lloyd Mitchell, navigator*

Canadian money is very similar to Newfoundland money, which was to be our next stop. And finally, the weather cleared up and we were off on April 19th across the Gulf of St. Lawrence, which was frozen over a stretch of 545 miles of ice. It took us three hours to make the trip. We thought it was cold at Presque Isle, but at Gander in Newfoundland, it was really cold. It looks as if I catch all the hospitals, but every time I go up, my ears swell up, because I got out too soon at Salina.

So, just as soon as we landed, Mitchell and I reported to the hospital with bad ears. Neither one of us was really sick, but our ears were in bad shape. As usual, they always put you to bed.
— *Lt. Ruben Neie, pilot*

From Presque Isle, Maine we went to Gander, Newfoundland, and from Gander Lake, we were going to ferry the planes across the North Atlantic. I remember I was in the hospital there at Gander Lake. I had a bad cold and we were flying altitude. Those old 17s, they didn't have compression. They were just open. So, flying altitude with a head cold is not recommended, and I spent two or three days or more there with ear problems.
— *Lt. Lloyd Mitchell, navigator*

APRIL 20, 1943

Have to pull guard here on ship all 24 hours. Steve started last night. This camp is a 50/50 position. One side is Canadian and the other side is American. CWACs here, too (Canadian Women's Army Corps). Submarine Patrol Division here, composed of PBYs, B-24s and B-17s, plus Pursuit Patrol.

Fixed our heater and all okay. Lt. Neie and Lt. Mitchell grounded for ten days on account of ears. It looks like we'll be here for quite a while. Went out to the Canadian side and inspected it. Had a nice time. Nelson on guard tonight.
— *Sgt. Joseph Kotlarz, gunner*

✤ Canada and Maine were both covered with about eight feet of snow and the nights were plenty cold. Pine trees and tall hills and clean lakes really make a picturesque country-side. In places, the snow would drift as deep as 30 to 40 feet.

Mitchell and I spent most of our time in the hospital playing Chinese Checkers and reading books. We were rather lucky to get to stay in the hospital because we had clean sheets to sleep on, meals in bed, and pretty American nurses who washed our backs every night with rubbing alcohol. The boys who stayed in the barracks did not have sheets.

— Lt. Ruben Neie, pilot

✤ A dreary day in the hospital. Read "All Cats are Gray." Thinking of Mabs and Brookum.

— Lt. Lloyd Mitchell, navigator

April 21, 1943

✤ Watched four "Hurricanes" take off in formation. Lt. Asper and Lt. Mendolson in town 70 miles away. Woke up late today.

Worked on the ship, just for a while today. Left Eddie, Dick, Lowell and Leo working on ship. Steve and I went to the hospital to see Lt. Neie and Lt. Mitchell. Both feeling quite well and expect to be released in 36 hours.

This camp is supposed to have been built by Germans. On account of recent sabotage, we have to guard our own planes.

Got a surprise going out on guard. Met Lt. Shelton and his crew here. Our crew figured they had gone over already. They stopped at Stephenville, Newfoundland for an engine change.

— Sgt. Joseph Kotlarz, gunner

✤ Ho-hum. Another day in the hospital. Read another book. Wrote Mabs a letter.

— Lt. Lloyd Mitchell, navigator

✤ Lt. Neie and Lt. Mitchell are in hospital. Ear trouble, so we won't be leaving for a while. Went over to Canadian side of post – big recreation hall and swimming pool. Went swimming with Nelson. Not bad. Canadian boys are a nice lot. Also some Highlanders here and some CWACs.

— Sgt. Dick Haseltine, radio operator

✤ S/Sgt. Malinowski also spent seven days in the hospital with a bad case of tonsillitis. Lt. Asper and Lt. Mendolson, knowing we were stranded for about ten days, took off for Cornerbrook. They stayed until they ran out of money and finally returned.

— Lt. Ruben Neie, pilot

APRIL 22, 1943

✠ Holy Thursday. Was on guard last night and just got in barracks. Steve went to hospital today on account of bad ears and cold.

Sure a lot of foreigners here on this field (civilians). Plane in tip-top shape and all okay, except oxygen.

Visited Steve, Neie and Mitch at the hospital. Went to Holy Thursday services at the recreation hall on the Canadian side and heard a French sermon.
— *Sgt. Joseph Kotlarz, gunner*

✠ Another day in the hospital. I'm tired. Maybe get out tomorrow. Read another book.
— *Lt. Lloyd Mitchell, navigator*

APRIL 23, 1943

✠ Good Friday. Loafed around today. Sure a lot of different outfits represented from the Canadian Army. Seems as if the different regiments wear different uniforms. The RCAF wears a blue outfit. Other parts of the Canadian Army wear a gray and an OD outfit. Looks as if we'll have to spend Easter Sunday here on account of Steve, Neie and Mitch.

Went to USO show this evening after church services. After watching the planes at the end of the runway, I can imagine what a thrill people get when we buzz them and hedge-hop. Went to the Station of the Cross and Good Friday services. Planes ("Flying Fortresses") leaving for the European Sector. Sure a sight, leaving a minute apart.
— *Sgt. Joseph Kotlarz, gunner*

✠ Still in the hospital. Wow! Read another book. Wrote a letter to Mabs and Brookum. Sure wish I could hear from them. It's awful lonesome when you can't get a letter from there.
— *Lt. Lloyd Mitchell, navigator*

✠ While I was in the hospital, one of the pilots, Capt. Fulton, bumped out one of his brake expansion tubes. So he asked me to give him one of mine, since I couldn't get out for some time.
— *Lt. Ruben Neie, pilot*

APRIL 24, 1943

✠ Holy Saturday – end of Lent. Fasted all morning; not even breakfast. Lt. Neie out of the hospital today. Lt. Mitchell won't be released until Monday.

Gave Capt. Fulton's plane our expander tube (brakes), since we won't leave for a couple of days, and we can wait for a new expander tube by transport.

Loafed around – best part of the day. Visited Steve this afternoon. Rest of the fellows who were left behind are grounded on account of bad weather. Seems as if only a day in a week is okay on that Transatlantic Hop. Capt. Ford and Lt. Shelton's crew left yesterday. We're the only ones left out of the 413th, although there are a few more crews out of the 96th Group.
— *Sgt. Joseph Kotlarz, gunner*

Another day in the hospital. Another book read.
— *Lt. Lloyd Mitchell, navigator*

Even after I got out of the hospital, I went back every day and spent most of my time with Mitchell.
— *Lt. Ruben Neie, pilot*

April 25, 1943

The Resurrection or Easter Sunday

Easter Sunday – Went to confession and mass this morning at the base theater, where the Americans have their services. Served at mass this morning. Capt. Sullivan (Chaplain) had 7 o'clock mass. Quite a few bases here in Newfoundland, the two best being Gander and Goose.

Addresses:
James D. Blake, CQ
420 W. Pierce, J-24949
Houston, Texas

Frank L. Tivavi
c/o Dixieland Hotel
Detroit, Michigan
— *Sgt. Joseph Kotlarz, gunner*

Easter Sunday! Still in the hospital. Read some, and wished that I could be with Mabs and Brookum. Wrote to Dad and Mom.
— *Lt. Lloyd Mitchell, navigator*

Lt. Neie out of hospital. Got another ship. Steve in from our ship. Wish we could get going. Maybe his crew pulled in and pushed out this weekend. Pulled guard. Slept in ship. Easter Sunday. Missed church first time in my life. Couldn't be helped, though.
— *Sgt. Dick Haseltine, radio operator*

April 26, 1943

Lt. Asper and Lt. Mendolson came back from Cornerbrook, where they were since we came here. Steve and Mitchell still in hospital.

Address:
Capt. Walter E. Flagg
430 22nd Street
Richmond, California

A year ago today, I left S. Omaha City Hall for the Army.
— *Sgt. Joseph Kotlarz, gunner*

APRIL 26, 1943

✠ Still in hospital. Got a pass and went swimming and played tennis. Should have written a letter. I'll get out tomorrow. I love Mabs and Brookum.
— *Lt. Lloyd Mitchell, navigator*

APRIL 27, 1943

✠ One year in the U.S. Army. Supposed to work on our plane today, but unable to do so, since our brakes (expander tube) hasn't arrived from the States. Lt. Mitchell discharged from hospital.

A year ago today, I was sworn in, and at 11:00 p.m., left for Fort Leavenworth.
— *Sgt. Joseph Kotlarz, gunner*

✠ Hooray! I'm out of the hospital! Expander tubes gone, and Malinowski in hospital, so we can't leave.
— *Lt. Lloyd Mitchell, navigator*

✠ Lt. Mitchell out of hospital. He and I played indoor tennis over in the Canadian Rec Hall. Played against two Canadian boys. Beat easily. Went swimming.
— *Sgt. Dick Haseltine, radio operator*

✠ Even though snow and ice covered the ground, we went swimming every day after we got out of the hospital in an indoor pool.
— *Lt. Ruben Neie, pilot*

APRIL 28, 1943

✠ Slept till 11:00. Wrote a letter to Mabs & Brookum. Went to Atlantic briefing.
— *Lt. Lloyd Mitchell, navigator*

✠ On guard last night. Just got up and ate breakfast. Went up to the library this morning.

Went out hiking with Lt. Neie, Lt. Mitchell, Lakey and Dick. Went out by Lake Gander and tested our carbines, and they're really the guns. It's really nice here on the hills near the lake – heavy timber (birch and pines) and snow. Four and five feet deep in certain timbered spots. Really had a swell time.

— *Sgt. Joseph Kotlarz, gunner*

APRIL 29, 1943

✠ Shucks, I guess I slipped up.

— *Lt. Lloyd Mitchell, navigator*

✠ Lt. Neie and Lt. Mitchell, Joe, Leo and I went out into the woods down by a large lake near here and practiced shooting. First time I had shot my carbine. She's a sweet gun. We shot at hunks out in the lake. Took off through the woods coming back, and darned near got mixed in the deep snow. Had fun, though. Read in the library all evening.

— *Sgt. Dick Haseltine, radio operator*

Passin' Time at Gander by Dick Haseltine

✠ Nothing doing today. Brake expander tube has not come in as yet. Our plane developed motor troubles, so the ship is being put in a hangar. Setting in new plugs in engine Number 4 and a new carburetor.

— *Sgt. Joseph Kotlarz, gunner*

APRIL 30, 1943

✠ Packed all our baggage as neatly as we could, then tied it down securely. We worked on it all morning and noon, up until take-off time. B-17s took off from this field one minute apart, flying singly across the ocean. About 40 planes took off all together. We took off at 1945. Circled the field several times, then headed toward the east. I flew in the nose with Lt. Mitchell and Lt. Mendolson. We flew about 2,000 feet above the ocean for quite some time. We saw a large group of icebergs one hour after leaving Newfoundland. After that, we saw quite a few more large ones floating about.

— *Sgt. Dick Haseltine, radio operator*

✠ Got the plane out of the hangar and found out that the brake expander tube came in, so we took it back in the hangar.

Malinowski discharged from the hospital.

White and Nelson working on brakes. Leo and myself changing plugs on Number 1 engine. Dick screwing up, as usual. Bunch briefed for flight to Prestwick, Scotland. Getting all set to leave. Packing ship and baggage.

Left with about nine other planes. Left the east coast of Newfoundland at 8:00 p.m. (1-1/2 hours ahead of Central Time). Left Gander AAB for Prestwick, Scotland.
— *Sgt. Joseph Kotlarz, gunner*

APRIL 30, 1943

✠ Packed our stuff hurriedly, at chow, set our watches 2:30 ahead, and at 2142 GMT, we took off and nosed out over the Atlantic toward England. Our first "make it or else" flight. Approximately ten hours later, we flew the ship over Ireland, and continued on to Prestwick, Scotland.
— *Sgt. Leo Lakey, gunner*

✠ S/Sgt. Malinowski got out of the hospital the day we left Gander. It finally worked out that Capt. Fulton and I both left Gander at the same time, and I got another brake installed about three hours before take-off. It was lucky, but I was real glad to leave Gander.

We took off on April 30 about 30 minutes before sunset for a night trip across the ocean for England. Our load amounted to 60,000, which took 2,700 gallons of gas to pull us across. The weather was bad, and we had to fly at 18,000 feet on instruments most of the night.

I was in bad need to use the relief tube before we landed, so I finally went back into the bomb bay and was so paining that when I started, I found someone had beat me to it and had not drained it, and the urine had frozen in the bend of the tube. Naturally, it ran over and I was in a hell of a shape. So, our luggage caught a good shower, but I got relief!

By the time we reached England, the sun was about one hour high again. It was my only time to take off in daylight, and flying all night and landing the next day at daylight. Lt. Mitchell did a good job of navigation across. He took a sun shot and said, "Five more minutes, and we will be over Scotland." And so we were! Our gas was too low to be comfortable, but we finally landed at Prestwick, Scotland about 9 o'clock on May 1st.

Several of the ships that took off from Gander the same day we did landed in Scotland because they were short of gas, and when we finally landed, one runway was blocked at Prestwick by one of our planes. The landing gear collapsed, but no one was hurt.
— *Lt. Ruben Neie, pilot*

✠ We were going to go to Ireland and strike a spot in Ireland, and then fly to Prestwick, Scotland. The weather was supposed to be good that night. There wasn't supposed to be any storms. So we took off, and the first thing you know, it began to get stormy. We had to start climbing, and the further we went, the worse the storm got, and the higher we had to climb. We had to get up to 20, 25,000 feet to get above the storm, and I started taking star fixes. That was all you had to navigate, when you were in a situation like that, was to navigate with the stars.

Now, celestial navigation is not too rough if you've got a stable platform to shoot from. What you do is, you have your sexton, and you knew the navigation of the stars. There's a number of navigational stars, and you knew your star, and you'd take your sexton and fix it in the stars in the sexton site, and click it. What you were doing is you were measuring the altitude of the star above the earth's horizon. That's what you were measuring. As long as you had a stable platform to shoot from, that's a pretty good method of navigation, because you'd shoot one start, and you had your tables that you'd go to, and you'd plot it on your map, and you would get an LOP – a line of position – which meant that you were somewhere along that line. You didn't know where – you were somewhere along that line.

Then you would pick another star, preferably 90 degrees from your first star. It didn't have to be 90 degrees – it could be 60 – but it had to be some distance from the first star. Then you would shoot it and get you another LOP. Then you would have to move your first LOP because of the time-lapse between your two lines of position. You'd take them at different times. Time was important. When you shoot that sexton, you look at your watch and get the time and write it down.

Then you would take a third line of position and, hopefully – if you did it right – you'd advance your first two lines of position, then you would have a triangle. That triangle was supposed to be pretty small, and you were supposed to be right in the middle of that triangle – your plane was.

But the problem was when you had an unstable platform, like an old B-17 in a storm, you had a lot of difficulty getting… You would have to take eight or ten sightings on one star and then take an average. You'd click your sexton and make a little mark, but you'd have to take an average.

Well, I started working on my star-fixing and, after an hour and a half, I got one triangle, and it was big. It was big, and that bothered me. I said, 'Man! It's not supposed to be that big!' Then I started work and, mind you, it was cold. You were flying, say, at 25,000 feet, and it's cold, and you are wearing oxygen masks, and you are wearing heavy gloves and heavy clothing, and you are gasping for breath – "haah-haah" – you know? I took a second fix and, it, too, was big. But it showed me – we are drifting north. We are drifting north of where we are supposed to be, and I kind of got alarmed. And I worked.

In another hour or two, I had a third fix and, it, too, showed me we were drifting 150, 200 miles north of where we were supposed to be tracking. And I remember going up to the pilot and telling him, "Hey, Rube, these don't look good. The plane is so bouncy, and it's cold, but this is all we've got." I said, "I did the best I could, and it shows me that we are 200, 250 miles north of where we are supposed to be." And I said, "If this is right, we are going to pass the British Isles, and we are going to land somewhere in the North Atlantic. Now, if it's wrong, and we don't make the correction that I'm going to recommend, we are going to go into France – Occupied France." I said, "But it's all we've got and we are going to have to go on it."

Rube said, "Okay, Mitch. You've done the best you can."

So I gave him about a 35- or 40-degree correction to the right, and we flew that a-ways for some time. And then – lo and behold! They had us on the Irish coast – they had a radio direction beam that they would send out into the Atlantic, hopefully, for planes to pick up – they sent the radio direction thing out. And when we got within hearing distance of that, we were pretty close. We made a small correction, but the radio engineer picked up that signal and told us we were coming in where we were supposed to on the Irish coast.

Well, I remember the sun was up then. The sun was coming up, and I took a shot on the sun and got an LOP. Then I used that radio direction signal for the other LOP, and where they crossed with where we were, I then estimated the mileage into Ireland, and we gave the guys an ETA – which is "estimated time of arrival" – and I missed it by two minutes.

Those guys thought I was the best navigator in the world! They didn't know how scared I was! Ha-ha-ha! They didn't know how far off we'd got before we made the correction. That was one of the scariest nights of my life. It was so cold, and I was so tired and scared, I prayed.

The U.S. lost a lot of planes ferrying them across the North Atlantic. Not long ago, I read about…I think there was about, oh, maybe ten planes that took off at the same time, and they hit storms, and most of the planes decided to go down to a lower altitude, closer to the ocean, and one or two of them started climbing, but those that went down lower to get below the storm, they were never heard from them again. Those that climbed made it. But we lost a lot of planes ferrying across the North Atlantic.
— Lt. Lloyd Mitchell, navigator

MAY 1, 1943

✠ Just before it got dark, we had to climb to 19,000 feet above a formation of clouds and a little storm. We stayed at altitude for about six hours. It was very cold because our heater was out. Strayed off course for several miles; otherwise, we were okay. As dawn broke, no one slept during the entire trip. We saw the clouds breaking up, and it wasn't long before we saw the English coastline. It looked very green and slightly hilly. We headed straight for Scotland. We landed at 0845 Scotland time. Prestwick, Scotland. Had dinner there. Took off 1645. Landed at 1800 in Grafton Underwood.
— Sgt. Leo Lakey, gunner

✠ Flew from Gander to Prestwick today. Left at 2210 BCT; arrived 0800 BCT. Sure sweated this one out. Drifted north about 100 miles. Saw Claude Turner and sent a telegram to Mabs by him.
— Lt. Lloyd Mitchell, navigator

✠ At 8:15 a.m., pass over Ireland. Entered Scotland and finally arrived at Prestwick AAB. Both Ireland and Scotland full of rich green fields. The arrangement of the base here is super-deluxe. Arrived here at 8:30 a.m. Entire flight from Gander, Newfoundland to Prestwick (2,200 miles) took around 13 hours. The North Atlantic Ocean sure a mass of ice and gloom, fog and low clouds. Sure hate to be forced down in the ocean, because a man could not survive.

Left Prestwick, Scotland in a five-plane formation for Grafton Underwood AAB near Kettering, England.

Arrived at Grafton Underwood AAB and joined the entire 96th Bomb Group. The base here is really dispersed all over the creation around. Wrote Bernice and Ma V-mail letter.
— *Sgt. Joseph Kotlarz, gunner*

✠ It was a beautiful scene – fluffy clouds piled high, and green, green fields below us. We landed there at Prestwick and were taken in a bus to a miniature "castle" where we ate chow (.40 Scotch!). After chow at 1:00 p.m., we attended a briefing, along with the other ships' crews that had made the Atlantic Hop, and learned that we were going to take off immediately for a different base in England.

Ours was Grafton Underwood, 70 miles from London – one field that has never been bombed. Landed there and found us a bunk. Everything is far apart, and everyone rides bicycles. Met Scotty and Andy, and they told me the R.O. undergoes pretty rigid training – had to pass an 18 W.P. and code check. Wrote V-mail to Jinny and Mom.
— *Sgt. Dick Haseltine, radio operator*

✠ Now, after we landed at Prestwick, Scotland, we went to one base where we only stayed a week or two.
— *Lt. Lloyd Mitchell, navigator*

May 2, 1943

✠ Reported to ground school today and got mail. Two letters – one from home and one from V. Aranda.

Latrines spread all over the place, but not washing bowls in them. Have to walk about two blocks to bath house.

All English, Scottish and Irish homes mostly built from brick and have real slate or stone floors. Rationing is really felt here, especially on fuel. Mess and eats here are okay, and plenty of them, too.

Began dismantling plane of different odds and ends not needed (de-icer tanks, glyco-tanks, bomb bay tanks, doors, etc.). Missed mass today.

Runways here are concrete and treated asphalt, with beautiful grass all around. Over 200 airports around this section of England.
— *Sgt. Joseph Kotlarz, gunner*

✠ Anniversary. Spent a quiet day at Grafton Underwood. Flew from Prestwick yesterday. Remembered vividly a year ago today. England is pretty.
— *Lt. Lloyd Mitchell, navigator*

Lloyd Mitchell and Joe Kotlarz Cleaning Guns

May 2, 1943

✠ Not too bad here. Real cold in the early morning. Everything is old and not so very clean. No comfortable bathing facilities. Everything is rationed.

We stripped our ship of all baggage and loose material, and they began to modify it for combat. Talked with some boys here (U.S.) that have been on missions – interesting. Enemy attacking from the front now. Found that Billy Mountains Gap is about 22 miles from here. Understand we're to be here for about ten days, during which time we go to school starting tomorrow.

Caught up on letters. Found four waiting for me here. Changed my American and Canadian money into English pounds (worth $4.00) – ten-pound notes, half-pound, etc.
— *Sgt. Dick Haseltine, radio operator*

✠ We ate dinner at Prestwick, and then five ships took off, of which one was us, for Grafton Underwood, England, to meet the rest of our boys. This was our first trip across England, which was covered with balloons. Yes, we were rather scared of them, but we finally became acquainted with their locations and never feared them. But I would hate to run into one of the steel cables that hold them in place! We landed at our new home a little before sundown and were very busy getting our beds and room together, and meeting our friends who we had not seen in 29 days. You see, with all the trouble we had, it took us 29 days to make the trip. But we were well paid for it, as we had loads of fun, experience, and per diem of $6 per day en route, which the boys that went across in two days did not appreciate.

The first thing I noticed was that everyone was riding bicycles instead of cars, and the few cars had the steering wheel on the right side and everyone drove on the wrong side of the road. But the longer you stay in England, the more you find the English people do things backwards. You should see them eat! They hold the fork in the left hand upside-down, and rake the food on top of it with the knife held in the right hand. Try it some time. I can't make it work.

Asper, Mitch, Mendolson and I all stayed in a building all by ourselves, and we really had a pretty good place to stay, but we had to walk or ride our bikes about three blocks to take a shower and eat. One day, I was Officer of the Day, and just to top it off, I was blessed with the GIs. Yes, I almost made it! But, to be frank, that was the first time I didn't make it since I was a very little boy. But then, I didn't have time to wear a six-gun, either, and that took some time to remove. Yes, I was embarrassed, but mostly relieved (25 years old).

Kettering was our town, about a six-mile ride, but full of pubs (honky tonks) and girls. So, we just spent most of our time there, except on pass. Then we went to London. The first 13 days at GU all we had was ground school, listening to the big shots tell us how it was supposed to be done. We also did our own airplane maintenance, because the Ground Echelon had not arrived by boat. Here again, I spent five more days in the hospital, but this time, I was absolutely sure my ears were cured before I even asked to be released, because I knew all that was going on was ground school and I had set through it several times before and was damn glad to get out of it!
— *Lt. Ruben Neie, pilot*

MAY 3, 1943

✠ Leo and I on latrine duty today. Saw an English Lancaster four-motored bomber for the first time. We have blackout time here – 9:00 p.m. each night. Each building has special curtains for blackouts. Cleaned guns and took off covers to have them slotted. The English tower control operators are really good. They really sound good. This is not our permanent base. We will meet ground crews around the 15th, somewhere within 30 miles of London. Got my weekly rations today.

On crap detail with Lakey today. Really nice and green around here, but rainy and always sort of a chill.
— *Sgt. Joseph Kotlarz, gunner*

✠ Nothing occurred around here. Went to ground school. Heard J.B. Lear got shot down. Went to town.
— *Lt. Lloyd Mitchell, navigator*

MAY 4, 1943

✠ Reported at ground school. See a lot of Short Sterlings and Lancasters, both heavy bombers. At 3:00 p.m. today, saw an 80-plane formation of B-17s headed for Germany. Before they hit the Channel, there were 112 B-17s, Spitfires and P-47s as escorts. Lecture on security in foreign lands.

At Kettering, had a good time with crew at a public house or pub. Later on, met Miss O.B. Woods, 6 Howard Street, Kettering (home), 491 London Road, Isleworth, Middlesex. She was with a Canadian and we sure had a swell time.

Went to town (Kettering) with Leo by convoy (trucks). Met. Lt. Neie, Lt. Asper, Lt. Mendolson, Eddie and Steve. Had a swell time.
— *Sgt. Joseph Kotlarz, gunner*

MAY 5, 1943

✠ Woke up and found out from J.D. Miles that Lowell, Eddie, Leo and myself were supposed to go on a gunnery mission.

The English were on a big raid last night and lost 35 bombers. So it must have been a big raid. Flew in 15-plane formation (high altitude). Used my heating suit. Saw a Halifax bomber that crashed last night (three miles from the field). Not a good sight. Two big burned-out patches on the field; the remains of the bombers and, at last, a few scattered odds and ends.

Came in from Kettering this morning at 4:00 a.m. and I am tired now. Flying time: 3 hours.
— *Sgt. Joseph Kotlarz, gunner*

MAY 6, 1943

✠ Going to ground school today. Got paid today. Wrote to Mabs. Wish I could get a letter.
— *Lt. Lloyd Mitchell, navigator*

✠ Supposed to fly this morning, but on account of bad weather, we went to ground school. Lectures on "escape" and general topography of England and Europe.

Received two back-mail letters – one from Bernice and one from Stanley, the kid brother.

Heard that Lt. Lear, our old co-pilot at Pocatello, was given up for dead on the bombing mission of St. Nazaire.
— *Sgt. Joseph Kotlarz, gunner*

MAY 7, 1943

✠ Went to ground school today. It rained all day. Wrote to Mabs & John. Cleaned my gun!
— *Lt. Lloyd Mitchell, navigator*

✠ Woke up at 6:30 a.m. and had calisthenics. Went out to briefing building for a meeting. Later, took Lt. Mitchell and Lt. Mendolson and gave them instructions as to separation of .50 caliber machine gun.

Plane has a leak in gas tank (engine Number 4). Undergoing repairs. Had a combat crew meeting and told detail of operations. The Colonel (Old) said we will start on our missions next week (diversion missions). Went up for five-hour flight till 8:00 p.m.

Saw a DeHaviland Mosquito (two-engine bomber) for the first time. As fast as a pursuit, and it's really getting famous for itself. Flying time: 5 hours. On guard tonight.
— *Sgt. Joseph Kotlarz, gunner*

MAY 8, 1943

✠ Still haven't assumed our ship as yet.

Went to a couple of lectures. Had my American money changed. English money rates as follows:

    Pound   = $4.03 to $4.07 (bill)
    10-shilling note = $2.00
    Half-crown = .50
    Florin = .40
    Shilling = .20
    6-pence = .10
    3-pence = 5-1/2 cents
    1-penny

Rainy and windy today, and grounded. On guard tonight 10:00 p.m. till 6:00 a.m.
— *Sgt. Joseph Kotlarz, gunner*

MAY 9, 1943

✠ Still at Grafton Underwood. Went into town with one of the "experienced" fellows last week and he taught us some of the ways of the English. We visited all the "pubs" in Kettering. They are somewhat like our beer parlors, except that better people frequent them. I got a mug of cider. Found that drug stores are "chemist shops." Hardware stores are "ironmongers." Barber shops are "hairdressers." Beginning to really like it here.

About every other night, the British bombers drone over and head way up out of sight, about 11:00 p.m. I was going out to guard our ship the other night when they went over. British searchlights probed the sky. It was really beautiful. About 3:00 a.m., I heard the planes come back a few at a time. Some sounded as if they were "limping." Some were low, others high, and our base lay silent and dark with no life, as if in prayer for the few that didn't get back. Suddenly, a ship roared overhead, landed, and then round again, followed by a far-away explosion, as it crashed. Learned the next day that it was a Halifax and its crew bailed out safely. Maj. Hand went on a diversion mission with another group the other day and they came back and told us about it. Interesting!
— *Sgt. Dick Haseltine, radio operator*

✠ On crap detail with Leo again. Got my weekly rations. Cigarettes are worth about .44 a package. I usually get the seven-package limit each week.

Went to Shelveston, England to study gunnery on the Hunt Trainer, used for range estimation. Went right in from Shelveston to Kettering and messed around.
— *Sgt. Joseph Kotlarz, gunner*

MAY 10, 1943

✠ Bernice baptized a year ago today.

Rainy and windy today (grounded). Had another tooth filled.

> **Addresses:**
> Lt. E.G. Shelton
> Route 2
> Plainville, Texas
>
> S/Sgt. Paul C. Dolman
> 7144 Jeffrey Avenue
> Chicago, Illinois
>
> Charles C. Demmber
> 4224 Madison Avenue
> Congress Park, Illinois

Iver W. Wenander
310 7th Street
Wausaw, Wisconsin

Went to town tonight and called on B. Woods. Sure had a nice time. Had a rabbit dinner in town. Came in at 11:00 p.m.

— *Sgt. Joseph Kotlarz, gunner*

May 11, 1943

✠ Flew today – two 5,000 – 35 degrees. Went to hospital this afternoon. That left ear again. Perhaps this week if I get out of the hospital.

— *Lt. Lloyd Mitchell, navigator*

✠ Briefed at 5:00 a.m. today and went up on high-altitude hop for about three hours in 54-plane formation (94th, 95th and 96th). 18 planes from each group.

> **Address:**
> Miss Bunny Wood
> c/o 6 Howard Street
> Kettering
> North Avis
>
> Home:491 D London Road
> Isleworth, Middlesex

I took our plane to Modification Center to install nose guns in bombardiers' compartments. Flying time: three hours. On guard tonight on Capt. Flagg's plane.

— *Sgt. Joseph Kotlarz, gunner*

May 12, 1943

✠ Still in hospital. Boresome day. Wrote to Mabs and Mom.

— *Lt. Lloyd Mitchell, navigator*

✠ Nothing doing today, so I caught up on some letter-writing and diary. Ready to go to town and, what happened, but an alert is on, and everyone is restricted to base.

— *Sgt. Joseph Kotlarz, gunner*

May 13, 1943

My group went on their first raid today. These damn ears kept me on the ground. Saw six fellows parachute from their plane. A gunner shot its right elevator off. I hope Joe Hudson made it okay. I hear the "Abbeyville Kids" caught hell. Capt. Rogers was killed.

— *Lt. Lloyd Mitchell, navigator*

MAY 13, 1943

✠ Finally, on May 13, our group went out on its first raid. I was not scheduled because I had two men in the hospital with bad colds – Lt. Asper and Lt. Mitchell. The mission was to bomb the famous Abbeyville Airport in France, but our boys, being inexperienced, all aborted when our leader, Col. Old, lost an engine and was forced to abort.

Just after the take-off, Capt. Rogers' waist-gunner was testing his gun, which ran away, and he shot the right-hand stabilizer clean off by the fuselage. Two .50 calibers struck the tail-gunner in the hip, knocking him cold. I was on the ground and saw the stabilizer fall off. The shot flew pretty good, and Capt. Rogers was able to fly it back over the field and ordered the men to bail out. The first man was the unconscious tail-gunner, who they threw out, tying a string to his ripcord. Then seven chutes followed, all landing safe. The pilot and co-pilot were then last seen flying toward the English Channel. By the time they reached the Channel, the ship was coming to pieces. They intended to bail out and let it crash in the water, but they were almost too late. However, they both got out in time before it flew all to pieces. They drifted rather far out over water before they landed and before a boat came, Capt. Rogers froze to death. But the co-pilot, Lt. Gorse, was rescued. He almost froze, also.

My top-turret man, S/Sgt. White, saved the life of the unconscious tail-gunner by shooting him with morphine and dragging his chute off him. The wind would have dragged the poor boy to death. This was a bad start, but we had to buckle up again and make up for it next time. Capt. Rogers was one of the best officers and pilots I have ever known.
— Lt. Ruben Neie, pilot

✠ Worked on our ship 'til 3:00 a.m., getting it ready (ammunition and 300-pound bombs). Ate breakfast at 7:30 a.m. and went back to sleep.

Went out tonight with B. Woods. Sure had a good time. Came in on 11:00 p.m. convoy.

21 ships took off on the mission. We did not go up on account of Lt. Asper and Lt. Mitchell in hospital. Capt. (337) Rogers' ship had a mishap. Waist-gunner discharged gun over the field and shot off complete right-horizontal stabilizer. All men went out in chutes. Tail-gunner was tossed on account of injuries. White and I first to pick him up, and he was pretty bad. White really a sensible and cool-headed man.
— Sgt. Joseph Kotlarz, gunner

✠ Up all night last night from 6:00 p.m. until 7:00 a.m. this morning waiting for bombs to load on the ship, but they didn't come, and we left and went to our barracks and slept until 10:00 a.m. Flying system called us to briefing, and we were told that our wait for a mission was over. This was it! We were to bomb an airdrome in France, and our whole crew eagerly listened to the briefing. Then our names weren't read to go. We sure were disappointed.

Formation took off and suddenly, so we watched. We heard a gun and then the right stabilizer fell off a bomber directly over us. The pilot kept it up and brought it over the field, and the crew bailed out. Some lived up to the U.S.A. courage, just as regular as could be. They jumped out. The waist-gunner shot the guns that took off the tail and

hit the rear-gunner in the @#$. They had to throw him out with a rope attached to his ripcord. Nobody hurt in landing. The ball-turret operator in the lead ship of the formation forgot his oxygen supply, and the whole formation had to turn back.
— *Sgt. Dick Haseltine, radio operator*

✠ Dry run for our crew – first mission for our crew was a flop. Our crew did not take part in this mission due to the fact that we had three men in the hospital: Lt. Mitchell, Lt. Asper and Lt. Mendolson.

The day was sunny and warm. One of the few nice days they have in this wet and cloudy country. Take-off was about noon. This was a bad start due to some of the crews starting their engines too late, not knowing exactly what position to fly, and waiting too long for the other ships after they left the runway. About half-way, a plane taxied off the runway and got stuck in the mud. That held up the entire group back for quite a while. In the meantime, the planes that did take off kept circling around the field. About their last time around the field, they were almost all in formation, except Capt. Rogers, who was just catching up. He was about 500 yards behind and about 1,000 almost above us when we heard a gun go off. Saw a tracer, and his right horizontal tail-fin came fluttering through the air. Capt. Rogers and his co-pilot kept the ship on an even keel. Made several wide turns over the field, or, rather, miles around it, because it was hard to fly with half of the tail shot off.

Two boys bailed out over another field – four over our field. Dominick the tail-gunner was hit in the spine when the gun went off. So, they tied a rope to his ripcord and the rope to the inside of the plane. They threw him out over the field. He was the first one to bail out over the field. I was at the tower watching them jump. Miles was coming down near the tower, so a few of us ran out and caught his chute after he hit the ground, to keep it from dragging him too far.

The officers must have stayed with the ship and jumped before it went out to sea to release its bomb load. While over the water, the plane must have gotten out of control, and they were forced to make a water landing. Lt. Gorse was picked up within one hour after they hit the water. Capt. Rogers was picked up about four hours later, frozen to death.

The entire group came back within two hours due to the delay in take-off, and other little mishaps. They did not even go up to high altitude. Saw the Channel for a few seconds, then turned back. The rest of the group went over and dropped their bombs.
— *Sgt. Leo Lakey, gunner*

✠ Each field had a bombardment group, a heavy bombardment group, and we had four squadrons. My bombardment group was with the 96th, and I was 413th Squadron. Each squadron had about 12 air crews. So, in a base, maybe you have about 48 air crews. One of the other squadrons, the gunner was – what they call – "clearing their guns." They are just kind of checking their guns out, .50 caliber machine gun. And one of them, a waist-gunner – his gun was supposed to be fixed so it didn't swivel that far – but he was checking his gun and swiveled it around and shot off the horizontal stabilizer of the old 17 – the tail. A big tail. Shot it off. Well, the plane was very, very hard to hold in the air without that horizontal stabilizer. So the pilot and the co-pilot flew and made a circle or two – a couple of circles – and bailed their crew out. Then the pilot, he couldn't control it enough to bring it into the airport airbase, and after he bailed his crew out, he tried to tie his plane up. He found something to try to tie it up to where he and the co-pilot could get out. The co-pilot got out okay, but the pilot, by the time he could get out, he was over the North Sea. Now, the North Sea is on the east coast of England. The North Sea lies between mainland Europe and the British Isles. He bailed out into the North Sea, and they found him about an hour later. He had found a buoy to cling to, but he was dead. You could last – the North Sea was cold – you could last about 20 or 25 minutes in the North Sea before hypothermia got to you. So, they found him dead, clinging to a buoy.

That was a failure. They never did get to the target. They had to turn around and come back. I've forgotten the details, but that mission didn't count – it didn't count as a mission. It was a failure, and the CO – the commanding officer – was very, very unhappy. He was a tough old bird. His name was Archie Old and he was a colonel then. Later he became a three-star general, I think – Archie did. And he really reamed the pilots out. He was very unhappy about it.
— *Lt. Lloyd Mitchell, navigator*

MAY 14, 1943

✠ 96th's first mission – flew 4 hours – Courtrai, Belgium.

Got up at 0600. Wash engines and wings. Briefing at 0730. Clean guns. Lt. Neie told us to get ready for our first mission about 0900. Got plane in shape in one hell of a hurry. We took off at 1000. Flew over field several times to get into formation. We were Tail-End Charlie of a 21-ship formation. The day was sunny and warm. Visibility very good. Met our Spitfire escort halfway across the Channel. Flew to Courtrai, Belgium and dropped 16 300-pound bombs on an airdrome from altitude of 24,000 feet. Very cold up there. Ice in oxygen mask. No ships attacked us. Spitfires did all of the fighting. Plenty of flak – 53 flak holes in plane. Landed 1400. Briefed. Cleaned guns after supper.
— *Sgt. Leo Lakey, gunner*

✠ Mission #1: bombing altitude 24,000 feet.

Briefed this morning. Told we were not going on a mission today, so we (crew) began cleaning the ship. Then Lt. Neie came in the plane and told us take-off time was 10:25. We had 16 300-pounders and our target was an airdrome in Belgium (Courtrai). Three groups (94th, 95th and 96th) went over (20 planes to a group), escorted by Spitfires. One of the other groups lost a plane (B-17). I saw two fellows bail out in chutes. Only five or six enemy aircraft intercepted us, but were taken care of by the Spitfires. Sure a sight for me. Anti-aircraft shells came near us and left us four small holes in our plane. No one was hurt. We came back at 2:00 p.m.

30 of our ground crew came here today. Loaded planes tonight with ten 500-pounders.

Air Task Force:
Target: (airdrome) Courtrai, Belgium

Kipling's Error
**ground crew l-r
Howard "Freddy"
Breson, Baird,
Byciewiez,
Wagner, Shell**

Planes dispatched: 34 B-17s with Spitfire escorts
Planes lost: two 17s
Seven enemy aircraft destroyed by Spitfire escort (82 tons bombs)
— *Sgt. Joseph Kotlarz, gunner*

✠ One of the first – I guess it was the first – combat missions that we flew on, I was sick. Again, I had ear problems. My ears were bothering me, and I was in the hospital with them, so I didn't get to take off with the crew that day. I was very unhappy. I wanted to do so, and I didn't get to do so.
— *Lt. Lloyd Mitchell, navigator*

✠ Number 1 – the very next day.

We were off to Courtrai, Belgium to bomb an airport, and this was my Number One! Yes, Asper and Mitchell are still in the hospital, and so is Lt. Shelton with pneumonia. So, I used his co-pilot, Flight Officer Collette, and navigator Lt. Hockin. We worked almost all night getting our plane in shape and loaded with ten 500-pound bombs and ammunition. The trip was very strenuous for us, being our first.

We came back with a .20mm cannon hole in the right wing, which hit the main spare, and calls for a new ship. We also got four other small holes from flak.

The fighters reminded me of red wasps when you knock their nest down.
— *Lt. Ruben Neie, pilot*

Waiting to undertake mission

MAY 14, 1943

 Mission #1 – Up at the first streak of light, and attended a briefing. This time, our crew (with navigator and co-pilot in the hospital, substituted with Shelton's navigator and co-pilot) was scheduled for mission.

We took off at noon and met other groups at the coast, and proceeded toward France. Halfway over the Channel, our P-47 fighter escorts caught up with us and stuck to us splendidly through the raid. Found and made the bombing run on Fort Rouge, and airfield at St. Omar. Dropped the bombs and headed for home.

I was standing by my gear and suddenly noticed pretty little fluffy clouds all around us. Took a moment for the fact to register that we were in actual anti-aircraft fire, and damn close, too. Our ship was hit and crashed. Only two men bailed out. The rest of us made it okay.

Landed here at Grafton and examined our ship – four holes – small one in outer right wing, one in right wing fuselage, one in rudder, and one in left stabilizer. Briefed, and cleaned our guns and ship.
— ***Sgt. Dick Haseltine, radio operator***

MAY 15, 1943

 My first raid, and it was the docks at Emden, Germany. The SC – Maj. Hand – said we did a good job. Not too many fighters, and quite a bit of flak. Rather an exhilarating feeling. The first out. None of our boys got it, but the other group lost six planes. 1/25.

Note: The number "1/25" refers to the number of missions completed and the number of total mission required to be completed before you were finished flying. Obviously, this was an important number to the flight crews. It is hard for me to imagine being

there and not being constantly aware of how many more times I had to "dodge the bullet."
— *Lt. Lloyd Mitchell, navigator*

✠ Number 2: Next day to bomb the docks at Emden, Germany. Mitchell couldn't stand it any longer, so he was with us today. But Flight Officer Collette reported with two extra pieces of armor plate for him and me to sit on, just in case stray bullets came our way from the bottom and – believe me – I will never go on another mission without my armor plate!

Flak and fighters were about the same as yesterday, but we slipped through without a hit. We (96th Group) never lost a man or plane. But the poor old 94th lost six planes and crews.

I also got to try out my new relief tube I installed, which can be used while sitting in my pilot's seat. It works fine, but my poor ball-turret man, S/Sgt. Malinowski, catches it all.

The next day, we took a rest and did more work on our plane for our Number 3.
— *Lt. Ruben Neie, pilot*

✠ Mission #2: bombing altitude 26,000 feet.

Briefing at 4:25 a.m. Left the field (Crew B-3) at 7:30 a.m. and rendezvoused on coast of England with three wings (nine groups). We left the coast of England for Emden, Germany, where we arrived at 11:00 a.m., and left the town in smoke and flames. Anti-aircraft fire was really thick, and ten minutes after we left the target, about 20 Focke-Wulf 190s attacked us. I saw one B-17 go down. We were on the left tail of the last element, and I tried to keep this Focke-Wulf from getting him, but it just couldn't be done. About 15 gun positions fired at him, but it wasn't enough.

We came in at 2:00 p.m. No casualties and no one hurt in our plane (ten 500-pound bombs). Some more of our ground crew came today (26,000 feet).
— *Sgt. Joseph Kotlarz, gunner*

✠ Second Mission – flew six and 1/4 hours – Emden, Germany.

Got up at 0300. Breakfast 0330. Briefing 0415. Clean guns and load ammunition. Take-off 0730. Sunny and warm. Visibility very good. Circle field several times. Tail-End Charlie in eight-ship formation. Three wings flew; 50 planes in all. Very cold. My oxygen mask froze. Stuck hose. Drop ten 500-pound bombs on ship and sub base in Emden, Germany. Plenty of flak and FW-190s. Shot at several of them. Everyone did plenty of shooting. 150 rounds of ammo used. I saw three of our 17s go down. Knocked hell out of target. No holes in our ship this trip. Land 1345. Briefing last 45 minutes. Everybody very tired. Clean guns after supper.
— *Sgt. Leo Lakey, gunner*

MAY 15, 1943

✠ Mission #2 – Seemed that I no sooner hit my bed when 4:00 rolled around and we attended another briefing. This mission was to bomb the industrial section in Emden, Germany. We did a diversion over the North Sea at high altitude, and it was so cold that we left long trails of smoke vapor behind us. Approached coast of Germany and was shot at as we passed over an island, but the fire wasn't accurate. Dropped our bombs, and the formation headed for home with compact formation. Fighters (Focke-Wulfs) hit us as we left the coast, and the fight lasted about a half-hour, but our formation wasn't attacked, so all we could do was put about at a distance. The vapor trail left by the maneuvering formation was a sight to see. Each ship left his own in a huge series of curves. Landed at Grafton. Cleaned guns, and we were debriefed.
— Sgt. Dick Haseltine, radio operator

MAY 16, 1943

✠ Rested up. My cold is awful. My ears are still bad. Another mission tomorrow. I should write Mabs.
— Lt. Lloyd Mitchell, navigator

✠ Not much doing today. Everyone tired from overwork and the two missions.

On that accident over the field on Thursday, the tail-gunner, Dominick (337th Squadron) was shot and seriously hurt. Capt. Rogers, the pilot, tried to land it in the English Channel and, as a result, lost his life. This was our first casualty, and also the first ship lost on our first operation (which was a complete flop).

Went to mass here at the base. Went out with O. "Bunny" Wood.
— Sgt. Joseph Kotlarz, gunner

MAY 17, 1943

✠ And here came Number 3 – Lorient, France, and its power house and U-boat pens. Plenty of fighters all the way into the target. We knocked the hell out of the target, but they almost got us, too. Lt. Conahan and Lt. Holcombe both went down over the North Sea. They were flying on my wing. We hate to see them go with their crew, but we couldn't help them. We should be happy it wasn't us.

Lt. L.B. Ward went with me as an observer. Lt. Asper and Lt. Mendolson stayed out all night before, and were off the ball all day because they were too sleepy. Asper did a piss-poor job as co-pilot, and Mendolson failed to get rid of his bombs. I finally had to salvo them from the cockpit. Lt. Ward, an old pilot, got so mad at Asper that he almost knocked him out of his seat and took over himself. It was also a very long trip, and we landed at a strange field in England so we could gas up and go home.
— Lt. Ruben Neie, pilot

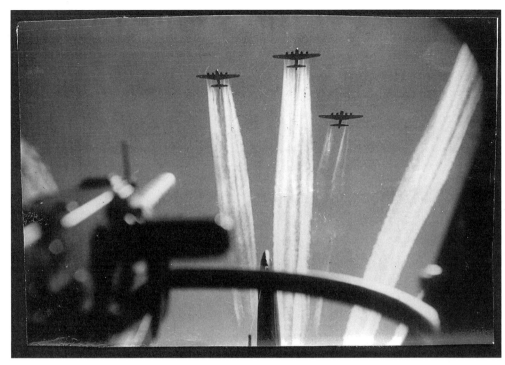

Flying Formation, from Gun Turret

✠ Mission #3 – bombing altitude 28,000 feet.

Woke up at 4:30 a.m. and got briefed at 5:00 a.m., and got plane all set. Left for a mission to bomb power plant and docks at Lorient, France. Attacked by FW-190s five minutes before we hit the target. Saw one B-17 go down. (Target was bombed okay and left in smoke and flames.) Focke-Wulfs again attacked us after we were through bombing. George Haslip (Capt. Ford's crew) got one FW from top turret. A.E. Beasley (Capt. McClatchy's crew) got one from ball turret. Landed at a field 30 miles from our base at 3:00 p.m. because we ran out of gas. Came into Grafton 5:00 p.m. About 50 planes took part in the mission. Spitfires escorted us part of the way. (Ten 500-pound bombs today.)

Sure tired. Bombed from 28,000 feet.
— *Sgt. Joseph Kotlarz, gunner*

MAY 17, 1943

✠ Third mission – flew six hours – Lorient, France.

Got up at 0430. Breakfast 0500. Briefing 0530. Clean guns and work on plane. Dress up very warm. Sunny and warm on ground. Take off 0900. No fighter escort. Flew several diversions on the way over the Channel. Visibility was very good. Plenty of flak, FW-190s, and a few Me-109s. Shot at several. Dropped ten 500-pound bombs on big sub base. Hit target. Saw several fighters go down in smoke. My oxygen mask

froze – suck hose. Altitude 28,000 feet. Very cold. Fingers on right hand almost froze. Saw one of our ships go down. Eight boys hit silk. On way home, our gas ran low, so we had to land on RAF field 40 miles from home. Waited four hours for gas. Got it and landed home 1700. Brief one hour. Clean guns after supper. Everyone very tired. 175 rounds of ammo used.
— *Sgt. Leo Lakey, gunner*

✦ Mission #3 – Same briefing procedure. Lorient, France – sub bases and power houses. Headed for France, a diversion back to England, and across to Lorient, France. Received inaccurate flak and reluctant fighter attacks. Good visibility, so we probably destroyed our target. Ran out of gas just 15 miles short of Grafton, and just made it to an incomplete ramp at Bruntingthorpe. Refueled and came over to Grafton. Boys seem glad to see us, as we left the formation early on our own, and they weren't sure what happened to us. Debriefed and ate. Froze my left hand. Blisters forming on middle finger. Nothing serious. Wish we could have gloves that were warmer.
— *Sgt. Dick Haseltine, radio operator*

✦ Today we raided Lorient, France. Power house was the primary target; U-boat pens, secondary. Whew! The fighters picked us up before we hit the target. Our bombs wouldn't release and we salvaged. The doors wouldn't close. I knew we were dead pigeons. The fighters tried to get us, but got Capt. Conahan and Lt. Holcombe instead. We were flying on their wing. 2/25.

Most of the time, individual bombardiers, we'd call them "Tombardiers" instead of 'bombardiers,' because you'd be flying formation, and when your lead plane would drop, then you would drop.

The raid on the German sub pens on the French coast that we were bombing – that was the same time that the bombardier was not able to release the bombs. We had to go out into the Mediterranean. (Note: This was probably the Bay of Biscay.) We didn't release the bombs in France, except on the target. We wouldn't take an alternate target, and we went out into the Mediterranean, and one of the guys finally got back there and got the bombs released, but couldn't get the doors closed. We were fighting to get our doors closed when one of Rube's friends – that he had gone to college with, his good buddy – he fell back to kind of protect us and they knocked him down. But, eventually, we did get our doors down and caught up then. But that was something else.
— *Lt. Lloyd Mitchell, navigator*

MAY 18, 1943

✦ Woke up and sure felt a lot better today.

Here in England, the English girls go out with American Negro soldiers and think it an honor to do so.
— *Sgt. Joseph Kotlarz, gunner*

✠ Rested up for tomorrow's mission. Cleaned my guns. I can take one of those guns apart easily now.
— *Lt. Lloyd Mitchell, navigator*

Eddie Nelson Closing Bomb Doors

✠ Then, on the 18th, we rested again and worked on *Kipling's Error II*, our ship, and loaded for the next raid.

By the way, maybe I should say something about the name of our ship. Five of us are from the West and five of us are from the East. And Kipling once wrote: "East is East, West is West, and never the twain shall meet." But we did meet, and making a damn good team! So, we called it "*Kipling's Error*."

We also have an insignia of the ten different states' emblems represented in one. (You will, no doubt, see a picture of it soon, if we can keep up the good work we are out to do.) The insignia is as follows: myself from Texas, a lone star; Lt. Asper from Oregon, a beaver; Lt. Mitchell from Oklahoma, a buffalo; Lt. Mendolson from Pennsylvania, a keystone; T/Sgt. Nelson from Minnesota, a gopher; T/Sgt. Haseltine from Maine, a pine tree; S/Sgt. White from New Mexico, a zia; S/Sgt. Malinowski from Ohio, a buckeye leaf; S/Sgt. Lakey from Illinois, a plow; S/Sgt. Kotlarz from Nebraska, an ear of corn.

Eddie Nelson Kicking Out Live Bombs

All of that put together makes a pretty nice insignia which really means something, whereas most names of planes have no meanings.
— *Lt. Ruben Neie, pilot*

MAY 19, 1943

✠ This one, we missed – Flensburg, Germany.

Got up at 0330. Breakfast 0415. Briefed 0500. Clean our guns and work on plane. Two-hour delay due to low fog. Taxi up to runway, then our batteries went dead. Everyone mad as wet hens because of our misfortune not to take off after sweating it out all morning, as we did. So, we just undressed and waited for the rest of the group to come back. They did a good job, dropping ten 500-pound bombs on a sub base in Flensburg, Germany. Flak was light, and very few fighters around. None of our ships was lost. Several FW-190s were shot down.
— *Sgt. Leo Lakey, gunner*

MAY 19, 1943

✠ Another raid (Mission #4) for our group. Our crew did not go. Just before take-off, our batteries went out, and we didn't go. The bombing mission was to Flensburg, Germany (shipbuilding and naval base for submarines).

Received 12 back-letters today.

All 19 planes from our group came in okay.
— *Sgt. Joseph Kotlarz, gunner*

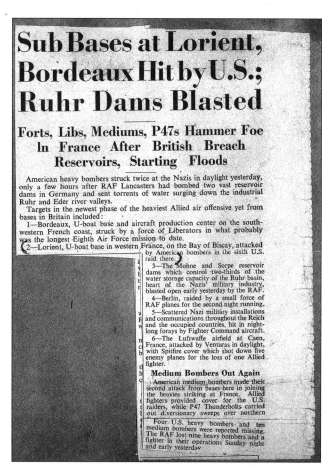

Sub Bases at Lorient, Bordeaux Hit by U.S.; Ruhr Dams Blasted

Forts, Libs, Mediums, P47s Hammer Foe In France After British Breach Reservoirs, Starting Floods

American heavy bombers struck twice at the Nazis in daylight yesterday, only a few hours after RAF Lancasters had bombed two vast reservoir dams in Germany and sent torrents of water surging down the industrial Ruhr and Eder river valleys.

Targets in the newest phase of the heaviest Allied air offensive yet from bases in Britain included:

1—Bordeaux, U-boat base and aircraft production center on the southwestern French coast, struck by a force of Liberators in what probably was the longest Eighth Air Force mission to date.

2—Lorient, U-boat base in western France, on the Bay of Biscay, attacked by American bombers in the sixth U.S. raid there.

3—The Mohne and Sorpe reservoir dams which control two-thirds of the water storage capacity of the Ruhr basin, heart of the Nazis' military industry, blasted open early yesterday by the RAF.

4—Berlin, raided by a small force of RAF planes for the second night running.

5—Scattered Nazi military installations and communications throughout the Reich and the occupied countries, hit in night-long forays by Fighter Command aircraft.

6—The Luftwaffe airfield at Caen, France, attacked by Venturas in daylight, with Spitfire cover which shot down five enemy planes for the loss of one Allied fighter.

Medium Bombers Out Again

American medium bombers made their second attack from bases here in joining the heavies striking at France. Allied fighters provided cover for the U.S. raiders, while P47 Thunderbolts carried out diversionary sweeps over northern

Four U.S. heavy bombers and ten medium bombers were reported missing. The RAF lost nine heavy bombers and a fighter in their operations Sunday night and early yesterday.

Bombers Blast Sub Bases

✠ Target: ship yards and power house at Flensburg, Germany. We were all set to go, but as we were taxiing out to take-off position, one of our battery solenoids stuck, causing a short-circuit, which stopped our hydraulic pumps and instruments, and, before we could find our trouble, it was too late to catch the formation, so we had to miss the raid. And, just as we expected, it was an easy one. No flak and no fighters. Just our luck! The target was knocked out completely. The next day, as usual, was rest day. But very little rest did we get because our ground echelon still had not arrived.
— *Lt. Ruben Neie, pilot*

✠ Today, the boys raided Flensburg, Germany. The shipbuilding yards and the power house was the target. Our brakes went out as we were taxiing for take-off. Sure would have liked to go. An easy mission. Very inaccurate flak and very little fighter opposition. The boys say they knocked hell out of both targets.
— *Lt. Lloyd Mitchell, navigator*

MAY 20, 1943

✠ Got up at 3:00 a.m. for briefing… I guess I made a mistake, because we slept late and just had a lecture this PM.
— *Sgt. Joseph Kotlarz, gunner*

✠ Got 13 letters today, and was I proud to get them!
— *Lt. Lloyd Mitchell, navigator*

MAY 21, 1943

Second Emden, Germany raid, and was it a rough fight! We had fighters continuously attacking for one hour. We took off at 9:30 and were over the target at 12:45. White got two FW-190s and Kotlarz got one. The damn fools came in so close, we could almost see the whites of their eyes. But we got home on time and in pretty good shape. One .20mm in wing, and a few flak holes, but no one touched in my ship.

Capt. Stevenson's ship caught fire from enemy shots. His ship went down. Nine chutes opened and one caught afire just as it opened. They were over the cold North Sea at the time. I hope they are POWs (prisoners of war), instead of fish food. The North Sea is so cold, a human cannot live over one hour in it. He was the third man to go down off our wing. I hope and pray they don't get any closer – or that close – anymore.

May 21st was Lt. Shelton, Lt. Moreland, Lt. Palusi., Lt. McMath, Lt. Rossman and my one-year mark since we got our wings. So, Lt. McMath got into the bourbon I brought from Canada and celebrated our birthday. Our bicycles – got too drunk to ride – we really had a time! We started to London, but Jack only got about five miles and went back on a truck. I went on to Kettering and found Asper. He and I went to London on our first three-day rest period. It was our first time in London and we had a hell of a time getting around and along with the crazy cab drivers and pub keepers. But we found two nice girls and enjoyed a nice three-day leave in the Russell Hotel of London. We visited Piccadilly Circus for our first time. I never have seen such rotten women in all my life. You have to carry a stick after dark to beat them off! It is about 99 times as bad as South Ackond Street in Dallas, Texas. Lt. N.A. Tanner of California spent most of these three days together. My girl's name was Miss Rae Gibson. She was small, black-headed and very nice and pretty. We went dining and dancing.

— *Lt. Ruben Neie, pilot*

 Mission #5 – bombing altitude 24,000 feet – Group #5.

Got up at 3:30 a.m. and briefed on mission to Emden, Germany. Target: submarine base. Left Kettering (Grafton Underwood AB) at 9:05 a.m. Attacked by 20 Focke-Wulfs five minutes before we hit target. One B-17 exploded; one hit by pursuits and seen going down. Left target and heart of town in flames. Two groups in this raid. We took the sub base and the other group took the town. Lot of anti-aircraft fire. We were hit by A-C fire and thought we were goners (two .20mm shells exploded in our wing in back of engine Number 4). Attacked by 30 FWs 15 minutes after we left target over North Sea. I got my first FW as he swooped in through the formation. We lost two ships out of the 96th Group. Came back at 3:15 p.m.

Capt. Ford's crew came in out of gas and cracked up at the end of the runway. Saw the two B-17s go down in Germany. Then, about 50 miles off the coast of Germany, I saw Capt. Stevenson's crew start burning up. The crew bailed out. One fellow's chute burned up as he left the ship, and he shot down in the Sea. This crew was one of our old 413th crews, and sure a bunch of good fellows.

— *Sgt. Joseph Kotlarz, gunner*

May 21, 1943

✠ The most nerve-breaking day of my life. We took off from here at 0930 and was over the target at 1245. The target was sub pens at Emden, Germany again. Fighters jumped us before we hit the target, and stayed with us about one hour. We lost one ship. Capt. Stevenson – pilot, Grover – bombardier, Mac Bowan – navigator. The ship caught fire about 30 minutes out from the German coast and nine chutes were seen. To leave it, one of the poor devils pulled his ripcord too soon, and his chute caught fire. He dropped like a rock. White got two Focke-Wulfs and Kotlarz got one. I bet they are not as easy the next time we go in. They were continually pouring in on the nose. I hope we hit the target. Got nine letters today. Oh, boy. 3/25.
   — Lt. Lloyd Mitchell, navigator

✠ Fourth Mission – flew six and 1/4 hours – Emden, Germany.

Got up 0330. Breakfast 0400. Briefed 0500. Clean guns and work on plane. Take off 0900. We flew left wing on lead ship. No fighter escort. Our target: eight subs under construction, several miles from the last target we hit. FWs hit us as we hit the coast, and stayed with us until 15 minutes after leaving the coast on the way home. Plenty of flak. Altitude 24,000 feet. Visibility very good. Dropped ten 500-pound bombs. Saw one of our ships go down over the target, and three hit silk. FWs were really thick. Shot at too many. Some were all black. Some were yellow tip wings, tail and nose. Saw their swastika on wings. We really had a hot time getting out. White claimed two hit and Joe one. Saw ship burn over North Sea. Nine hit silk. Our right wing was hit by two .20mm and exploded and missed gas tank by three inches. Flew all the way back, expecting it to burst into flames at any minute, but it didn't. We were very lucky.

Land 1515. A few minutes after we landed, Capt. Ford came in with all four engines cut off and crash-landed. Four went to hospital. Briefed one hour. Clean guns after supper. We were told our ship was out of commission due to the big hole in the right wing.

The 96th lost one plane in the North Sea.
   — Sgt. Leo Lakey, gunner

✠ Mission #4 – Briefed, and after a couple of delays, took off. Target was Emden again. Maintained low altitude and headed out over the North Sea. Headed toward target, diversion back, and climbed to 24,000 feet in the frigid air. This time, our ship, *Kipling's Error*, was wing ship off the lead ship instead of Tail-End Charlie, as we previously had been. We approached the target, and I stood by my gun during the bomb approach. We were almost on target when a burst of anti-aircraft fire caught a ship behind us on the nose, and I watched the bomber keel over slowly and nose down out of my sight. Then the fighter hit us with attack after attack, sneaking along the outside until far ahead of us, then in toward our nose. Our bomb doors were stuck, so our ship was their target. Saw only one ship close and he was not so fast. I didn't have twice to blink. Looked like a rag blew by my face. Then something kicked *Kipling's Error* in the belly, and I looked out and saw a large hole in our right wing. Lt. Neie called Steve in the ball turret to watch for gasoline leaks, but couldn't see any, so we just held our breath. By now, we were 15 minutes out from the German coast and still being attacked. Suddenly, Eddie yelled, "Got 'em!" and soon after, Joe's guns chattered, and he claimed a fighter, too. We were all pretty scared, but gating like hell. Guess the waist-gunners and I and the pilot and co-pilot were worst off, as we couldn't get away from them. Finally, they faded from the sky and we were soaring our way homeward.

Then the ship that George Harrington was in, on our right wing, caught fire and plunged down into the sea. We counted eight chutes opening before it went out of sight. I switched my emergency SOS signal on so the rescue squad in England would get a bearing on them, and as I listened, I heard another ship sending in their position. As I watched George's ship fall, I felt all sickish inside. I came damn close to crying, but I was too cold.

Finally, got off oxygen and Nelson came forward and I crawled up the bomb bay door. Landed without mishap, and watched the others limp in. Capt. Ford's engines out and he just made it onto the ramp. His flap was shot away and his brakes out – he crash-landed at the end of the runway, but all were safe. Andy (R.O.) was hit by flak from ankle to shoulders, and two gunners had minor injuries. The whole group was on the edge, and I, for one, thank God for being able to drink that hot coffee again, instead of being out in the cold sea like George was.

We were debriefed. Eddie claimed two ships and Joe one. Later, we learned that some of George's had been picked up – only six of them – names unknown. Rather than stay around and let the whole damn fight prey on our minds, most of us went to town after cleaning our gear.

Kipling's Error may have to be scrapped or have a wing replaced. They couldn't see how it had stayed up for this trip, but when I read Jinny's letter and read "I pray for you every day," I told them why we made it back. The ship that hit us came up from under and fired two .20mm into our wing. One went through; the other exploded inside and perforated the wing with small holes. If Steve's turret hadn't been covered with leaking oil, the plane could never have got in like that. "Live and Learn" should be changed to "Learn and Live." We've never felt fear of that sort before. Much of it was due to being half-frozen, hindered by oxygen masks, radio headsets, mikes, parachutes, bomb doors stuck, the sight of ships going down close to us – but we know one thing for sure now. If ever *Kipling's Error* knows fear, it'll be a fighting type of fear to the last man! All guns were blazing continually. As a crew, we were tops, and feel that we've been through a good lesson in the School of Experience.
— *Sgt. Dick Haseltine, radio operator*

May 22, 1943

✠ Supposed to be on pass till Sunday, 8:00 a.m. Noon today, found out entire Wing has a pass until Monday 1800 (6:00 p.m.). Went downtown and just messed around.

Not very much of a write-up in the paper about last day's (Friday's) raid.

Our plane (*Kipling's Error*) was hit by two .20mm shells, which just missed the #4 tank and hit a main, and now it is condemned and due for the sub depot for repairs. We sure were lucky on this trip.
— *Sgt. Joseph Kotlarz, gunner*

May 23, 1943

✠ We're on leave now. We are off until Monday at 1800. Sgt. Haseltine and I played tennis all day. I really enjoyed it. Wish Mabs could have been playing with me.
— *Lt. Lloyd Mitchell, navigator*

✠ Went to confession and mass in a Catholic church in Kettering. Took Lt. Neie's bicycle and just roamed around town.

Have come to the conclusion that the English people are not as superior and high-class as they think.

— *Sgt. Joseph Kotlarz, gunner*

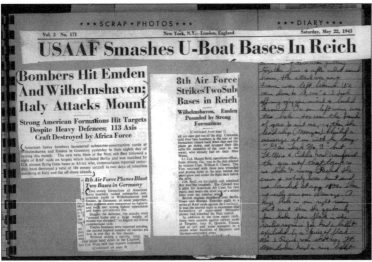

**Bombers Smash
U-Boat Bases**

May 24, 1943

✠ A very rainy, disagreeable day. Went to Kettering to the OM. Slept until 1300. Tomorrow back on duty, I suppose.
— *Lt. Lloyd Mitchell, navigator*

✠ Took life easy today. Rainy here, as I am catching up on a lot of sleep.

Carbine #153480. Parachute #530776.

The Focke-Wulf I reported shot down was also claimed by two lieutenants. Waiting for some confirmation on who got it.

Sent Bernice $65 by cable.
— *Sgt. Joseph Kotlarz, gunner*

May 25, 1943

✠ Practice Mission – flew 1-1/2 hours – northern part of England.

Got up at 0645. Breakfast 0715. Briefed 0800 to 0830. Work on plane and guns until 1050. Prepared for take-off. Take off 1100. Flew left wing of lead ship. Three-ship formation. Drop 12 100-pound practice bombs in northern part of England near the coast. Very cold up there. Near 25 below zero mark. Flew at 20,000 feet. Visibility very good. Used some other crew's ship. Ours still out of commission. Land at 1230. Carry our flying equipment to shack near our own ship.
— *Sgt. Leo Lakey, gunner*

✠ Bad weather, so we're taking it easy. Went up on practice bombing mission from 10:00 till 12:00 in 828 (Lt. Tanner's ship). The English are really far behind in regards to new homes and modern buildings. The different type of machinery I've seen so far would be classed obsolete. And, last but not least, the English are not as educated as the present-day American.

Flying time: two hours.
— *Sgt. Joseph Kotlarz, gunner*

MAY 26, 1943

✠ So far for the 96th, in its five missions, has only lost two planes, one of them catching on fire. Got our new plane today. The number of it is 42-3180. It's a new ship and in fairly good condition.

Saw B. Wood for the last time. Had a swell time tonight.
— *Sgt. Joseph Kotlarz, gunner*

MAY 27, 1943

✠ We moved to a new base at Great Saling, where we met our ground echelon, and I think they were almost as glad to see us as we were to see them. From now on, they do the maintenance and ground work, and all we have to do is go fight the Jerries, as we refer to the !@#$ Germans.
— *Lt. Ruben Neie, pilot*

✠ Moved to Great Saling today. Had 13 letters waiting for me. Most of them from Mabs. Cleaned my guns. We have a new ship now. Two .20mm explosives ruined the other one's right wing. Wrote to Mabs.
— *Lt. Lloyd Mitchell, navigator*

✠ Shipped all equipment to new base at Andrews Field. Buzzed the base before we left for Andrews Field. Left Grafton Underwood Army Air Base for Andrews Field. Arrived 12:00 noon. Andrews Field is the first American field in England. Can't see too much in it as yet. I think Grafton Underwood had it beat.

Sent B. Wood a letter.

Andrews Field – Great Saling. Great Saling is a drop in the bucket. Just a village.
— *Sgt. Joseph Kotlarz, gunner*

MAY 28, 1943

✠ Didn't do much today. Cleaned my guns and fooled around. Ran into Lloyd Umberger, one of my OU friends. He joined our squadron in New Jersey.
— *Lt. Lloyd Mitchell, navigator*

MAY 28, 1943

✠ No mission today. One of our nearby groups had an accident and the mission was called off.

Always thought the English were modern, and were the most intelligent of all nationalities, and now I find out England is not modern, and they use machines here that would be obsolete in the U.S.A., and that the people here are not as educated as we are in the U.S.A.

Worked on our ships all afternoon, checking guns, etc.

Flying time: 4:30 hours.

Got my rations today (seven packs of cigarettes, two bars candy and one pack of razors, etc.).

Named our new plane *Kipling's Error II*, and it's okay, too.
— *Sgt. Joseph Kotlarz, gunner*

MAY 29, 1943

✠ No more than settled at our new base, and we were all alerted for a very important naval store and depot at Rennes, France, which we knocked hell out of. The visibility was good, but the camouflage and flak was the worst we had ever run into – I mean, for us. It was damn good for the Jerries. We flew Tail-End Charlie. That is low man of the low square of the low group. So, we caught holy hell. Poor taxpayers – we will have to have another ship. We had Number 3 engine on fire for a while, but put it out. We also got three gas tanks shot out, and our wing and stabilizer shot up. In fact, we were very lucky to get home. But S/Sgt. White was on the ball again and saved most of our gas by transferring it into a good tank. When I last saw my good friend, Lt. Jack McMath of Denton, Texas, he was coming along fine and on our way back. But he suddenly disappeared. I hope he is safe and will come walking in soon to report for duty. He was really a swell fellow – one of my classmates.

New ship – *Kipling's Error II*, Number 25885, and what a honey! My boys have it fixed up to a "T" for the next mission. Lt. Mitchell and Lt. Mendolson added lots of armor plate in the nose. It makes me feel much safer, too. Not too much to do until June 11th.
— *Lt. Ruben Neie, pilot*

✠ Fifth Mission – flew five to six hours – 96th Sixth Mission – Rennes, France.

Got up at 0700. Target: industrial factory in Rennes, France. Sunny and warm on ground. Work on guns and plane. Take-off 1300. Did some diversions. Flew at 22,000 feet. Very, very cold. Several Spitfires escorted us into target. Plenty of flak and FWs before and after hitting target. Visibility very good. Flak and FWs really gave us hell. Fired 700 rounds. Hit two. Our ball turret was out due to Steve passing out. No oxygen. His hose was bent. Saw about 50 FWs. Drop ten 500-pounders. About 60 17s in our formation. Saw several enemy planes burn up. Saw two 17s go down and only one hit silk. Several boys hit. Went to hospital. Our crew okay. Our ship was hit all over. Number 3 engine knocked out. Hole in Number 4 gas tank and Number 2 tank. Holes in left wing, radio room, tail and right wing. Very lucky trip home. Ship out of commission. It was our second ship and made just this one mission with it. I burned out my barrel. The FWs we saw were yellow nose, wing tips, and tail also yellow. Rest was silver. Others were pure black. Other ships hit as bad as ours. On the way home, we saw over 100 Forts going into a different target. We landed at 1830. Looked the ship over and wondered how it ever flew back. Briefed after supper, then went back and cleaned guns until 2300.

Saved piece of flak and shell from this raid. The 337th lost one plane. Shylocks in that crew.

A .20mm shell stopped in gas tank behind Number 4 engine. The gas ground crew got it out and kept it.
— *Sgt. Leo Lakey, gunner*

✠ Mission #5 – Recently moved to Great Saling, about 50 miles from London, and at 8:00 a.m. we were briefed for our first mission from this base. We have a new ship, *Kipling's Error II*, and at 11:00 a.m., we lifted her up and pointed her nose toward France. Rennes was our target and we were left wing on a lead ship of the lower element at 22,000 feet. I felt tops after a brief sickness from gas from a Spam sandwich. It had passed, and my gun worked fine when I test-fired it.

At approximately 1530, we passed over the French coast, and our fighter escort left us, and three or four minutes later, Joe reported the FW's climb up to intercept us. As we neared the target, we flew through a small amount of anti-aircraft fire, and then got shot from quite a distance. "Bomb doors down!" "Bomb doors away," and we all veered toward home – and into the hottest fight we've ever seen yet!

The "ack-ack" fire was a beautiful job – it was bursting on a lot of sides of us, above and below and, at the same time, the Magi planes attacked us. Our ball turret was covered with oil so Steve couldn't see a thing, which left us helpless from attacks below. Number 3 engine was hit hard and running away, and the enemy spotted our trouble and in they came from all sides, one at a time. My ammunition stuck in the box, so I was a busy lad – shoving my ammunition can onto my gun, finding a plane coming in over the tail, following him with tracers until he faded from sight beneath the tail, reloading and repeating. Joe's guns jammed, but Eddie and I watched the tail until he got it fixed. Every once in a while our ship would lurch, as a shell or spray of ack-ack would hit us, but all that seemed unimportant with those Focke-Wulfs coming at us. The crew was pulling together fine, and after what seemed hours, the attack was over and France was left behind.

We came down to 10,000 feet and I took off my oxygen mask and looked around. On our left wing were two holes, and too near the tanks of gas to suit me. Then the lead ship (Morgan) blinked a message at us with his lamp: "Gas leak, Number 3," but Lt. Neie had transferred the gas out of that tank, so we didn't worry. Checked the crew and nobody was hurt, and we landed at approximately 1800. Then we really saw our damage: a huge hole in our right wing that went through the gas tank; four holes from flak in the radio room. Joe had a bullet explode by a piece of flak; Number 3 engine was shot up. Lt. Mendolson had a nice bullet hole in the window of the nose, and the payoff was when we learned that, while over the target, Steve had passed out from lack of oxygen. He was out for about 20 minutes. Eddie, Lakey and Steve all claimed planes shot down. *Kipling's Error II* is definitely out of commission, but not her crews. Matthews was wounded in the hand. Roche got hit pretty bad, too, but no one was killed. So, we felt pretty good.

Briefed, and off to chow and to bed. Chow here stinks. We had to watch ourselves or we'll line up in front of the garbage pail instead of going inside!
— *Sgt. Dick Haseltine, radio operator*

MAY 29, 1943

✤ Mission #5 – bombing altitude 22,000 feet – Group #6.

Woke up late today and briefed at 9:30 a.m. Target of mission: a pre-fabricating plant (naval and submarine) at Rennes, France. Left Andrews Field (Great Saling) at 1:00 p.m. and rendezvoused at coast with two other groups. Saw about five different groups go to a different target en route. Had P-47 escorts up till five minutes before (1:00 p.m.) and, immediately after they left and when we began our bombing run (4:00 p.m.), we were attacked by FW-190s, about 50 or 60 of them. Steve (ball turret) passed out due to lack of oxygen. Both of my guns went out, and I sure thought we were goners. Good gunnery due to ball turrets and tail turrets from other ships kept us from going and getting shot down. Came in 6:20 p.m. (all 96th ships okay).
— *Sgt. Joseph Kotlarz, gunner*

MAY 30-31, 1943

✤ Slept most of today. Got three letters – two from Mabs and one from Johnnie. Wrote some letters.

Handwritten diary note by Lt. Lloyd Mitchell

May God's blessing be with Stevenson, Holcombe, McMath and their crews. They were good Americans.
— *Lt. Lloyd Mitchell, navigator*

MAY 30, 1943

✤ Went to 7:00 a.m. mass today. Offered mass for yesterday's raid, when everything seemed so hopeless. Sure tired today. Our ship, *Kipling's Error II*, due for sub depot, so we'll get a different ship.

On yesterday's mission, we were hit in quite a few spots. One .20mm shell went through Number 2 engine gas tank. Another .20mm shell went through Number 4 engine gas tank. A third .20mm shell went through the leading edge of the wing between co-pilot and Number 3 engine. Sure a mess, and due for the sub depot for repairs. White transferred the gas out of Number 1 and Number 4 tanks for safety. Number 3 engine started leaking oil from a hit and began burning, but somehow it stopped. A shell hit my ammo box and jammed my ammunition. A lot of other hits and holes on ship.

— *Sgt. Joseph Kotlarz, gunner*

MAY 31, 1943

✠ Memorial Day officially celebrated in the United States. Nothing doing here today. Had a meeting at 9:00 for practice mission, but we (crew B-3) were not in on it, on account of not having a plane.

On Mission #5, I saw two B-17s go down. So far, the 96th has lost only three planes over enemy territory, and three on this side (England). This was our toughest mission. Over 60 FWs attacked us and it was really rough.

Had my first air raid today and slept through it. Went to town tonight. Just another town to me. All you can do here is get drunk.

So far, the 413th hasn't lost a ship over enemy territory or any of the crews.

— *Sgt. Joseph Kotlarz, gunner*

JUNE 1, 1943

✠ Attended an intelligence lecture by Capt. Ullman. It was interesting. Gen. Anderson came in and gave us a brief congratulatory speech. He said we've done fine – better than the group we had replaced. Even better than the crack 305th, which makes us about the best in the E.L.O. Also mentioned something about initiatives coming up.

— *Sgt. Dick Haseltine, radio operator*

✠ Nothing special doing today.

After a member of the combat crew (enlisted man) goes through with five missions, he gets the "Soldiers Air Medal." I'm eligible for it now.

Had a special meeting and lecture by Capt. Ullman on "Escape." Also, had a guest on the program today, a one-star general, Gen. Longfeller, who gave us a nice welcome speech.

On this last raid, the 96th really took a hammering, 'cause when we got back, most of the ships were out of commission. The Germans really lost a lot of FW-190s in this raid. 307th Squadron lost one.

— *Sgt. Joseph Kotlarz, gunner*

JUNE 2, 1943

✠ Rained all day. Wrote letters and loafed.

— *Lt. Lloyd Mitchell, navigator*

JUNE 2, 1943

✠ Supposed to have a practice mission today, but called it off. Weather has been rather bad. Lost of a couple of days on account of we're not doing any flying at all.

Most of the fellows have their own bicycles here. Transportation is tough here, so bicycles will solve the problem. Every member in our crew has a bike except Lakey and I, who share Steve's bike (RAF bicycle).

Combat crew meeting with the Lt. Col. (Old) presiding. According to the colonel, the 96th has a pretty good record so far as bombing is concerned, and for bringing its ships back.

Went to Braintree, England tonight.

— Sgt. Joseph Kotlarz, gunner

JUNE 3, 1943

✠ Ascension Day.

Went to mass today on the base. Had ground school till 9:00 a.m. Bad, rainy weather today. Most of the combat crew did not attend ground school, so they got penalized and have to march to chow and class. Lakey and I have been going every day and are in the clear.

Payday today: 22 – 10 – 7.

Went to town (Braintree) tonight. Ate at the Red Cross Club, and had a fairly good time.

— Sgt. Joseph Kotlarz, gunner

JUNE 4, 1943

✠ Perfect weather today. Expected to have a mission, but called off for some reason or another. The 96th received a citation for its efficient work, which included good bombing (precision 50% hits), good gunnery, and bringing back the planes (no plane losses). So far, only three planes have been lost due to combat, which is a very good record.

Eddie White, our assistant engineer (top turret), has two Focke-Wulf-190s to his credit officially, and both destroyed.

Fellows in barracks made a collection ($5 apiece) and bought a radio-making kit like home here. Went to Braintree tonight.

— Sgt. Joseph Kotlarz, gunner

JUNE 5, 1943

✠ Ground school this morning from 8:00 to 9:00 a.m. on "escape" (Ullman). On the May 21st raid to Emden, Germany, the FW-190 I got was not confirmed. So, I still have my first one to get (officially), although I'm satisfied, as I had the satisfaction of seeing my tracers go through the FW-190.

Lord Haw-Haw (German propagandist of English birth) came over the English radio, even before 15 of our ships came over, and announced their arrival. At one time in Grafton Underwood base, he broadcasted that our clock was 15 minutes slow, and it was! How he gets his information is uncanny.

Went to confession tonight.
— *Sgt. Joseph Kotlarz, gunner*

JUNE 6, 1943

✠ Practice Mission – over Channel.

Got up 0500. Breakfast 0600. Briefed. Used someone else's plane, so we had to lug all of our flying equipment from our hut halfway around the field to get to this plane. Checked the guns and dressed up for a practice mission. Take-off was at 0900. Flew at 7,000 feet. Weather not so good. I flew in the tail-gun position. As we got over the Channel, the weather closed in. Just a few seconds before it did close in, we saw six ships headed toward the English coast, each with a balloon above it to protect it from diver bombers. We turned back as soon as we hit the rain and flew through the clouds all the way back. Landed at 1:30. Turned in my parachute to be re-packed.
— *Sgt. Leo Lakey, gunner*

✠ Had a briefing this morning and went up on a flight from 9:00 till 11:00 a.m.

Before we left Grafton Underwood Air Base, Lord Haw-Haw told the 96th they would get a "warm reception" when they got to Andrews Field. This all came over the radio. Up till this time, we haven't been bombed as yet. Chemsford, 18 miles away, got bombed before the air echelon got here.

Went to town, Braintree, and later to Chemsford. Chemsford was the first bombed English town I've seen. They have barrage balloons all over the city, but even for the bombings, it's really nice.

Flying time: two hours.
— *Sgt. Joseph Kotlarz, gunner*

JUNE 7, 1943

✠ Our crew on alert today. Went to ground school from 8:00 to 9:00 a.m. Foggy this morning, and all planes grounded.

Clearing up now and really sunny, like after a shower.

Bad weather settling in again.

Rumors are floating around camp that we will leave Andrews and go to a field near the coast.

Went to a few of the scattered villages here near camp: Little Dunmow and Dunmow.
— *Sgt. Joseph Kotlarz, gunner*

JUNE 8, 1943

✠ Ground school 8:00 to 9:00 a.m. Received two letters from Bernice and one from Cy, and one from Joe and Anne.

Addresses:
B.A. Wells
Louise, Kentucky

Jean St. Clair – A.R.D.
College Park, Maryland

Went on a practice mission for three hours. Flying time: three hours.
— *Sgt. Joseph Kotlarz, gunner*

JUNE 9, 1943

✠ Learned today that when they dug into *Kipling's Error II*, they found an unexploded .20mm cannon shell. Talk about luck!!!
— *Sgt. Dick Haseltine, radio operator*

✠ Ground school this morning. The fellows bought strawberries last night and saved me some, so I had fresh strawberries for breakfast.

It is final that we will leave Andrews Field, near Saling.

The mechanics on our ship, *Kipling's Error II*, found an unexploded .20mm shell in Number 3 gas tank. So, we really were lucky to get back from the Rennes, France raid.

Flew from 3:30 to 5:30 on a practice formation flight. Flying time: two hours.

Lt. Mitchell eating strawberries

Went to Large Dunmow, a small town five miles away.
— *Sgt. Joseph Kotlarz, gunner*

JUNE 10, 1943

✠ Packing, bagging and getting all ready to leave here. Our crew will leave by train. Went swimming at the pool at Braintree and almost froze.
— *Sgt. Joseph Kotlarz, gunner*

JUNE 11, 1943

✠ Today we raided Wilhelmshaven. We were supposed to hit Bremen, but there was a front over the target, so we hit the secondary target. The 94th and composite group hit Cuxhaven. My first picnic. Didn't even see a fighter, and the flak was very light.

We took off from Saling and landed at Snetterton Heath. You've got to get your mouth just right to say "Snetterton." This was close to the "Robin Hood" forest that you read about. That was just a story, but I think the name of the forest was in "Robin Hood," and there was where we took off and did our combat missions.

Joe got a fighter. 5/25 or 1/5.
— *Lt. Lloyd Mitchell, navigator*

✠ Scheduled for Bremen, Germany, but went to Wilhelmshaven, Germany instead. It was supposed to be a rough raid, but it was our first real pushover. No fights, and very little inaccurate flak. But, what do you know! We took off from Great Saling and were ordered to land at our new base, Snetterton Heath. We did so and found everyone had moved while we were on the mission.
— *Lt. Ruben Neie, pilot*

✠ Mission #6 – bombing altitude 25,000 feet (five 1,000-pound bombs).

Woke up this morning and told we were to leave on the 9:30 train. Went by truck to the railroad station four miles from Andrews Field and boarded train, only to be called off to go back to Field on account of a mission. Had a briefing at 12:15 and told our target was to be Bremen, and in the event it was closed in, the secondary target would be Wilhelmshaven, Germany. Left the field 3:15 p.m. over the North Sea and came in over the coast of Germany, intercepted by more two-engine fighters who ran away, directly after an FW-190 came in and was shot to pieces (time: 1826) by Steve and me. Saw only four single-engine and double-fighters through entire mission. Visibility was poor over Germany, so we made for the secondary target, Wilhelmshaven, Germany (Dielard Engineering Works and Submarine Pens). Direct hits were scored by our group on pens and oil tanks and works.

We were in line with the 94th and 95th Groups. Sure a lot of Fortresses making raids today. Counted five groups as we were entering Germany, and seven as we left. Leo Lakey counted around 200 Fortresses. We came back to our new field and were really given a welcome. We carried five 1,000-pound bombs and bombed from 25,000 feet. The mission was a complete success.

The name of this new base is Snetterton Heath AAB, and it's located 18 miles from Norwich. It's really spread out, but nice. Lots of flowers around, and poppies blooming, and rabbits running and playing around; the thought of combat ruining the scene.
— *Sgt. Joseph Kotlarz, gunner*

JUNE 11, 1943

✠ Sixth Mission – flew six hours – 96th Seventh Mission – Wilhelmshaven, Germany.

This mission was called off very early in the morning. Got up at 0515. Breakfast 0545. Formation at 0800. Rode the trucks down to the railroad, waited there for a while before the train pulled in. We were in our cars a few minutes before the colonel came in with an order for all combat crews to go back to the base to carry out that scrubbed mission. We were rushed back in a hurry, briefed, ate dinner, then we ran all over the field looking for flying clothes because ours was shipped out earlier in the day. After we found some flying clothes, we worked on our guns, or, rather, in our regular positions in someone else's ship named Rikki Tikki Tavi, because our ship, *Kipling's Error*, is still undergoing repairs from its last raid.

We took off at 1515 and flew low until an hour away from the target. The weather was cloudy most of the way, but the visibility was good. On our way over, we saw hundreds of 17s coming back from Germany. As we got over Germany, the flak was very light and we only saw four fighters. We flew above the scattered clouds at an altitude of 25,300 feet, and it was very cold. There were no fighters around, so I had a good look at Germany and our other groups dropping their bombs.

I saw over 200 B-17s while in German territory. We dropped five 1,000-pound bombs on Wilhelmshaven, Germany. Saw several airfields, but no fighters came up, probably due to the fact that all other groups before us fought them out and shot them up.

On the way home, about 20 miles from the German coastline, we saw a 17 go down from another group. It was about two miles behind us. As its engines started to burn, it pulled out and, somehow, the fire died down, but he was badly hit and headed for the French coast. Two fighters spotted him and fought with him for a few minutes. After the fighters left, the 17 went into a dive and one man hit the silk. After he bailed out, it went into a spin. It hit the water with a big splash. All we could do was just watch and feel a little sorry for the crew that met its end there in the North Sea. The rest of the trip home was rather quiet after seeing that.

We landed at our new field at 2115. A very pretty field with poppies growing all over. After landing, we were briefed, had a sandwich and some tomato juice, which hit the spot. We did not bother to clean our guns because after we found our clothes and our sleeping quarters, it was well past midnight, and we were very tired.

Post note: Some of the boys reported that they saw a B-17 flying – or, rather, trying to slip into our group – but before they could identify it, it peeled off and flew back toward Germany. Our guess is – and a good one, at that – it was captured in Germany at one time or another, fixed up, and is being used to try and fly into our tail-end of any formation and knock off the Tail-End Charlies. From now on, we will have an identifying mark on each plane, and shoot down all the others.
— *Sgt. Leo Lakey, gunner*

✠ Mission #6 – Packed and ready to leave Great Saling. Took truck coming to train, and no sooner boarded train, then we were ordered back to the base (combat crews). Went back and was briefed at 12:45. Ships were loaded with five 1,000-pound bombs, which were to be dropped on Bremen or secondary target.

Bombs Away

Took off at 3:15 and headed out over North Sea. Interrupted by some two-engine fighters over the coast who weren't too eager to fight. Joe and Steve doubled up on one and pumped tracers into it until it exploded. Really was a tame mission for our flight. The group behind us really caught hell. I saw one Fortress go down in flames, and another that just slowed up a bit after being hit.

We landed at our new base, Snetterton Heath. Really spread out. Flowers and red poppies blooming all over the place. Looks good to me. Some group – the 96th – running a raid and moving at the same time. Norwich is 18 miles NNE of field. Lots of little rabbits running around here. Can this be war-torn England?

— Sgt. Dick Haseltine, radio operator

JUNE 13, 1943

Kiel, Germany shipyards. My crew was not scheduled, and I guess we were pretty lucky, because we lost Lt. McKell, Lt. Rossman and Lt. Webster's crews, besides one co-pilot, one radio man, and one bombardier killed. The 96th was attacked about 30 minutes from the English coast on the return. Everyone was all relaxed, not expecting anything, and, all at once, the Jerries hit, and hit hard. We lost three ships, the 94th lost ten, and the 95th lost nine ships and crews. Capt. Young was the pilot of the dead co-pilot. He was hit in the chest by flak, killing him instantly. I went through the ship after it landed and found small pieces of flesh all over the cockpit and nose. Capt. Young retired after this mission. He is now operations officer of the 337th Squadron. His engineer helped him fly the ship home. This was our heaviest loss so far.

— *Lt. Ruben Neie, pilot*

JUNE 13, 1943

✠ Mission #8 (Group).

Woke up at 1:30 a.m. today, had breakfast at 2:00 a.m., and briefed for bombing mission to Kiel, Germany (complete submarine works and assembly plant and harbor). We (Crew B-3) did not go on account of no ship. The planes took off at 6:12 a.m. and came back about 1:30 p.m. The 96th Group met a lot of fighters, both twins and single-engine pursuits, and lost three planes. We suffered two casualties (339th Squadron). A co-pilot and a waist-gunner were dead, and a radio man was seriously wounded. The 95th lost ten planes out of 18 planes. It was really rough on all groups, and, to top it off, visibility was poor and the target was not hit. I was supposed to go with Capt. Ford's crew, but Lt. Neie and the rest of our crew objected to it, so I didn't go.

> **Resume of Mission #8:**
> Air Task Force target: Kiel, Germany (sub pens and install.)
> Planes dispatched: 108 B-17s; 17 B-24s
> Bombs dropped: 302 tons
> Planes lost: three 17s and 6 24s
> 52 enemy aircraft destroyed
>
> First Wing: LeMans, France
> Target: Rhone and Rhone Aero-Engine Warehouse
> Six groups dispatched – 108 B-17s
> E/A downed: three probable; three damaged
>
> Secondary effort:
> Three groups – 40 B-17s
> Diversionary sweep – North Sea
>
> 4th Wing: LeMans, France
> Target: Rhone and Rhone Aero-Engine Warehouse
> 4 groups – 84 B-17s
> 726 – 500-pounders on target
>
> Escort:
> Eight Squadrons – P-47s (Thunderbolts)
> 17 Squadrons Spitfires
> — *Sgt. Joseph Kotlarz, gunner*

✠ Got up at 2:00 a.m. and ate breakfast and attended a briefing. Our crew was not scheduled to go, so we hung around just wishing we could go. The group took off at 6:12 a.m. and briefed back at 1:30 p.m. The group was surprised about 40 miles from the English coast, coming back, by two-engine fighters. Three ships were shot down, but all of the 413th ships returned. I followed a ship that had landed to its disposal area, and I was going to help unload the wounded. They were taking a body out of the nose

Briefing at Snetterton

(co-pilot). I reached up to catch his shoulders as they lowered him out, feet first, but there were no shoulders there. They were just torn away by a .20mm shell that entered the top of the cockpit. His radio operator was also seriously wounded. Poor pilot was crying. Must have been a terrific strain coming back with his buddy dead beside him! A waist-gunner's head was blown off in the 334th. The 95th group lost ten planes out of 18. Rough battle, but the Germans paid for it, too.

— *Sgt. Dick Haseltine, radio operator*

June 13, 1943

✠ An unlucky day for the USAAF. We were supposed to raid Kiel, but the weather was too bad and they dropped their bombs in the North Sea. Fighters attacked in two waves. The last squadron of fighters intercepted the 17s about 30 minutes from the English coast and caught them unawares. Three B-17s collided. We lost three ships – McKell, Rossman and Webster. In addition to that, three men in our group were killed – one co-pilot, radio man and waist-gunner. I wish I hadn't saw the ship where the co-pilot was killed. Blood was dripping like oil from under the fuselage. There were bits of meat scattered all over the cockpit. The other groups lost more heavily than we. I'm glad my crew didn't go this time.

Guys got shot up and killed, bleeding all over the place, and I'd watch them wash the blood out of the plane – you know, clean up the planes. I wasn't doing it myself. It wasn't infrequent that they'd come in with some of the crew dead. Planes were still flying, but they'd get some of their crews killed. They'd shoot flares and you'd see the flares going off – as they were coming in, they'd shoot flares, so they'd have the ambulance and the doctors ready at the landing.

I've come to the conclusion that anyone lasting 25 missions is very, very fortunate.

God rest the souls of these American flyers.
— *Lt. Lloyd Mitchell, navigator*

JUNE 13, 1943

✠ 96th's Eighth Mission – dry run for our crew – Kiel, Germany.

Got up at 0130. Ate breakfast 0200. Briefing at 0230. We did not fly because we could not get a plane. So we hung around operations until 0600. Then we went back to bed. We had fresh eggs for breakfast, first ones since we left the States. They really hit the spot.

Our group lost two planes. Three men were killed – a co-pilot, radio operator, and a right waist-gunner – from the 338th and 337th. Our squad all came back. The weather over the target was cloudy. The flak was light, but the fighters were really tough. They dropped five 1,000-pounders.

Our new plane came in this evening right after supper. We went out and worked on our guns and helped to get it in flying shape. Over several hundred B-17s took part in this raid. Plenty of planes.
— *Sgt. Leo Lakey, gunner*

JUNE 14, 1943

✠ Went to communion at 3:30 p.m. yesterday on the base. Yesterday was a really gloomy day.

Got another new ship yesterday evening. According to word from Headquarters of the Wing, the 96th Group came out okay, and one of the best in yesterday's raid. Went on a practice flight in our new plane over the coast. Encountered bad weather – sleet, snow and rain, with lightning hitting us twice. What a trip! Came in at 4:00 p.m. New plane is okay.

Lt. Col. Old made full-fledged colonel this week.
— *Sgt. Joseph Kotlarz, gunner*

✠ Practice Mission – flew 2-1/2 hours – North Sea.

Test new ship. Take-off at 1330. Flew through several cloudbursts and clouds. Flew up to 18,000 feet. Very cold up there. Test-fire all our guns over North Sea. This will be our third ship to use in combat.

Guns and performance of ship was satisfactory. On our way home, flew into two lightning flashes – made plenty of noise and bright red flashes, enough to scare the hell out of us.

We landed at 1600 in a slight rain. Cleaned guns, then went to chow.

We are up for an operational mission tomorrow. On this hop, we flew into a squadron of P-47s. They played with us for about a half-hour. They sure did buzz us.
— *Sgt. Leo Lakey, gunner*

JUNE 15, 1943

✤ Ground School from 8:00 to 10:00 this morning on "evacuating plane."

The mission scheduled on June 4th was called off because the 94th had an accident in which a 500-pound bomb dropped and 22 fellows were killed beside the few planes out of commission.

Went out on a 24-hour pass. Got the 5:00 p.m. train for Cambridge. Came in Cambridge about 7:30 p.m. Got a hotel room with Steve. Called in to see if there would be a mission in the morning, but all okay on account of bad weather. Woke up and went to the Red Cross Club and took a shower and had breakfast. Went out sightseeing over the college campus. Sure a nice town.

> Met a Polish soldier:
> Mieczystaw Kutisa
> 24 Portugal Street
> Cambridge, England
>
> After July 1st address:
> P-175
> Polish Forces

Had dinner with him, and also a few drinks. He is supposed to send us (Steve and I) the Polish emblem and souvenirs. Exchanged American coins for stamps with him, and we both were satisfied. Came in from pass at 5:00 p.m.

— *Sgt. Joseph Kotlarz, gunner*

JUNE 15-16, 1943

✤ My crew spent a 48-hour pass in London. I bought a new uniform and spent 24 pounds, but did have a good time. The damn trains here are hell to ride. They go at least 20 miles per hour and don't let you know when you get to a station. So, on our way back to Echols Road, we were all asleep and forgot to get off. But we did get off at Attleborough, five miles too far. It took about three hours to get back to the post.

— *Lt. Ruben Neie, pilot*

JUNE 16, 1943

✤ I spent today in Norwich with Sgt. Haseltine. Sure did enjoy myself. We visited two different museums and ate lots of strawberries. We biked over there last night from camp. We rode 50 miles all together. Yesterday, met a very pretty Scottish girl, but somehow there was something about her I didn't like. I think, perhaps, she had witnessed too much war. She was very hard. I hope and pray that I don't become that way. I didn't stay with her but two or three hours. Mabs. She is the first girl I ever met. Sweetheart. I'm lonely, but I'll always be faithful to you. You are the only woman I'll ever know.

— *Lt. Lloyd Mitchell, navigator*

JUNE 17, 1943

✠ Another one of those damn practice missions which we hate much more than a real mission, mainly because they don't count up on our total directly, but, indirectly, it makes our life insurance – namely, good formation!

I did not go to Ground School and had to report to Capt. Diltz and Maj. Hand. They both pissed me off, but I forgot what they said by now. A chewing doesn't hurt me anymore, whether I know I was in the right or wrong.
— *Lt. Ruben Neie, pilot*

✠ Had Ground School from 8:00 to 9:00 a.m. Cambridge was full of students of ministry. Never saw so many in my life. Also, it seemed that every block had a church or two. A Panzer division of 25,000 Polish troops is stationed at Cambridge. The Poles wear a standardized English uniform, with "Poland" engraved on a piece of cloth one inch by three inches, and sewed one inch from the top of each shoulder end. So far, I've seen Czechs, Poles, French, Norwegians and Canadians.

Flew for two hours this afternoon. Flying time: two hours.
— *Sgt. Joseph Kotlarz, gunner*

✠ Flew on a practice mission. Biked with Haseltine. Wrote a letter to Mabs.
— *Lt. Lloyd Mitchell, navigator*

JUNE 18, 1943

✠ Practice Mission – flew 2-1/2 hours – local loop – the Welsh Channel. (Note: This was probably the Bristol Channel, not the Welsh Channel).

Flew with Lt. Turner and Lt. Collette. I flew in the tail-gun position. He made a beautiful take-off. We took off at 0915. Flew in an 18-ship formation, Tail-End Charlie. Few more times up and he will make a good first pilot. Flew at 6,000 feet. It was cloudy and rough. Not too cold up there, although I wore all of my flying clothes. Several of the ground crew were with us. Landed at 1145. Very beautiful landing. Take flying clothes back to our own ship.

It started to rain about 1230 and hasn't stopped yet. The time now is 1930. Too much rain in this country to suit me.
— *Sgt. Leo Lakey, gunner*

✠ Supposed to have a meeting at 8:45 a.m. with general from wing.

In the raid on Kiel, Germany, Sunday, June 13th, the 94th Group lost nine ships and the 95th lost ten ships, and our group lost three ships. The 384th Group at Grafton Underwood hasn't made one mission and has lost six ships since they left the States.

On the May 21st raid, Capt. Stevenson's crew was one of our old crews at Pocatello and was transferred to the 337th.

George Harrington
Dan Seigling
Harold McGillavery
Joe Bargis
Don Manchester

May their souls, and all of the souls of the faithfully departed, rest in peace.

— *Sgt. Joseph Kotlarz, gunner*

JUNE 19, 1943

✣ We were almost to Germany but the groups were late on scheduled time of rendezvous, so Wing radioed the recoil sign to abandon mission. So we all turned around and came home.

— *Lt. Ruben Neie, pilot*

✣ Weather was rather bad, last few days. Supposed to go up on a practice flight, but decided to take it easy and didn't go.

Went out on a night pass, visiting all the nearby towns, and finally ended up in a small town (Bamham). Went to a dance there.

— *Sgt. Joseph Kotlarz, gunner*

JUNE 20, 1943

✣ Practice Mission – local loop.

Got up at 0600. The sun was shining – the first time in a long while, so it seems. Ate breakfast at 0700. Briefed at 0800. Check guns and ammunition. Take-off was at 0930. We were third ship in lead formation. I rode as tail-gunner. A little cloudy in spots but otherwise, it was good flying weather. Several P-47s buzzed us for a few minutes. This country really is pretty from the air when the sun is out. We flew over bombing range and dropped five 100-pound practice bombs. Went up to 5,000 feet. Not too cold up there. We landed at 1130. Put away our flying clothes, checked guns, and went to chow.

— *Sgt. Leo Lakey, gunner*

✣ Went on a two-hour flight this morning from 9:00 to 11:00 a.m. Went to 3:30 p.m. mass here on the base. Left on a bicycle tour of the surrounding towns.

— *Sgt. Joseph Kotlarz, gunner*

JUNE 21, 1943

✣ Dry run – somewhere in Germany.

Got up at 0400. Ate breakfast 0430. Briefed. Our crew was split up to fill out other crews. White and I to fly with Lt. Jerger, Joe and Nelson with Lt. Tanner, Mitch with Capt. Ford, and Mendolson with Capt. Flagg. We were all hot under the collar when

we found out we were split up to fly with these different crews. All of us expressed our feelings to the operational officer about the entire affair. After it was said and done, we still had to fly with these crews. Take-off was to have been at 0800, but was called off again at 1300 due to the weather. We changed planes twice and cleaned the guns in each. Certainly was a screwed-up affair. Lt. Neie put in several growls.
— *Sgt. Leo Lakey, gunner*

JUNE 21, 1943

✠ Woke up at 4:30 a.m. for briefing for a bombing mission. Our crew was not scheduled as a crew, but some members were scheduled with other crews. All of our crew were disgruntled with Capt. Diltz, the operations officer. Everyone came to words of disgust with Capt. Diltz.

Mission finally scrubbed on account of bad weather. The ship Steve and I shot up on the Wilhelmshaven (June 11th) mission was credited to me as damaged.

Went to mass here on the base and served for the occasion.
— *Sgt. Joseph Kotlarz, gunner*

JUNE 22, 1943

✠ Today, we bearded the lion in his own den. We bombed a synthetic rubber plant in Huls, Germany. This is located on the northern end of the Ruhr (better known as "Happy Valley"). Results seem to be good. Flames were shooting 10,000 to 15,000 feet in the air. This plant produces 20% of Germany's rubber. I don't know how many planes we lost. I saw four go down. Morrison failed to return. He and his crew seemed like awfully nice fellows. Russell also failed to return. I'm pretty sure most of the boys bailed out. I'd much rather see them bail out over Germany than the North Sea. Haseltine and White claimed a fighter each today. We flew with the 94th Group today. They are a bunch of !@#$. May God's blessings be upon Morrison's and Russell's crews.

P.S. We must complete 30 missions now!
— *Lt. Lloyd Mitchell, navigator*

✠ Seventh Mission – flew 4-1/2 hours – Huls, Germany – synthetic rubber factory.

Got up at 0200. Bright moonlight. Ate breakfast at 0245. Had eggs sunny-side-up. Second time in England we ever had fresh eggs. We were briefed at 0330. This briefing wasn't so very good, because they would not tell us enlisted men what the target would be – or, rather, what city or town. They did tell us it was in the Ruhr Valley and that it was a big rubber manufacturing factory.

This mission, our entire crew flew together, also in our own plane. After briefing was over, we rode out to our plane and cleaned our guns with the aid of a flashlight. It was rather chilly, so after my gun was cleaned and my ammunition checked, I put on my second pair of socks, long-handle underwear, and my heavy woolen sweater all under my coveralls. A few minutes after we took off, which was at 0700, I put on my entire flying suit, Mae West, and parachute harness.

A few minutes after that, Lt. O.C. Asper, our co-pilot, called us over the interphone and told us what the target would be. It was a rubber manufacturing factory in Huls in the Ruhr Valley, near Essen – 20 miles southwest of Essen. Just before we left the English coast, we put on our oxygen masks and started to climb, slow but sure, until we reached our bombing altitude of 24,000 feet. Over the Channel, we test-fired our guns.

Several B-17s turned back due to engine failure. Our ship was okay. We flew Tail-End Charlie with the 97th Group. They had a very poor formation.

The first flak we hit was at the coastline. It was medium and inaccurate. Also, the enemy fighters picked us up there and fought us all the way into the target, and out to the coast where our Spitfire escort picked us up and scared the Germans away.

During the fight, I only fired 200 rounds. They came in from the nose and right side of the ship. The other boys in our crew had all the fun. So I just watched the fight, saw the bombs do all their damage, and kept my feet and fingers from freezing. It was about 25 below zero up there. We dropped five 1,000-pound bombs. As we made the turn after dropping the bombs, I could see the smoke and fire. The smoke rose above the clouds which were about 10,000 feet, and I saw about six different big fires in and around this big smoke cloud. From what I could see, the target was hit right in the center. I saw the smoke about 75 miles away from the target on our way home. We were the last group to hit the target. Visibility was very good. A few scattered clouds were around, but not enough to hinder us in any way.

From what I saw of the Ruhr Valley, it looked very beautiful. Farther to the east was where the RAF bombed that dam. We could not see it. The river looked swollen, but I couldn't see whether it overflowed the banks or not, due to that RAF bombing.

We were attacked by a great number of German planes – some old and some of the newer ones. We saw some FW-190s by day and night fighters, some MF-109s and Me-109s, and also, several two-engine planes, namely, JU-88s. They fought us up until our escort picked us up over Holland, which was a great load off our minds. When they saw the Spitfires, they high-tailed it back into Germany. About 75 Spitfires met us. It was a very welcome sight.

Going home over the North Sea, I counted 156 B-17s going back home. There were more I did not see. I also saw a B-17 go down in Germany. One of our crews was lost over there somewhere. It was Lt. Morrison's crew, a new crew making its second mission.

We stayed on oxygen just until we got over the English coast. We hit the coast at about 12,000 feet. Somehow, we beat our own group in after the 94th left us. We circled the field several times, then landed at about 1130, hungry and sleepy. Took off our clothes and made a beeline for the interrogation room, where we had several jam-and-Spam sandwiches with hot cocoa. They tasted darn good.

After telling all we did and saw, we went back out to the ship, cleaned our guns and reloaded with ammunition. We also found one little flak hole in our left wing, about one inch in diameter. After I got back to the barracks, it was 1600, so I sat down, wrote this little experience and, in a few minutes, I'll eat supper, wash, and hit the old sack for a good night's rest.

— Sgt. Leo Lakey, gunner

JUNE 22, 1943

✠ Mission #7 – Briefed at 2:30 for bombing mission to Huls, Germany, fifth most important target in Germany. We were loading ten 500-pound bombs and took off at 7:00 a.m. Up over the North Sea (is there a more hated body of water in the world?) and over Germany, about 75 Me-109s and FW-190s intercepted us just before we hit the target. Made our bombing run, dropped them, and streaked for home amidst heavy flak barrages that took its toll of B-17s. Then fighters hit us again. Two groups of two each came in high over the tail. Eddie got one and I hit another. We saw them both fall and burst into flames. The target was a synthetic rubber plant and we made direct hits. Such smoke and flames high into the clouds! Lt. Morrison's crew was lost – our first 413th lost. Flak got them. Met by Spitfires after one-and-a-half hours over Germany territory, and came on home safely in their escort. Their appearance just puts enemy fighters to flight.

— Sgt. Dick Haseltine, radio operator

✠ We went over the Ruhr. We called the Ruhr "Black Valley." They had the Ruhr heavily defended. They had a lot of their manufacturing done in Ruhr. The flak burst was the danger for us – the flak seldom demolished a plane, but the danger was it would knock out two engines. Now, the plane could keep up formation with three, but if you had only two, you could fly but you couldn't keep up with the formation, and that was sure death, to be left out there by yourself, because those fighters – four or five of them – would just rotate. I mean, here is a plane, and they could just come in. They would just go like that, and, after two or three minutes, a little plane – you would just see it burst into flames and go down. So, that was the danger. Of course, if you got a direct hit with flak, it gets you, but the danger is where you couldn't stay up with the formation.

— Lt. Lloyd Mitchell, navigator

✠ Mission #7 – bombing altitude 24,00 feet.

Woke up at 2:30 a.m. for bombing mission to Huls, Germany. This target is classed as the fifth most important military target in Germany (ten 500-pound bombs today). Take-off was 7:00 a.m. Four of our crews flew with the 94th Group. Saw quite a few B-17s go down. About 75 fighters intercepted us (Me-109s and FW-190s). We were over Germany and the enemy territory over one hour-and-a-half. Sure tough on the crews. Heavy anti-aircraft fire stopped a few 17s. It was the heaviest flak I've ever seen so far. Two of the planes in our formation went down in Germany. Direct hits were scored and flames shot up a mile high. I counted over 180 B-17s myself, and that wasn't all. Landed at 1:30 a.m. Lost our first plane from the 413th today, two out of the 96th group.

Resume of Mission #7 (Huls):
Escort: in going to Germany

8 squadrons – P47s outgoing to base
23 squadrons – Spitfires
3 squadrons – Typhoons

First force: Huls, Germany
Target: synthetic rubber manufacturing
10 groups dispatched; 235 B-17s dispatched; 16 B-17s lost to E/A and A/A
46 enemy aircraft destroyed
21 enemy aircraft probably destroyed
35 enemy aircraft damaged
Two personnel killed; 16 wounded; 35 missing

Second force: Antwerp, Belgium
Target: [?]
2 groups dispatched; 42 B-17s; 4 lost to E/A and A/A
One killed; three wounded; 40 missing
191 100-pound bombs dropped
One E/A destroyed; one E/A probable; nine damaged

Resume of Mission #9:
First Wing Air Force: LeMans, France
Target: aircraft engine warehouse
Groups participated: not known
103 planes dispatched (B-17s)
254 tons of bombs

Additional First Wing
Target: aircraft factory
Groups participated: not known
61 B-17s dispatched
145 tons of bombs

Fourth Wing Air Force
La Pallice, France
Target: sub pens and installations
Groups participating: four
71 B-17s dispatched

Eight B-17s mission from all three operations, with claims of enemy aircraft shot down.
52 destroyed – 15 probable, 22 damaged.
— *Sgt. Joseph Kotlarz, gunner*

JUNE 23, 1943

✠ Dry run – flew four hours – along coast of France.

Early morning mission was scrubbed. Got up at 0630. A few minutes later, we went back to bed. Got up again at 0930. Went down to the ship and cleaned guns and loaded ammunition. Rode back to the barracks, got my mess kit and went to the chow hall, and, from there, to the barracks for a few minutes. We were briefed at 1330. After briefing, we went out to the ship again, checked our guns, and also flying equipment.

**Living Quarters
at Snetterton**

We waited around the ship until 1615, at which time we started up our engines. At 1630, we took off. The weather was rather cloudy and chilly so, a few minutes before take-off, I put on all of my flying clothes.

We started to climb to altitude about 20 miles before leaving the English coast. All of us put on our oxygen masks at that time. We test-fired our guns a few minutes after we reached 18,000 feet. Guns were okay. We flew along the French coast about ten miles away. Over the Channel, the weather was clear and visibility was good. But over the French coast, it was very cloudy. We flew along the coast for quite some time, trying to find a hole in the clouds, but no soap. So, orders from Wing came through to turn back. All of us were highly peeved when we had to turn back after sweating it out all day long, but we don't control the weather. On this mission, we carried ten 500-pounders. We flew back along the English coast on the Channel side, about 2,000 feet above ground. Flew east of London. Again, we were Tail-End Charlie during this mission.

It was not too cold up there. Only a thin film of ice formed on the oxygen masks. A few degrees below zero. We landed at 2030, taxied up to our parking strip, undressed, oiled the guns, and went down to be interrogated. Had a few sandwiches and one cup of cocoa. Tasted pretty darn good.

After interrogation, we headed straight for the barracks. Received a letter from Stanley and Red Nellesen, read them, and then voice over the tenny said it was 2230. Time for blackout. Curtains to be put up. Also time for me to hit the sack.

— *Sgt. Leo Lakey, gunner*

JUNE 23, 1943

 Mission #10 for the Group.

Woke up at 8:00 and told there would be a mission today. Went out and checked guns, etc.

On yesterday's mission, Spitfires (RAF) escorted us back about 20 minutes after we hit the target. About 90 Spitfires all together. And later on (half-hour), about 40 Typhoons came along to help. All enemy fighters disappeared as the Spits came in. Briefed on mission to France.

Flying time: four hours.

Left Snetterton Air Base and rendezvoused with 94th and 95th Groups, and just came within a half-hour of the target, and were ordered back. The weather seemed to be closing in. Came back to base 8:30 p.m.

> **Resume: Mission #10**
> Mission I: Villacoublay, France
> Target: [?]
> Six groups: 116 B-17s dispatched
> E/A claims: 15 – 7 – 6
> Three 17s lost
> Bombs dropped: 600 100-pounders; 810 500-pounders
> Casualties: one killed – three wounded – 21 missing
>
> Mission II: LeBourget, France
> Target: air supply depot (Me-109s)
> Four groups: 84 B-17s dispatched
> E/A claims: 41 – 27 – 32
> Four B-17s lost
> Casualties: 16 injured; 41 missing
> Bombs dropped: 819 300-pounders
>
> Mission III: Amiens - Gilsy, France
> Target: [?]
> Three groups: 64 B-17s
> Casualties: 6 – 3 – 10
> E/A claims: 9 – 3 – 2
> One B-17 lost
> Bombs on target: 852 100-pounders and 269 300-pounders.

— *Sgt. Joseph Kotlarz, gunner*

JUNE 24, 1943

 Flew a practice mission today. Washed my clothes. Should have written Mabs.

— *Lt. Lloyd Mitchell, navigator*

JUNE 24, 1943

✠ Ground School this morning from 9:00 to 10:00 a.m.

> **Address:**
> M/Sgt. Joseph A. Gracelet
> 121 Warwick Avenue
> West Warwick, Rhode Island

Nothing doing special today.
— *Sgt. Joseph Kotlarz, gunner*

✠ Another 48-hour pass and to London again, as usual. And, just our luck, the boys went to Bremen, Germany on a very easy mission, and also on one to LeMans, which was just as easy. Lt. Shelton aborted on the Bremen mission and was jumped by 25 FWs on his way back. Three men were wounded and his ship was really shot up. But the main thing is, he made it by flying home through cloud cover.

Met my classmate, Lt. Buster Peek, in London. He was on leave after ditching successfully on his ninth mission. He also broadcast home the night of June 16th. He only lost one man, and he was dead before they ditched. He died at his gun station.
— *Lt. Ruben Neie, pilot*

✠ Dry run for our crew – saw German coastline.

Woke up at 0130 and told us we wouldn't have to fly. We were peeved because we were scheduled to fly this mission. Had our guns and rest of ship in tip-top shape. Lt. Jerger flew it because his ship wasn't in commission, and we have the most missions in so far, being high crew with seven.

After Capt. Ford's crew cleared out of the barracks, which was about 0215, we went back to bed.

Take-off was about 0500, and it was rather cloudy. On the way over, the weather got worse. Just before they saw the German coast, they flew over a convoy of German ships. One group dropped its bombs on this convoy. Our group tried to get into Germany, but it was too darn cloudy. So, they turned back and tried to find the convoy but, in the meantime, it sailed out of sight – what was left of it. Just as they turned around, Lt. Shelton got lost in a cloud for a few seconds and ran into four FW-190s. His ship was shot up a bit, but they shot down three of the four planes. His fourth engine was shot up, so he feathered it. Right wing seven feet from the tail-end, had a four-foot hole in length, 1-1/2-foot hole in width in it. Several small ones in the tail, fuselage and radio room. Gorman, tail-gunner, was hit. Not bad. Christian was hit around the right ear and right eye. Not bad. Maule was hit in the arm. Not bad. All three are in the hospital now and will be there for a few days.

In the meantime, their ship is out of commission. They were the only ship fired upon by enemy fighters, and not one ship in our group dropped its bombs, so we don't know whether it will be counted as a mission or not. Shall know in a week or earlier. Everyone was peeved about the whole mission, but, again, the weather was against us.

Kipling's Error III

This noon, we had to dress up in class uniform, march down to the hangar, and heard a speech given by Lt. Gen. J.L. Devers and Maj. Gen. Ira C. Eaker and Anthony Eden, telling us what a grand job we were doing, and a bunch of other compliments. After their speeches, they looked at Lt. Shelton's plane. I didn't hear what they said, but I have a fairly good idea what they were thinking of, looking at those big holes in the wing and tail. Period.

— *Sgt. Leo Lakey, gunner*

June 25, 1943

✠ Mission #11 for the Group.

This was supposed to be to Kiel, Germany. Bad weather prevented the group from dropping bombs (visibility poor). Anthony Eden made a speech today. Just another propaganda stunt (3:00 p.m.).

The group hit a convoy off the German coast. Lt. Shelton's group got lost in the clouds and was attacked by enemy aircraft. The crew downed and destroyed four FW-190s. Three of Lt. Shelton's crew were slightly hurt.

We were not scheduled (b-3). Left for a 48-hour pass this morning. Arrived in London at 9:30 p.m.

Resume of Mission #11:
First wing: Hamburg, Germany
Target: [?]
Eight groups: 107 B-17s dispatched
Casualties: one killed; nine wounded; three missing
E/A claims: 32 destroyed – seven probable – three damaged
One B-17 lost

Fourth wing: Hamburg, Germany
Four groups: 84 B-17s dispatched
E/A claims: 28 destroyed; seven probably; 33 damaged
One B-1 lost.

Diversionary sweep: Amsterdam
Two groups: 41 B-17s Holland
— *Sgt. Joseph Kotlarz, gunner*

JUNE 25, 1943

✠ Gen. Devers and Gen. Eaker commended us today in a forward review after the group returned from an unsuccessful mission to Kiel, Germany. Bad weather forced them back. Lt. Shelton's crew were separated from the formation and were attacked, and three of the boys were hurt slightly. Maule had three holes blasted in the top of his radio room. He must carry a damn charm with him – talk about luck! He has his share.

Given a 48-hour pass this evening. Took a train with Steve for Braintree to pick up some clothes he left there, and to buy some drawing materials for me. Missed connection at Bishop's Stratford, and had to stay there all night. All hotels asked that we be in by 11 o'clock, and we didn't want that, so we had no place to sleep until a middle-aged couple invited us to stay at their home.
— *Sgt. Dick Haseltine, radio operator*

JUNE 26, 1943

✠ The boys went on a raid. Bad weather. They brought the bombs back.
— *Lt. Lloyd Mitchell, navigator*

✠ Dry run for our crew.

This was our pass day, which I spent with Pat Connors and the rest of the Fresno gang. Our group took off about 1530. Weather was a little cloudy. They flew a few miles in France; met no fighters or flak. Also, no bombs were dropped. They landed about 2030 and got credit for a mission.
— *Sgt. Leo Lakey, gunner*

✠ Mission #12 for the Group.

Woke up early and went to Kettering. Called on the Lewis family. Came back to London with B. Wood who showed me the town. Soldiers of every nationality here: Polish, Czech, French, Canadian, Norse, Greek, Scotch Highlanders, Belgians, Dutch and colored troops. Arrived in London from Kettering 1:10 p.m. London just another big town. Rode the subway here and really had a grand time. Met B. Wood's family and they were pretty nice.

Last night, stayed at the Mastyn Club (Red Cross). It costs about 30 cents for a night's lodging here at any Red Cross Club, and meals are usually about 20 cents.

Came in and stayed at the Red Cross Club (Columbia).

Mission today: northwest France. Target unidentified.
— *Sgt. Joseph Kotlarz, gunner*

JUNE 27, 1943

✠ I have been in Norwich since Friday night. I had a pretty good time. Ran into a Scottish lassie by the name of Margaret Brown. Went horseback riding and cycling. I went to church this morning. A very interesting speaker. He seemed very certain that, in the future, we would war against Russia.

Oh, great God in Heaven – what is the sense and meaning to life? What good is this struggle now if it only leads to a greater one? Will my unborn son have to go through this agony of hell and war that myself and millions of others are going through? A bit irrelevant, I suppose, but if one knows in advance that he is to die soon, how do you go about preparing for it? Do you forget all restraints of the emotions, and do as the old physical man wants to do, or do you cling to the Christian ideals and remain faithful to the teachings of the Holy Bible? This is a very great problem for me.
— *Lt. Lloyd Mitchell, navigator*

JUNE 27, 1943

✠ On the 27th, when we got ready to pay our hotel bill at the Gravenor House, it cost Lt. Asper, Mendolson and myself 19 pounds, which included damage on one chair. But we had fun, and what are we to use the money for here anyway?
— *Lt. Ruben Neie, pilot*

✠ Woke up at 6:00 a.m. and ate breakfast and went to 7:00 a.m. mass at a nearby church.

Met B. Wood and Eddie White at the Rainbow Red Cross Club. Went on a sightseeing tour. Had a swell time running around. To me, London is just another big city. Talked Polish with quite a few Polish soldiers. They think my Polish is perfect.

> **Address:**
> Donald C. Hasty
> First Lt. A.C.
> Communicating Officer

4346 Berkley Avenue
Chicago, Illinois
Oakland 6267

Just hardly made the train home.
— *Sgt. Joseph Kotlarz, gunner*

JUNE 28, 1943

✠ St. Nazaire, France. Screwed again, as usual. Late from pass, so Capt. Diltz (chicken) wouldn't let my crew make the mission. But K.E. went. Lt. Ward, a very good pilot, flew it and got only one small flak hole. They met no fighters. The sub pens were completely demolished by 2,000-pound Black Busters. Tokyo tanks were filled, because the ten-hour mission required more gas than our usual six-hour missions. The total weight of each plane at take-off was 62,000 pounds. All ships returned. Lt. Jerger's waist-gunner was wounded in the back by flak. My crew was royally pissed off because we did not get to go, and don't think we didn't let Diltz know about it.
— *Lt. Ruben Neie, pilot*

✠ Dry run for our crew – St. Nazaire, France.

Got up about 0700. Briefed at 0830. Lt. Ward's crew to fly our ship. Our entire crew was peeved off again because we wouldn't fly this mission. They took off about 1145. Flew two 2,000-pounders with Tokyo tanks filled up – a long trip, most of it over water. Will be back about 2130. That is the time they landed. Bombed St. Nazaire, France. All of our ships got back okay. Kwansky, right waist-gunner in Lt. Jerger's crew, was hit in the arm by flak. Weather was very clear over France and chilly here in England.
— *Sgt. Leo Lakey, gunner*

✠ Mission #13 for the Group.

Woke up this morning at 7:30. Briefing at 8:30 a.m. for bombing mission. Our crew not scheduled for the mission. Good reason we're not going because we're all tired from our 48-hour pass. Today, the bomb load consisted of two 2,000-bombs. Each plane had 2,800 gallons of gas, so the trip must be a long one, and a vital target. For the first time on our missions, the Tokyo tanks were used. They're located on outer edge of wing tips, left of Number 1 tank and right of Number 4 gas tank. Take-off time was 11:50 a.m. Not expected in till 9:00 p.m. Target: St. Nazaire, France.

Bombs: two 2,000-pounders.
Entire flight was a success, and it took only ten hours.
Bombing altitude: 23,000 feet.
— *Sgt. Joseph Kotlarz, gunner*

JUNE 29, 1943

✠ Slept late waiting on a late briefing and, finally, it came. Third attempt on LeMans motor works and missed the target again. The target was covered by clouds, so no fighters, and flak was light. The mission counted, but we really didn't do any good.
— *Lt. Ruben Neie, pilot*

✠ Today we raided LeMans, France. The motor works was the target. We had luck in that there was a cloud cover just extending to the target, but visibility over the target was excellent. I'm afraid we missed the primary target. No fighters, and very little flak. I like this kind. They have lowered the number of missions to 25 again. 7/25.
— *Lt. Lloyd Mitchell, navigator*

✠ Mission #8 (Group #14).

Woke up late today and told there would be a mission. Bombing altitude: 22,000 feet. Bombs: ten 500-pounders.

Group photographer took shots of us just before take-off. Briefed for bombing mission to LeMans, France. Take-off was at 5:15 p.m. Bombed the target at 8:05 p.m. No flak (anti-aircraft) or fighters seen. Came back at 10:30 p.m.

Flying time: 5:15 minutes. Lot of diversion raids, one of the reasons we encountered no fighters. Ninety Spitfires escorted us back. About 120 B-17s took part in this raid.
— *Sgt. Joseph Kotlarz, gunner*

JUNE 29, 1943

✠ Mission #8. Late mission today. Briefed at 2:00. As we were preparing to take off, a photographer took our pictures. Went to LeMans, France. Take-off at 5:15 p.m. Altitude 22,000 feet. Easiest mission yet. No flak, no fighters. Nearly 120 B-17s with us. Looks like Germany is pulling out of France to protect Germany. I dread our next raid over Germany. Ninety Spitfires escorted us back. We arrived at 10:15 p.m. Briefed, and off to bed!
— *Sgt. Dick Haseltine, radio operator*

JUNE 30, 1943

✠ Payday, and everyone changes from broke to good humor again. This happens every month. I took M/Sgt. Chilton, a line chief, up in 25183 for a test flight. He took the B-17 off and landed it. It was a pretty good job, too. We buzzed the hell out of several fields and trains. Naturally, getting lost without a navigator, but T/Sgt. Haseltine brought us back home on QDMs.
— *Lt. Ruben Neie, pilot*

✠ Woke up and really felt good after yesterday's mission.
— *Sgt. Joseph Kotlarz, gunner*

JULY 1, 1943

✠ Our first party in our club. Norwich women came by the truckload, and not bad to look at. I got just a little too much to drink, and had a little trouble with Lt. Hetrick, but we are good friends again. We tangled up with the stove and proceeded to move it.
— *Lt. Ruben Neie, pilot*

✠ Laundry is done for free for the enlisted personnel, providing it doesn't exceed nine pieces. Also, dry cleaning is done free two times a month.

Ground School this morning.
— *Sgt. Joseph Kotlarz, gunner*

JULY 2, 1943

✠ Dry run for all – somewhere over French coast.

Got up at 0300. Breakfast 0400. Take flying clothes out to ship, clean guns by the light of a flashlight. Check ammunition. Had two 2,000-pound bombs in bomb bay and Tokyo tanks filled with gas. Take-off was to have been at 0700, but it was delayed 30 minutes at the last moment. At 0730, after we had our engines warmed up, ready to taxi up to the runway, it was called off for another hour. At the end of that hour, it was called off again after having engines warmed up again. For the third time, it was postponed and then scrubbed, the time being a few minutes past 11:00. After waiting that long, we were glad it was scrubbed. Scrubbed due to bad weather.
— *Sgt. Leo Lakey, gunner*

✠ Mission to LaPallice, France. Got up at 3:00 a.m., briefed at 4:00 a.m., and stood by our ships until 11:30 a.m. when the mission was scrubbed. We started our engines four times, and every time was ordered to delay. We were loaded with 2,000-pound bombs and 2,800 gallons of gas. The flight was to be 11 hours. So, after we came back to our barracks, Lt. Shelton and I played ball, boxed, and took two showers. Lt. Mayhand took a newsreel of Shelton and me boxing.
— *Lt. Ruben Neie, pilot*

✠ Woke up at 2:30 a.m. for mission to France. No mention was made of the target, but it must be far, because our Tokyo tanks are filled with gas. Take-off was supposed to be at 7:19 a.m. After waiting from 3:00 a.m. till 11:00 a.m., the mission was scrubbed. Came in and went to bed.
— *Sgt. Joseph Kotlarz, gunner*

JULY 3, 1943

✠ Practice Mission – flew 4-1/2 hours – Atlantic Ocean.

Briefed at 1030. Weather sunny and warm. A few clouds in the sky. Take off 1300. Put on flying clothes just before we left the English coast. Also, put on oxygen mask.

It was rather cold up there at 18,000 feet. Dropped four 100-pound practice bombs on a target near the coast. About one dozen Spitfires buzzed our formation for about 20 minutes. All of us got in some tracking practice. We landed at 1730. Put a little oil in the gun. Our crew is up on the alert list for tomorrow's mission, if the weather is good, which we hope it will be.

— *Sgt. Leo Lakey, gunner*

Nothing doing here today. Went on a practice mission from 12:44 to 5:25 p.m. Flying time: 4:30 hours.

— *Sgt. Joseph Kotlarz, gunner*

July 4, 1943

Firecrackers and fun over LaPallice, France. The mission was a success. 11-hour flight, very heavy flak, but only saw one lone fighter, and he had enough sense to keep his distance – the way we like to see them. Tokyo tanks came in handy. S/Sgt. White flew part of the way home. He can fly pretty damn good formation. He could bring the ship home in an emergency – I know. He is a very dependable man to have on a crew.

— *Lt. Ruben Neie, pilot*

Independence Day! Today, a year ago, I graduated from Kelly Navigational School. Today, we raided LaPallice, France. The target was the sub locks. Perfect visibility, and I think every group of bombs hit the target. We had some flak fairly accurate, but saw only one enemy fighters. 8/30. Damn it. They changed it to 30 again.

— *Lt. Lloyd Mitchell, navigator*

Got up at 0200. Breakfast 0230. Briefing 0300. Told us just where we were going and what route we were taking. Target is the U-boat pens at LaPallice, France. The weather over England was cloudy and foggy. We took off at 0600. It was just beginning to get daylight. Put on all of my heavy socks and underwear and wool sweater before taking off. We flew at 2,000 feet for awhile. Then, we had to climb up above the overcast, which was 6,000 feet. All of England was covered all over with clouds. We left England at the southeast tip and flew over plenty of water. The entire trip was about 2,000 miles long.

The clouds were with us until about 25 miles from the target, just about the time we started to climb to altitude. It was very cold up there. We flew at 23,000 feet over the target. The flak hit us a few minutes before hitting the target. The flak was thick, but not very accurate. The target was very plain to see – we even saw several small boats and one big battleship. I saw the target hit by at least half of the bombs of the entire flight. We dropped four 1,000-pound bombs. Our ship had the squadron camera in its camera pit. Dick took care of the camera. As we made the left turn, the target was well covered with bombs. Visibility was very good over and around the target. We encountered one enemy fighter and he was so far away, he was safe, but, still, we all opened fire on him. Don't know if we hit him or not. I fired about 40 rounds on this mission. After we came down from oxygen, some of us tried to sleep. I couldn't, so I took Steve's place in the ball turret for several hours. I fired about 30 rounds from the ball turret. I also rode up with Mitch and behind the pilot and co-pilot. Eddie flew for awhile.

We landed at 1700. The weather being very cloudy and overcast, more so than this morn. Put away my clothes. Ate several Spam sandwiches; also drank some cocoa. Interrogated, and then went out and cleaned my gun. Now it's time to go to bed. It's about 2000. The entire gang is tired.

— Sgt. Leo Lakey, gunner

JULY 4, 1943

✠ Mission #9. 24 years old today. Celebrated my birthday by getting up at 3:00 a.m., being briefed, and took off with Tokyo tanks for LaPallice, France to destroy their submarine pens. We went out over the Atlantic and headed south, came in fast over the target, and dropped our bombs in spite of heavy flak barrage, and lit out for home. The mission took 11 hours – what a long ride, but we really ruined the target. I had to take pictures of the results, and then transfer gas during the bomb run (gulp!).

Briefed, and off to town to a dance. Good to go out – relieves your nerves somewhat. We carried four 1,000-pound bombs. We put "Ria and Bob" on one, and Mitch dedicated one to his wife. I'll wait until a raid over Germany with 1,000-pounders before I write "To Hitler from Jinny" on it.

— Sgt. Dick Haseltine, radio operator

✠ Mission #9 – four 1,000-pound bombs – Group #15.

Woke up at 1:45 a.m. and briefed for bombing mission to LaPallice, France. Target: submarine pens and lock. Left at 6:05 a.m. and rendezvoused with 94th, 95th and 100th Groups (21 planes per group). Arrived at target 12:00 noon, and proceeded with bombing. Only one enemy aircraft intercepted. Anti-aircraft fire was heavy near target, and pretty accurate. Bombing altitude: 23,000 feet. We had our Tokyo tanks filled with gas, carrying a total of 2,790 gallons of gas. The entire mission was over water, and took approximately 11 hours. Came in at 5:00 p.m. Flying time: 11 hours.

— Sgt. Joseph Kotlarz, gunner

JULY 5, 1943

✠ Group practice mission. Also dance at Bantom last night. I had a date with the shortest girl in my life. Miss Fisher was 19 years old and five feet tall. When I took her home, she said, "You may kiss me on the cheek." So I went home four miles, in the rain – all wet.

— Lt. Ruben Neie, pilot

✠ Today I received three packages. Candy from mom. A bible and candy from Johnnie. They sure were welcome.

— Lt. Lloyd Mitchell, navigator

✠ Went out and cleaned guns, and then had a group formation and were presented our Air Medals by Col. Nilson. We had to go up "in a military manner," one by one, salute and receive a handshake, etc. Received a swell birthday card from Jinny and one from her mom. That made me feel better than receiving my air medal. Caught up on some letters tonight.
— *Sgt. Dick Haseltine, radio operator*

✠ Woke up late today. Went out and cleaned guns.

Entire 96th combat crew formation presentation of "Purple Heart Medals" and Air Medals. I received mine (Air Medal).

> **Address:**
> William E. Moore
> Captain A.C.
> 568 Hally Avenue
> St. Paul, Minnesota

— *Sgt. Joseph Kotlarz, gunner*

JULY 6, 1943

✠ Two practice missions today. Also rode an English motorcycle, which really gave me the blues for a new Harley-Davidson.
— *Lt. Ruben Neie, pilot*

JULY 7, 1943

✠ C.E. White (Eddie) got another confirmation of a plane, possibly destroyed on the Huls mission. R.E. Haseltine (Dick) got one confirmed as damaged on the same raid.

Sent Bernice $140 by Special Service (20-day service).
— *Sgt. Joseph Kotlarz, gunner*

JULY 10, 1943

✠ LeBourget Airfield in the outskirts of Paris. Just as we were reaching our bombing altitude, our Number 2 engine went out and, unable to keep up on three engines, we aborted (for our first abortion). The boys really hated to turn back, but it was all we could do. But we felt better when we found out that the whole group aborted. But Capt. Flagg got his ship and men shot up pretty bad. One hole in his ship was big enough to ride a small Shetland pony through.
— *Lt. Ruben Neie, pilot*

✠ Today we started on a raid to LeBourget an airfield on the outskirts of Paris. We had to turn back at the coast because of engine trouble. Capt. Flagg turned back after he had crossed the French coast. He was jumped by about 25 fighters. He knocked down eight of them and sure got powerfully shot up, and one was hurt seriously. "Wabbit twacks."

— Lt. Lloyd Mitchell, navigator

July 10, 1943

✠ Almost a mission – flew three hours – LeBourget, France.

We got up at 0100. Cold and a few clouds visible. Ate breakfast at 0130. Briefing 0200. After briefing, we went out to the ship and cleaned our guns by the aid of our flashlights. The weather on the ground didn't look any too good, and it was rather chilly. After cleaning my gun, I put on all of my heavy underwear and flying suit. Nelson, our right waist-gunner, did not make this trip with us because he is in the hospital with a bad eardrum. A kid by the name of M.R. Lord from the 338th flew as our right waist-gunner. We took off at 0520, being Tail-End Charlie in high middle squadron of nine ships. The entire group started to climb to altitude a few minutes after all the groups got together. We hit 25,000 feet about one hour after taking off. It was very cold, about 30 below zero, leaving vapor trails all over the sky. A few minutes off the English coast, our Number 3 engine went out. All we could do is turn back and feel peeved off, for not being able to make this mission.

We landed at 0820. Oiled our guns, then put away our flying clothes. Rest of the crew went to the barracks. I hung around the ship waiting for the boy to get back with my bike. About 0920, Capt. Flagg came in shooting off three red flares and landed in one big hurry. The ambulance took three of the boys to the hospital: Lt. Millican with an arm wound – not bad; St. Salinsky was hit in the leg – not bad; Sgt. Wagner was hit below the left eye and his injury wasn't bad. Their ship was hit all over – a two-foot hole a little behind the left waist-gunner. Number 3 engine was shot up and propeller was feathered. Several .20mm came in through the tail and went through the entire ship, leaving big holes in the fuselage in the waist and radio room, and came out in the nose. Wings were hit with flak. Ball turret was hit. Our guess is there are about 300 holes, all sizes, in the entire ship. They were attacked just as they were leaving the French coast after leaving the entire formation due to engine starting to go bad. The boys claimed to have shot down seven to nine FW-190s. It will be several weeks before they are confirmed by the Wing.

The rest of the formation flew over the target, but did not drop any bombs because a solid layer of clouds about 12,000 feet covered the target area. The target was a few miles northeast of Paris. The enemy fighters weren't many. Flak was very light.

After watching all the planes land, I went to the barracks to get some sleep. It is now 1900 and raining. Will eat, shower, then go back to bed. We are alerted for tomorrow again.

— Sgt. Leo Lakey, gunner

✠ Briefed at 2:30 a.m., took off at 5:30 a.m., loaded with ten 300-pound bombs. Target: LeBourget, France – an airdrome. We assembled over a point near London with the rest of the group, and just as we were about the head out over the Channel, our Number 3 engine went out and we had to abort. I sent a message into the Wing telling them that we were returning to the base. First time of contradiction. Landed here at 7:00

and went to bed. Group returned at 10:15 – all came back – visibility over target was very poor. Capt. Flagg had to abort 15 minutes from target and started back alone. FWs and MEs hit them and they had a running battle. They made it okay with only three men slightly wounded. Solinsky in the ball turret got it in the leg, and then shot down the ship that got him. Morgan, R.O., shot down two ships in spite of a .20mm shell that hit the fuselage, exploded, and the hull of the shell continued on and entered his ammunition box, exploded an incendiary bullet, continued on, and pierced his leather flying pants, topped his unmentionables, and dropped harmlessly inside his pants. No harm done. Another shell tore a hole big enough to jump through in the waist-gunner's position, splattering one very slightly with small pieces. Lt. Millihire, bombardier, got a slight wound in his right forearm. Some affair when as many planes of the German Air Force can't stop one B-17. Can't even tell any of their crew. Lordy, and a lot of prayers were sure sent up plenty today. The plane I "shot down" was only damaged, according to a notice posted this week.

— *Sgt. Dick Haseltine, radio operator*

✠ Mission #16 (Group) – ten 500-pound bombs.

Woke up at 1:30 a.m. and briefed for a bombing mission to LeBourget, France. A big sub depot and airdrome. A very vital target for the maintenance of airplanes. Three-hundred B-17s were to take part in this raid. We had an abortion off the coast of England. Our Number 3 engine gone out , and Number 1 supercharger went out. The mission was not a success on account of poor visibility. None dropped their bombs. Lot of enemy aircraft were encountered (estimated 60 fighters). Capt. Flagg's crew had an abortion 25 miles inland (France) and had to turn back. They encountered a bunch of enemy fighters and destroyed five. Three of the crew wounded, but not seriously. The plane had more than 200 holes in it. A complete wreck. Bombing altitude: 25,000 feet.

— *Sgt. Joseph Kotlarz, gunner*

July 11, 1943

✠ Went to church at Attleboro with Lt. Mitchell – really a nice speaker – enjoyed it a lot.
— *Sgt. Dick Haseltine, radio operator*

✠ Went to 5:00 p.m. mass here in the official base chapel. Visited Diss, England on an evening pass.
— *Sgt. Joseph Kotlarz, gunner*

July 11 and 12, 1943

✠ Two practice missions, two dances, got my bicycle stolen, and test-hopped a new plane and, of course, some sack time.
— *Lt. Ruben Neie, pilot*

JULY 12, 1943

✠ Received word from Bernice that she invested in a $100 bond for the money I cabled her at Grafton Underwood. Due to a misunderstanding and a mistake, it was sent to my house.
— *Sgt. Joseph Kotlarz, gunner*

JULY 13, 1943

✠ Woke up for a practice mission at 3:00 a.m. after the real McCoy was scrubbed. Signed on per diem for the trip here.
— *Sgt. Joseph Kotlarz, gunner*

✠ Got up at 3:00 a.m. for an early mission, but it turned out to be a practice mission for five long hours, which cost us an entire engine change. Letters from home – Marvin and Lillie, and four pictures of Dad, Mother, Oliver and his colts.
— *Lt. Ruben Neie, pilot*

JULY 14, 1943

✠ We raided the air depot at LeBourget today. There were 300 fighters up after us. We claimed five. The target was obliterated. We got two bullet holes in the nose. Ward's crew got shot up pretty badly. Hinkle will never fly again. He may have to have his hand amputated. 9/25. Holstead was hit in the lung. He is through with this war.
— *Lt. Lloyd Mitchell, navigator*

✠ Tenth Mission – flew six hours – LeBourget, France.

Got up at 2430. Breakfast at 0115. Briefed at 0200. We were told about the entire mission. When we got to our ship, we were told it was out of commission due to a bad supercharger on Number 1. A few minutes later, we were given Capt. Ford's ship, *Ol' Puss*. Cleaned guns and loaded ammunition by the light of a flashlight. The weather was being clear all the while. A new gunner, Sgt. Novey, flew in Nelson's place. Put on my heavy underwear, socks, wool sweater and Mae West before taking off. Take-off was at 0510. We were Tail-End Charlie, again, of an 18-ship formation. Four groups flew over this one target. Put on my heavy flying clothes half-hour before take-off. Put on oxygen mask one hour after take-off. We hit high altitude just before we left the coast. A few times there, we were caught in the vapor trails of the front-end of the formation. The vapor trails of the group above us were very pretty indeed. A few miles out over the Channel, we test-fired our guns. All were okay. 20 Spitfires were our escort from the middle of the Channel to halfway to our target.

As soon as they turned back, the Germans hit us coming out of the sun. They were a mean bunch of devils, but brave – in a crazy sort of way. Diving right through a formation, then coming out of it, they would burst into flames. Several got through. The flak was heavy in spots. I saw two B-17s go down before we hit the target. Five men hit the silk. The German Air Force threw almost everything at us: FU-880s, Me-110s, FW-190s, Me-109Fs and 109Es. Some of these were her night fighters. They stayed with us for one hour. I never saw so many of them before. We figure there were about 100 of them giving us the works for that hour.

Our target was a big airfield and air supply depot a few miles northeast of Paris. We flew at 23,000 feet, dropping our 16 300-pounders from that height. As we turned after dropping our bombs, I had a short look at Paris, seeing the Eiffel Tower and a few streets. Then, back to shooting at the Jerries. Our crew claimed eight hits. I helped get two of them; White, two; Novey, one; Steve, one; Mendolson, one; and Joe, one. During this one-hour battle, we shot up 5,000 rounds of ammunition. I shot up about 725 rounds.

The Germans are darn good flyers and take a chance on almost everything. A good deal of them will never get the chance to try it again. I saw several of them corkscrew their formation. Some were hit; others weren't. They didn't try this too often. Our ship was hit by flak about 12 times, putting a hole 12x3 inches in the plastic nose, and several in the wing and tail. A .20mm came there by us in the waist, missing us by about five feet. When it hit the wooden catwalk, it sent a shower of splinters all over us – not hurting us, but giving us a little scare. The bullet hit Novey's parachute and stayed in it, ruining a good parachute. It's a good thing we had an extra parachute along.

Our new Spitfire escort met us in about the same place as the other escort left us. Sure were glad to see them. When they came into sight, the Jerries high-tailed it for home.

Visibility over the target, and for miles around, was unlimited. Sun was very bright and no clouds anywhere (except England). As we hit the English coast, Capt. McClatchy and St. Moore landed at the first air base they came across. Engine out in each plane – several more due to go out soon.

The weather in England is cloudy. We flew at 2,000 feet. We landed at 1105. Were interrogated. Had several Spam sandwiches. All were dog tired. Cleaned our guns. Our crew was interviewed by an American woman writing for *Liberty Magazine*, Betty Gaskill.

Also on this trip, Mr. Peter Masefield flew for his first trip in a B-17. He is the foremost English expert on aircraft and how and why they perform. He is the boy who said the 17 wasn't worth a damn some years ago. But after today, he changed his mind and gave the boys credit for the work being done by it here in England.
— Sgt. Leo Lakey, gunner

✠ Mission #10: Half-shut eyes blinked sleepily at the briefing offices at 1:30 this morning, and learned that we were to get a good look at Paris today. Bombing LeBourget, France – an airfield and sub depot used much by the Germans. Take-off at 5:15 a.m. 16 300-pound bombs. Met 94th, 95th and 100th Groups, and proceeded to France. We were escorted to a certain point in France, then went on alone. The minute they left us, 100 enemy planes attacked us (109s and P&Gs, FW-190s and MEs). At our I.P., two 17s went down. One reared up and then twisted to the earth. I got all the shooting I wanted. The better lasted from our I.P. continued through our bombing run and up until when we picked up our escort again on the coast of France. Ran out of ammunition and started shooting with my camera. Rather do that than just stand there. As for seeing Paris, all I saw was the blue sky above it, full of buzzing planes. After landing, learned that Asper got a slug to the sleeve of his jacket. He was riding in the nose as Capt. Ditlz went as co-pilot. Our substitute gunner (ours was sick) got a .20mm in his parachute, but nobody was hurt. No ships lost. Excellent bombing results. Flak was very, very heavy and continued for nearly half an hour. Who knew last year at this time that I would be standing on this framework of a B-17 with bursting hunks of steel, just sweating them out. Pete Masefield – leading authority on air power, author, and news commentator – rode with our group on the raid. Before this raid, the B-17 bomber was just a lot of hoopla. But with Masefield, now all he had was praise. He couldn't have picked a tougher mission.

— Sgt. Dick Haseltine, radio operator

July 14, 1943

✠ Somewhere – I don't know where I picked this up or whether it's true or not – but someone was talking to a general who was over the 17 crews and said that "17s were just *bait*." They didn't send the 17s out for the damage they could do, but they used them for bait to bring up the German fighters so that our fighter planes could knock them down. I read that somewhere, and it raised a lot of controversy with the B-17 people, you know? As if we were just out there as pigeons just to attract the fighters. Stephen Ambrose, one of the leading WWII historians in the U.S., has documented in his books that the 17s did the heaviest damage. We did a lot of damage to the German war effort, not only in knocking German fighters down, but knocking out refineries, aircraft factories, and other things. We missed a lot, but I know we hit quite a bit, too. But it kind of riled the B-17 boys to think we were just being put up there as cannon fodder (per Lloyd Mitchell interview years later).

— Lt. Lloyd Mitchell, navigator

✠ Mission #10 – 300-pound bombs (16) – bombing altitude 23,000 feet.

Woke up at 1:30 a.m. for bombing mission to LeBourget, France (a military airfield and sub depot for German fighters in France). Encountered or, rather, left the field (take-off) at 5:10 a.m. Rendezvoused with the 94th, 95th and 100th Groups (21 planes to a group) and proceeded to France. Had escort of Spitfires to a point in France. On their departure, was immediately attacked by 100 enemy fighters (Me-109s, FW-190s and Me-210s). Saw two B-17s go down at I.P. One looked as if it was hit by flak, the other seems like it was out of control. Both crashed (one just blew apart). Sure tough fighting. Did not even get a chance to see Paris. Came back at 11:05 a.m. The bombing tally was good. All planes returned safe. Capt. Diltz went along with us today. Lt. Asper was observer and almost got a slug.

— Sgt. Joseph Kotlarz, gunner

✠ Up at 1:00 a.m. for breakfast. LeBourget, six miles from Paris for the second time. Capt. Diltz went along as co-pilot, and Asper went as gunner in the nose where he got a piece of flak through the shoulder of his jacket, but didn't touch him. This was a very tough mission because of the sun in my eyes, very heavy flak, and we had to

Kipling's Error III Flight Officers, l-r Capt. Neie, Lt. Mendolson, Lt. Mitchell, Lt. Asper

shoot seven fighters down before they got us. It was a real fight. Lt. Ward and Capt. McClatchy both landed in England, but short of our field. McClatchy had one engine out. Lt. Ward had two engines out – one smoking – and five men wounded. His bombardier, Sgt. Henkel, lost his eye and will never fly again. Neither will his navigator, Lt. Nalstead, who got shot in the leg and lung. The co-pilot got it in the foot.

Our pass is due, but all passes are canceled. It looks as if something is cooking.
— *Lt. Ruben Neie, pilot*

JULY 15, 1943

✠ Woke up at 7:30 a.m. and told there would be a mission and briefing would be at 10:00 a.m. Briefed at 10:00 a.m. for mission to Courtrai, Belgium. Target: airfield. Twenty-four 100-pound fragmentation bombs. Bombing altitude: 24,000 feet. Mission scrubbed at 12:30 – 35 minutes before take-off time.

Had a Mr. Masefield (English air authority) go with us on yesterday's raid. Before yesterday's raid, the Flying Fortress was a poor ship, in his estimation. Now, it's a super bomber (Masefield went with another squadron).

Yesterday was one year ago that I flew in a B-17. Four of us flew together on our anniversary: Capt. Diltz, co-pilot; Lt. Neie, pilot; Haseltine, radio man; and myself, tail-gunner.
— *Sgt. Joseph Kotlarz, gunner*

July 15, 1943

✠ Three dry runs – all scrubbed.

Got up at 0700. Breakfast 0730. Briefed 1000. Clean guns. Ate dinner. Went back out to plane. Weather this time was sunny and warm. About 15 minutes before take-off, 1300, the mission was scrubbed. Everyone peeved off. Rain noon.
— *Sgt. Leo Lakey, gunner*

✠ Up very early again for a mission on two airports in France. We were loaded with 24 100-pound bombs. But it was scrubbed just before take-off.

Dance at Old Buckingham. Date with Pvt. Pauline STC.
— *Lt. Ruben Neie, pilot*

July 16, 1943

✠ I was interviewed in the barracks here today by Mrs. Betty Gaskill of *Liberty Magazine*. A real pretty girl. Nice personality. She wants to write an article about me. I don't know why. I can see how she'd get a story from Capt. Ford or Lt. Ward, or some of the other boys who have had to fight it out above with the Jerries, but she seemed to think she could, as I was all she wanted to know. Then Cpl. Roah took pictures of me on our plane. Rather embarrassing, the whole thing.
— *Sgt. Dick Haseltine, radio operator*

✠ Good luck! Betty Gaskill, *Liberty Magazine*.

Supposed to have been a mission today, but it was scrubbed.
— *Sgt. Joseph Kotlarz, gunner*

✠ Up at 10:30, briefing at 12:00, but it was a practice mission again.
— *Lt. Ruben Neie, pilot*

✠ Sunny and warm. Clean guns at 1000. Ate dinner 1100. 1145 the mission was scrubbed. Scrubbing these missions like this is getting some of the boys down.
— *Sgt. Leo Lakey, gunner*

July 17, 1943

✠ Today, we made an attempt at Hamburg. The targets were the engine factories there. Clouds prevented us from going into the target. We were jumped on the coast by fighters. Shelton was flying Number 2 on Flagg, and we were Number 3. All of a sudden, *Short Stride* gave a tremendous lunge. Went up 500 feet, and then flipped over on its left wing and started plunging seaward. We thought sure he was a goner. They managed to limp back home, but four of the boys had bailed out, thinking that the ship was going to crash. They landed in the North Sea about 25 miles from the coast – Kaufman,

Maule, Gorman and the Tennessee guy. I pray that they were picked up. The right life raft had been hit and fell out onto the elevator, which threw the ship out of control. Hockin tried to bail out and was caught in the nose door. He was half in, half out, with Number 2 prop missing. His head was out about six inches and the jagged remains of the bomb bay doors staring him in the face. Underneath was the frigid North Sea, which you can last about two hours in. Can you imagine such a gruesome nightmare? With the assistance of the engineer, Chris, he managed to get back in the plane. We got our flap controls shot off with a .20mm. 10/25 or 2/5.

Shelton was one of Rube's best friends, and we were coming home from a raid on one of the German ports. We were going after, I guess, submarine pens, and I remember going in. I was watching out front of us, and there were two cloud layers, and you could see the cloud layers coming together. You could see them there – they were coming together and, so help me, that lead plane took us instead of backing and going around – he took us right into that. And the first thing you know, there were 200 or 300 planes in the cloud covers. And Rube jammed those throttles forward, put it in climb, and come out of it, and then turned around and we went back. They broke up the formation, those clouds did. Well, the Germans were waiting for us. The German fighters were watching us when they realized what had happened, and they were pot-shooting us with JU-88s, and one shell hit Shelton's plane and released a raft. They had rafts there. If you had to ditch, you might be able to get into a raft. And it released the raft and wrapped itself around the vertical stabilizer. It threw the plane into a tight spin, and the bombardier and the navigator were trying to get out of the nose, and the bombardier got out. We were over the North Sea. He was never heard from again because he drowned. I am sure he was drowned, and if he didn't drown, then the North Sea would kill him, because he'd last about 15 to 20 minutes in the North Sea. But then, after losing several thousand feet, Shelton managed to drag it out, and then limp back to the base, and just as he landed that plane, a propeller came off and sliced through the nose. You can see the hole in the nose. I've often thought of that.

In between two cloud layers... I think we were going to Peenemude, which was a German submarine pen, and there were a lot of planes out, perhaps 250 planes. I remember distinctly getting into Germany and seeing two cloud covers come together. We were flying between, but you could look out and see cloud layers coming together, and that dumb so-and-so that was leading us led us right into it when they came together. And you can imagine having 200 B-17s flying in thick clouds.

Rube, our pilot, was a very good pilot. He didn't panic. That was one thing. Rube could keep his head. I remember Rube slamming those damn throttles forward and taking off on the Wing and climbing. He was trying to get away from the rest of the 17s. He climbed and then he started home. He turned around because he couldn't see any other planes. Then all of them did. They just scattered like a flock of quails. Planes scattered everywhere. We lost some cracking into each other.

We started home and the Germans knew what had happened. They were after us. The fighters – the German fighters – were after us because they realized what had happened. The pilots, then – they began to gather back into formation. They forgot. Generally, they flew with their own group. Not this time. Every time one plane could see another one, they'd start to come together and start flying in formation. Those blame German pilots were out there, pot-shooting us. Some Junkers 88s, they were twin-engine and half a cannon. I remember, they hit one of our planes and knocked the… The planes had rubber life rafts on the sides of them. If you had to ditch in the water, maybe you could get one of those life rafts loose and get in them, hopefully. The bullet hit that blame thing and it knocked it back on the vertical stabilizer, and the rubber life raft wrapped around the stabilizer and sent that blame plane into a steep spin, and the old plane was spinning out of control, going down into the North Sea. Several of the guys bailed out and were lost and never heard from again. One of them was my good friend, Lambert, a bombardier. He bailed out. Some of them couldn't get out. When those old planes went into a deep spin, the gravity – you know, the spin and the gravity would throw you back. With the gravitational force, you couldn't get out.

Well, Lambert got out and two fellows got out, and we never heard from them. Well, the pilot – he managed to bring that thing under control after losing several thousand feet, and managed to limp home with that old plane. As it came in landing, one of the props fell off and cut the nose in two. Cut the nose right in two. They were lucky there wasn't anybody left in the nose. They were all in different parts of the plane. But that was one of the meanest missions I remember, and I've always felt hard toward whoever was leading us, that they could be dumb enough to be leading us between two cloud layers.
— **Lt. Lloyd Mitchell, navigator**

July 17, 1943

✠ Hamburg, Germany – Shelton's story. We were hit by a swarm of fighters and was forced to turn around just as we reached the German coast. We almost lost two engines and did have to have one engine changed on *Kipling's Error*. Lt. Shelton was flying along beside me during the air battle when his life raft popped out, lodging on his stabilizer and forcing his ship into a dive. It dived so suddenly, I saw ammunition, guns and parachutes fly right out of the window. Five of his men bailed out, and Lt. Hackin almost got out, but he lost 12,000 feet in the dive, air speed unknown. He finally got the ship under control and brought her home, with the life raft still hanging on the stabilizer. And, to top it off, when he landed, the Number 2 propeller flew off, almost cutting the B-17's nose off.

When I saw him go down, I gave him up for a goner. We sent in his position, but was filled with joy to see him coming home just behind me. We are all hoping the five men who bailed out are alive if they are POWs in Germany.

Celebrated with a dance in the Officers' Club tonight.
— **Lt. Ruben Neie, pilot**

✠ Mission #11 – bombing altitude 25,000 feet.

Ten 500-pound bombs (communion before mission).

Woke up at 2:30 a.m. and briefed for mission to Hamburg, Germany. Target is the Bloehm and Voss Airplane Factory. Take-off time was 5:40 a.m. We were fill-ins and Tail-End Charlies, as usual. We did not drop any bombs on account of bad visibility. Met some 100 FW-190s and sure had some tough fighting. They attacked us six at a time (six fighters on one plane). Our group (21 planes to a group) took part in the raid. We were third group in line. I got me one FW-190 and put in a claim for it. The last group got attacked the most. This was a real tough fight for me. Lt. Shelton's crew had something go wrong with their plane, and it went out of control. They parachuted off the German coast, and must be prisoners if they survived the jump. The rest of the crew came back on a battered plane. Our plane came back in poor condition. One bad engine and another bad supercharger on another. The rest of Lt. Shelton's crew were okay. J.D. Miles and Lt. Hawkins got banged up pretty well. Christian, Strain and Lt. Shelton are okay.

— *Sgt. Joseph Kotlarz, gunner*

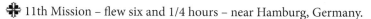 11th Mission – flew six and 1/4 hours – near Hamburg, Germany.

We were on a mighty mission. Got up at 0145. Ate breakfast 0230. Briefed at 0315. Sky was real clear due to a full moon. Cleaned guns by the light of a flashlight. Our ship was first standby ship. Just before the last ship took off, one of the earlier ones to have taken off flew over the field with one prop feathered. We got the go-ahead signal. Warmed up the engines, piled in our flying equipment, taxied up to the runway in one big hurry, gunned the engines for a few seconds, pushed the throttles forward, and away we went for a beautiful take-off, which was at 0515. While Lt. Neie was catching up to the formation, we were dressing. He caught up, which was about 20 minutes after taking off, and we were dressed and ready for action, which we got. More of that later. S/Sgt. I. Novey flew again in Nelson's place.

About 50 miles out from the English coast, it started to get cloudy. The farther we flew, the cloudier it got. We test-fired our guns about 100 miles out from the English coast. All guns okay. Lt. Neie was having trouble with one of the engines, but told us – in his reassuring manner – that everything was under control, which it was. We put our oxygen masks on about one hour before hitting the German coastline. We kept climbing until we were 27,000 feet high, and the clouds below us were almost a solid mass. Our lead bombardier was taking a chance that Hamburg would not be so cloudy. To our disappointment, it was a solid mass of clouds. We turned back a few miles before we thought we could get there. Visibility above the clouds was unlimited, and the sun was very bright. The enemy fighters hit us just as we got over the islands before flying over the mainland. At one time, we saw about 40 fighters. They would climb way up above us, come in at our tails and out of the sun, four to six at a time, shooting and twisting at the same time. Joe and Novey claimed a plane apiece. The flashes from their guns looked like their leading edge of the wing was on fire. Those old .20mm can really sling the lead. I didn't get very many good shots because another group was on our left wing. We also had some flak shot at us for a few seconds as we got a little glimpse of the islands. It was very inaccurate. The fighters stayed with us for about 45 minutes, pouring lead into us, but they got the worst of it. I saw three of their planes go down in fire, and only one of ours went down that I saw. Several of these boys bailed out, though.

About five minutes before the fighters left us (they flew around us like a bunch of angry hornets – they always do), Lt. Shelton, who was flying on our right wing, suddenly pulled out of formation. We did not know it at the time, but a life raft was jarred loose by the top turret. It hit the horizontal stabilizer, damaging it so to make it go into a steep dive of about several thousand feet, also doing the loop at the same time.

It pulled out of it quite a ways below us. Now, the Number 2 engine went haywire, so it started to dive again. Just as it started to dive, four of the boys hit silk – Manley ("Ridge Runner"), Frank Gorman ("Atlanta Peach"), Maule ("Static Happy") and Lt. Kaufman, the bombardier. All of these boys were and still are (wherever they may be) darn good pals of mine. We were together for so long. Just before we took off, their ship parked next to ours and we did some friendly joking. Now, nine hours later, they are no longer with us. Our hope is they were picked up by the Germans because they bailed out about ten miles out of Germany, rather than freezing to death in the North Sea. I believe that everyone saw them bail out and said a little prayer of some kind. I know I did.

After these four bailed out, Lt. Shelton, by some miracle, brought the ship under control. The rest of the crew was ready to bail out. It was brought under control just in time. He flew back with three good engines, minus his four men. In the meantime, our Number 3 engine conked out. We also struggled to get back home. Lt. Neie doing a marvelous job of flying.

On the trip back home, we were rather blue because after seeing those four boys bail out and their ship disappear into the clouds, we gave them up as being lost. At that time, we did not know it was under control as it went through the clouds. Lt. Shelton told us this after we landed. While all this was going on, Novey froze several fingers on his left hand. It was about 30 below up there. We had a tough time of it to keep from freezing our feet and hands. Our feet were numb with cold. Novey was almost in tears, it was paining him so. We both took a few minutes off from our post. The fight was over. I took off my gloves and rubbed his hands for about 15 minutes, then had to give up because both of mine were getting stiff. So, I gave him my gloves and I put on his. In a little while, we were down to 5,000 feet. We worked on his hand for a while longer until the danger of the entire hand freezing was past. Only several fingers were numb when we landed. I haven't seen him since. He went to the hospital. Sure hope it's only frostbite instead of several frozen fingers. Will know more about him later.

We landed at 1130. We were the last ship to land. We taxied into our parking space. Had our flying equipment out, ready to leave for the interrogation room, when in comes Lt. Shelton, whom all of us had given up for lost. Everyone on the field stopped whatever they were doing and silently cheered for his safe return. As his ship hit the runway, his Number 2 prop fell off, ripped a hole in the fuselage in front of the pilot, four feet long and two feet wide. Also, the life raft was still wrapped around the tail. The colonel, and, it seems, the entire field, was out there to greet him as he and his crew came out of that plane. They had that sad look on their faces because of losing four of their crew members. So did the rest of us. After hearing their story of the entire affair, we went to the interrogation room. Told them all we saw. Had several Spam and cheese sandwiches. Went out to the plane; cleaned our guns. In a few minutes, it will be time for supper, then for a good long sleep. Some of the boys are now sleeping.

The mission was a flop. No bombs were dropped. We carried ten 500-pounders. Too cloudy. Several Forts went down. Quite a few enemy fighters went down. Shot up 350 rounds. One .20mm shell went through the left wing four feet from the fuselage. Dent in rudder.

— *Sgt. Leo Lakey, gunner*

JULY 17, 1943

✠ Mission #11 – 2:30 in the morning is a hell of a time to inform a guy that he's going on our toughest details – to Hamburg, Germany (gulp!) to bomb the Bloehm and Voss airplane factory with ten 500-pounders. Take-off was at 5:40 a.m. Our crew thought we weren't going and were standing outside our ship, watching the take-off, when one B-17 passed overhead with a feathered prop. We hustled into *Kipling's Error III* and found ourselves Tail-End Charlie again. Abandoned operation and started to turn back. Just then, six FW-190s and some FU-88s (twin-engine fighters) attacked us, followed by six more, etc., etc. – six at a time. Joe got one FW-190 and Novey got one. I burned up nearly all my ammunition, but they were always too far away, and when they'd come in, they'd dip below our tail, and I couldn't see them. Scotty's crew (Lt. Shelton) were on our right wing when their life raft came out (came by way of the top turret) and caught on their tail. The plane started down, out of control, and Frank Gorman, Buford Manley, Lt. Kaufman and Scotty bailed out. Then Shelton got the ship under control and came into the base about five minutes after we landed. While taxiing in, Number 2 prop whizzed off and sliced into the nose. Nobody hurt.

— *Sgt. Dick Haseltine, radio operator*

JULY 18, 1943

✠ Got up at 0200. Breakfast 0230. Briefed 0300. Destination: Germany. Use 337th ships. Clean guns and load ammunition. Five minutes of 0600 take-off time. It was scrubbed. All went back to bed.

— *Sgt. Leo Lakey, gunner*

JULY 18, 1943

✠ Woke up at 1:45 a.m. and briefed for mission to Germany (city unknown). Target: Daimler-Benz Factory, manufacturers of airplane engines. Bomb load: ten 500-pounders. Bombing altitude: 21,000 feet. Went to communion before mission. Mission canceled ten minutes before take-off. We would have been over enemy territory for at least four hours. Went for 8:00 a.m. mass on the base, and then went to sleep.

— *Sgt. Joseph Kotlarz, gunner*

✠ Kassel, Germany. The mission was scrubbed at the last minute, and we were glad of it, because we were to fly a ship from another squadron, and it was in no shape to fly in a combat mission. Shelton and I went to Norwich, and I met Miss Barbara Grunton.

— *Lt. Ruben Neie, pilot*

JULY 19, 1943

✠ Went to church with Mitch. Prepared for a mission, but was scrubbed this morning.

— *Sgt. Dick Haseltine, radio operator*

JULY 19, 1943

✠ Bad weather.
— *Sgt. Joseph Kotlarz, gunner*

JULY 20, 1943

✠ Bad weather. Flew from 10:00 to 11:00 testing and slow-timing new engine. Sure did a lot of hedge-hopping. Flying time: one hour.

Left with Frank Kuczar to visit Thetford, England (12 miles away). Never saw so many Polish soldiers as I did tonight. Had a swell time talking with them.
— *Sgt. Joseph Kotlarz, gunner*

JULY 21, 1943

✠ Bad weather. Woke up at 10:00 a.m. Flew from 12:00 till 4:30 as engineer. Flying time: 4:30 hours.

Went out with Steve to Hampton and met a couple of Polish fellows. Supposed to get some souvenirs from them as soon as they get back from maneuvers (on Sunday, July 25th).
— *Sgt. Joseph Kotlarz, gunner*

JULY 22, 1943

✠ Beat the 339th Squad 13 to 2 in a softball game.
— *Lt. Ruben Neie, pilot*

✠ Bad weather. Woke up and really feeling okay.
— *Sgt. Joseph Kotlarz, gunner*

JULY 24, 1943

✠ Today we went to Bergen, Norway. Target was clouded over, and we brought the bombs back. Elaborate later. Norway was cold, bleak-looking country. High snow-capped mountains, and there were several huge glaciers, which made excellent checkpoints. The fjords were very numerous. 11/30.
— *Lt. Lloyd Mitchell, navigator*

✠ Bergen, Norway.

Shelton, Turner, Asper and myself came back from Norwich late, missed the briefing, and almost missed the mission. I reported to Maj. Hand and Maj. Cotter and they finally let me go.

Norway was covered with beautiful clean lakes and high mountains covered with snow and ice glaciers. The target was covered by clouds, so we did not bomb. The flight was eight hours and ten minutes.
— *Lt. Ruben Neie, pilot*

✠ Twelfth Mission – flew three hours – Bergen, Norway.

Got up at 0300. Breakfast 0400. Briefed 0430. Clean guns and load ammunition. First take-off delayed 30 minutes. Take-off was at 0815. Put on heavy underwear and socks before take-off. Weather over England was cloudy, and all the way over. Put on oxygen mask two hours before target. What we saw of Norway, it was mountainous and plenty of snow. The target was covered over with clouds. No bombs were dropped. No flak. No enemy fighters. Very cold, about 30 below zero. The sun above the clouds was very bright. Halfway home, the clouds thinned out, saw a big convoy nearing England. No clouds over England. Land at 1620. Ate Spam sandwiches and drank some cocoa. Interrogated; cleaned guns. Flew 22,000 feet.
— *Sgt. Leo Lakey, gunner*

JULY 24, 1943

✠ Mission #12 – Briefed at 2:30 this morning, and cleaned guns and loaded ammunition. Take-off was at 7:30. Out over the North Sea, and at 12:15, we were over the target in Norway – submarine pens. The target was obscured by clouds, so after circling around for a bit, looking for an open slot through which to drop our bombs, we had to head for home. Arrived at the base without any mishaps at 1600. Hope this mission counts for us.
— *Sgt. Dick Haseltine, radio operator*

JULY 24, 1943

✠ Mission #12. Woke up at 3:30 a.m. and briefed for bombing mission to Bergen, Norway. Eight 500-pound bombs. Bombing altitude: 22,000 feet. Target: submarine pens. Take-off was at 8:00 a.m. Norway sure a rugged country, full of jagged mountains and glaciers. Visibility poor, so did not try to drop bombs. No anti-aircraft fire or fighters. Came in at 4:30 p.m. Entire trip covered over 1,200 miles. Most of it was over water. Sure is a gloomy trip. Whether or not we get credit for the mission remains to be seen. Three wings were supposed to bomb the target. I only saw one wing. The target is an important one. First time I saw a glacier. Our plane caught on fire just before we left. No damage.
— *Sgt. Joseph Kotlarz, gunner*

JULY 25, 1943

✠ Today, our target was Warnemunde, Germany. It lies just south of Sweden. Target was clouded over, and we struck at Kiel. Results seem to be very good. 12/30 = 4/10 or 2/5.

Smoke pots were going full blast and were very effective. The other wing hit Hamburg. The RAF had just bombed it the night before with 700 bombers. I'll bet it is really a mess. I saw one B-17 crew ditch today. It looked like a smooth job.
— *Lt. Lloyd Mitchell, navigator*

JULY 25, 1943

✠ Thirteenth Mission – flew eight hours – Kiel, Germany.

Got up 0600. Breakfast 0630. Briefed 0730. Clean guns and load ammunition. Take-off time was called off twice. Almost missed this mission. Just as the other ships were taking off, our Number 4 engine started to act up. So, Lt. Neie turned off all the engines and let the ground crew work on it. In a few minutes, they had it fixed. In the meanwhile, the entire group had taken off. They scrubbed us, but Lt. Neie talked them into letting us take off, providing we could find an empty space up there, which we did.

This time, I put my heavy clothes on after we took off. We were on oxygen for about four hours. We flew at 23,000 feet. About six Me-110s and 210s hit us near Wilhelmshaven, staying with us for about 30 minutes. Flew across Denmark. Flying around northern Germany for several hours. Flak was thick in spots. Our first target was covered by the clouds, so we went to Kiel, Germany. There wasn't very many fighters up after us, but these twin-engine fighters stayed out about 1,700 yards and shot .37mm at us. Some came very close to us. It was very cold up there. We dropped ten 500-pounders on Kiel. Several miles past the target, we saw huge columns of black smoke about 4,000 to 8,000 feet high. It was very dense. Looked like a very good job of bombing. Visibility was very good above the clouds. The clouds were about 12,000 feet high. Several fighters hit us as we were leaving the coast, but not for long. Halfway out over the North Sea, two Forts caught fire, and they crash-landed in the sea. All of the boys got out and into their life rafts. Their position was radioed in. Now we are hoping they will be picked up soon. These two ships were from another group. Looked like duck season over Germany with so many 17s. Several groups caught quite a few enemy fighters.

We landed at 2015. Interrogated. Had a real supper of fresh eggs and steak. After supper, we went straight to the barracks. Too tired to clean guns. Alerted again for tomorrow, so now, to bed.

We were on oxygen for about four hours. The scenery a little north of Germany was rather interesting, seeing plenty of little islands and water. Saw several big ships standing idle in a small harbor.
— *Sgt. Leo Lakey, gunner*

✠ Mission #13 – Target today was originally Warnemunde, Germany. Our wing was to make a diversion to draw the fighters away from the first Wing who were going on a bit after we went in. Completed our diversion and succeeded to draw away some twin-engine fighters over the German coast. Turned around and headed back over North Sea, cut across Denmark and down to Warnemunde. Visibility was poor, so we went over Kiel and bombed it. Left huge fires behind us on harbor installation. Flak and fighters shot down a few B-17s, but we were unharmed.
— *Sgt. Dick Haseltine, radio operator*

✠ Warnemunde, Germany – It closed in, so we got Kiel, Germany instead. Only saw two fighters.

— Lt. Ruben Neie, pilot

✠ Mission #13 – Target: Warnemunde, Germany, Focke-Wulfe Airplane Factory. Kiel bombed instead of original scheduled target on account of poor visibility. Bombing altitude: 23,000 feet. One wing of four groups (84 planes). Ten 500-pound bombs (demolition). Take-off time was 12:15 p.m. Other wings bombed Bremen and Kiel. We were the first wing over to draw away and we did draw away the twin-engine jabs. Met them over the German coast. Over enemy territory three hours. Could not see our target, so we came back via Kiel and finished the job the other wing started. Our group hit harbor installation and the heart of the city. Left huge fires and havoc. Saw one plane catch on fire and crash. Another made a water landing in the North Sea, and we saw both life rafts. So, part of the crew is okay. (Fired 780 rounds.) Flying time: eight hours.

> **Resume of Mission #13:**
> First wing: Kiel, Germany
> Target: Glohm and Voss Yards (diesel engineering factory and works)
> Six groups: 123 B-17s dispatched
> E/A: 38 destroyed – six probable – 27 damaged
> Casualties: one killed – five wounded – 150 missing
> 15 B-17s lost
> Bombs on target: 400 500-pounders; 176 250-pounders; 680 100-pounders
>
> Secondary effort: three groups of 59 B-17s
>
> Fourth wing:
> Target: Deutsche Werke Shipyards
> Six groups: 141 B-17s dispatched
> E/A claims: six destroyed
> Casualties: one killed – three wounded – 40 missing
> Four B-17s lost
> 462 500-pounders; 116 250-pounders; 756 100-pounders; 179 500-pounders
> on airfield near Kiel, Germany.

— Sgt. Joseph Kotlarz, gunner

JULY 26, 1943

✠ Today we bombed Hanover. The target was a synthetic rubber plant similar to the one we bombed at Huls. The flak was terrific over the target. There were lots of fighters. Mendolson got one. We lost one crew – *Spino* of the 337th. Flak knocked out two engines. All of them parachuted safely into Germany. One crew bailed out over the North Sea. I've got a flak piece as a souvenir. It missed my head by inches. 13/30.

— Lt. Lloyd Mitchell, navigator

JULY 26, 1943

✠ 14th Mission – flew seven hours – Hanover, Germany.

Got up at 0330. Breakfast 0400. Had fresh eggs. Briefed 0500. Clean guns and loaded ammunition. Put on heavy underwear and socks before take-off. Weather was clear all the way. Put on oxygen mask two hours after take-off. Test-fired all guns. All were okay. Hit 24,000 feet a few minutes before over German territory. The fighters stayed with us the entire time we were over Germany, which was about two hours. They would come in at our tail three to six at a time, all their guns blazing. The only time they did not hit us was when the flak gave us a few good scares. The flak was very thick, well-aimed and plenty of it. Over the target, we dropped five 1,000-pounders from 24,000 feet. Visibility was very good. Also very cold. There were about 200 Forts over this target, and near vicinity. We sure did raise Cain with our target. I saw plenty of black smoke several thousand feet high a few minutes past the target. Over the target, the flak was really thick. Several came close. Just as we left the target, a flak burst hit a few feet in front of our nose, jarring the entire plane. Lt. Mendolson, our bombardier, was thrown over backwards, bumping his forehead, and a piece of flak two inches long and about a quarter-inch thick cut his shoulder strap on his left shoulder – one more inch lower, and it would have ripped a good-size hole in his shoulder. He sure was lucky. He has the flak, which he dug out of the ceiling.

Several B-17s were hit very bad. Some done by flak, and some by fighters. I saw five of our Forts go down – half of the boys bailed out. Saw one 17 explode in the air. No one bailed out of it.

The fighters stuck with us until we were well out over the North Sea, about 50 miles from Germany. One 17 flew home with half of its tail shot off. We lost *St. Spino's* crew over Germany. I used up 600 rounds. Lt. Mendolson and Steve claimed a fighter. Land 1500. Interrogated. Quite a few of the boys got sick due to a meal. Clean guns after supper. All very tired. Flak holes in left and right wings, nose, tail and bomb bay. None very serious. Will be ready to fly tomorrow. Saw one Fort ditched.

— *Sgt. Leo Lakey, gunner*

✠ Mission #14 – No sooner in bed than they got us up again. Target: Hanover, Germany. Rubber and tire products. Outputs 80% of Germany's rubber products. Put Jinny's name on one of the five 100-pound bombs. As we crossed the German coast, about 150 fighters intercepted us and, from there, in to our target and back out of it – it was a running battle. Two-and-a-half hours of steady fighting. In spite of them, we made a good run on the target, dropped our bombs and headed for the North Sea again. Flak over the target reached up as a solid wall and took its toll of Fortresses, but we sailed through safely. How? I don't know. I've never seen flak so heavy and accurate. Got a few holes in the ship – that's all. Nobody hurt. Good results were reported of the bombing. Returned at 3:00 p.m.

— *Sgt. Dick Haseltine, radio operator*

✠ Mission #14. Woke up at 3:30 a.m. and briefed for bombing mission to Hanover, Germany. Rubber Tire and Products Corporation. Its output of tires is 80% of all in

Germany. Bombing altitude: 24,000 feet. Bomb load: five 1,000-pounders. Intercepted by 25 two-engine fighters and over 125 single-engine jabs. (Me-110s, Me-109s and FW-190s). From the time we hit the coast of Germany till we hit the target and came out of the North Sea (2-1/2 hours), 54 planes were on our wing. Another diversion group (B-17s) hit Hamburg, while medium bombers hit Holland, Belgium and France. The 8th Air Force went out in all of its strength today. We were the lead group (middle). All attacks were on the low and high grades. Last one plane from the 96th. Flak (anti-aircraft) was heavy as hell in the vicinity of the target. Take-off time was at 8:00 a.m. Return: 3:00 p.m. Flying time: seven hours.

Resume of Mission #14:
Fourth wing: Hanover, Germany
Target: synthetic rubber and tire manufacturing
Six groups: 121 B-17s dispatched
E/A claims: 40 destroyed – nine probable – 28 damaged
Casualties: four killed – 22 wounded – 126 missing
Sixteen B-17s lost
Bombs on target: 160 1,000-pounders; 393 500-pounders; 150 100-pounders

First wing: Hamburg, Germany
Target: M.A.N. Diesel Engine Works
Six groups: 121 B-17s dispatched
E/A claims: five destroyed – one damaged
Casualties: one killed – three wounded – 20 missing
Two B-17s lost.

— *Sgt. Joseph Kotlarz, gunner*

✠ We finally got 18 ships off, of which six aborted and one was shot down, and 11 went over the target. This was our roughest one yet. Fighters hit and stayed with us for two-and-a-half hours, continuously attacking, and over the target was the heaviest flak yet. It was so thick, you could hardly see through it. We got eight flak holes in our ship. *St. Spino* got hit by flak over the target and went down. 11 chutes opened.

Lt. Mendolson got hit on the shoulder and his head got scratched by flak, which knocked him on his ass, but did not hurt him. His jacket was ruined.

— *Lt. Ruben Neie, pilot*

JULY 27, 1943

✠ Loafing around today. Resting after our three missions.
— *Sgt. Joseph Kotlarz, gunner*

✠ No mission. Rest.
— *Lt. Ruben Neie, pilot*

JULY 28, 1943

✠ Day of the Clouds – Oschersleben.

I hate to write about today. The hurt and suffering is still too vivid. We started to Oschersleben and, due to poor leadership and poor weather, we got between two cloud layers. We were just off the coast of Denmark when this happened. The fighters had jumped us like before. We got into the clouds. There were seven groups of us, all on the same level, when the clouds got so thick that the formations were forced to break up, and it was everyone for himself. There were FW-180s, Me-110s and FW-189s flashing in and out of the clouds everywhere you looked. Jerry must have seen our predicament from his radar and sent up everything he had. We came out of it okay, but our group lost seven planes. We lost Capt. Fulton's crew: Anderson – pilot; Humke – navigator; Wolford – bombardier. Maj. Emerson was with them as leader of our group, and Dean Howell was assisting Dave Humke in navigation. Nance's crew went down: Gorse – co-pilot; Joe Hudson – navigator; Mac – bombardier. Then there was covert crew Wilcox (him and four of his crew were picked up later). I can't think of the other crews. Oh, yes – there was Hughie Moore's crew: Ault – co-pilot; Hodges – bombardier. The only crew of our squadron lost. I wish there was some way of commemorating these brave men. I lost some of my best friends today.

Joe Hudson – him and I had an agreement that the first one to go down, the other would take care of his stuff. He was a really swell guy. Then there was John Gorse, Dave Humke, Dean Howell, John McIlvaine (his wife is expecting a baby the first of August). Hughie Moore's wife has a baby. Monroe (Moe) Coleman was a very good friend of mine, as was Ault. We never heard from that crew again. I suppose a person mustn't think too much of the cold North Sea and the watery graves of all these brave American airmen. 14/30 or 7/15.
— *Lt. Lloyd Mitchell, navigator*

✠ 15th Mission – flew six hours – west coast and Oschersleben, Germany.

Got up at 1:30. Breakfast at 2:00. Not so very good. Briefed 2:30. Cleaned guns and loaded ammunition by aid of a flashlight. Our ship just came into commission at midnight and the bombs were completely loaded a few minutes before take-off. Put on my heavy underwear and socks just before take-off. We were the last plane to take off because we were Tail-End Charlie again. Flying on Capt. Flagg's left wing. Since early last night, the RAF kept a steady hum going over into Germany. When we got up the searchlights were on, searching the clouds for them to guide them to their home base. At one time, I saw 15 bright paths of light searching the clouds. We put on our oxygen masks about two hours after take-off. Take-off was at 5:45.

We hit altitude a few miles off the German coast. The weather was very cloudy. When we neared the German coast, the clouds were very dense, just about the time we were to have gone into Germany. The fighters hit us, diving at us out of the clouds. They raised Holy Cain with us there in the clouds while we were fighting them off. The clouds got so thick and heavy that we could not see the plane in front of us. So, in the next few minutes, not being able to see a plane, everyone broke formation for safety's sake and scattered for several miles. It was one hell of a grand mix-up, with about 80 planes out of formation, lost in the dense clouds. It's a miracle we came through it. Several times, we fell a couple a hundred feet, almost out of control, but, again, our pilot, Lt. Neie, pulled us through, with some darned good cooperation from our co-pilot, Lt. Asper. Two darned good boys.

Just before we hit the dense clouds were the fighters, about 75 of them, who kept pouring on the lead. I saw three-quarters behind us a little above explode in the air, while still in formation. It seems the lead ship was hit in the bomb bay, setting the incendiary bombs off. No one in that ship knew what hit them. The explosion was so terrific, it blew the ship all to pieces, hitting the other two wing ships, setting them on fire. All three ships went down in a mass of flames. A very sickly sight to see.

As we came out of the clouds, we saw 17s all over the sky. Some were dropping their incendiary bombs all over the coastline in order to get more speed. We kept our bomb load. All of the planes were loaded with 12 100-pounders and six 500-pound incendiary bombs. A very dangerous load to carry. When the fighters left us, I saw a 17 ditch about 75 miles from the German coast. Lt. Moore ditched about 50 miles from the English coastline. We should hear from him in a day or two, if they all got out okay, which we hope they did.

All told, we lost eight Forts on this raid. Our biggest loss so far. Most of these crews were knocked down near Germany. No telling when and if we'll ever hear from them. We flew at 18,000 feet. The trip home wasn't any too cheerful. Ships from five different groups flew in our formation. That's how bad the mix-up really was. We landed at 1145. Packed our clothes and found several holes in the fuselage, very small. Ship still in commission. Had a Spam sandwich and cocoa. Interrogated. Went out and cleaned my gun. After supper, I'll be ready to hit the hay. Sunny and warm on the ground. Sun bath while writing these pages.
— *Sgt. Leo Lakey, gunner*

✠ Up at 1:30 a.m. Target: Oschersleben, Germany carrying incendiary bombs. At coast of Germany, met by nearly 200 fighters and, at the same time, ran into clouds. Ships attacked by fighters behind us were going down in flames. One exploded and took two others with it. Then we ran into the clouds, not intentionally, and couldn't see anything. Nerve-wracking. Nearly 100 B-17s in formation, ten yards apart and not being able to see. Finally, after knowing that every second we were going to collide with other ships, we broke out and found ourselves alone. After a time, we found Capt. Flagg's ship and, gradually, as other ships would break through, we built up a formation again and headed home. Landed, and six out of 20 planes returned. In our squadron, we lost Lt. Moore's crew. Others straggled in one at a time. Some touched into the rest of the wing and flew over the target and dropped their bombs. We wanted to go back, but Capt. Flagg was the leader, as we had to follow him. All during the fight, I had my eye on the bombs, ready to yell, "Salvo!" if they were hit, because if they were hit, it would be [?] and we'd be [?].
— *Sgt. Dick Haseltine, radio operator*

JULY 28, 1943

✠ Mission #15. Woke up at 1:30 a.m. and briefed for mission to Germany (Oschersleben). Take-off was at 5:42 a.m. Rendezvoused at coast with three other groups and proceeded to Germany. At the coast of Germany, we were met by 150 single-engine fighters and 25 twins. In the fight that followed in the clouds, I saw three 17s go down. Our wing (four groups, 18 planes to a group) got all lost in the clouds, and we came on into the base at 11:30 a.m. Bomb load was six 500-pound incendiary bombs and 12 100s. A very dangerous load. The reason why I saw three 17s go down – one ship lost out of the 413th. Seven out of the group. Bombing altitude: 18,000 feet. We were 45 minutes from the target when we got lost. All B groups must have had a lot of losses.

On Mission #15, the target was not reached on account of bad weather and all the fighters that were intercepted. Some Forts made it to the target, but whether the target was hit remains to be seen.

Met two girls from London at North Lupton.

Miss Jane Smoker
356 Kensington Place
London, S.E. 11

Resume of Mission #15:
First wing: Kassel, Germany
Target: Fiesler Aircraft Factory
Nine groups: 182 B-17s dispatched; seven B-17s lost
E/A claims: 27 – 15 – 22
Casualties: 15 wounded – 71 missing
Bombs on target: 340 500-pounders; 160 250-pounders; 80 100-pounders

Fourth wing: Oschersleben, Germany
Target: aircraft factory
Six groups: 120 B-17s dispatched; 15 B-17s lost to A/A and E/A
E/A claims: 83 – 34 – 63
Casualties: 26 wounded – 154 missing
Bombs on target: 238 500-pounders; 24 500-pounders; 48 100-pounders

Escort (to base): P-47s and 10 squadrons of Spitfires.
— *Sgt. Joseph Kotlarz, gunner*

✠ Oschersleben, Germany – Everything went fine until we all got lost in a cloud and no one could see anyone, and, at the same time, 300 fighters attacked. We had 148 B-17s flying in one cloud in all directions. I wouldn't have given two shillings for our chance to get out of the cloud without colliding with some other ship. Several just missed us. We were carrying incendiary bombs, and I saw one plane blow up and burn. We lost the following crews: Maj. Emerson, Capt. Fulton, Lt. Hetrick, Lt. Moore, Lt. Nance, Lt. Wilcox, Lt. Deshotel and Lt. Covent. This was our biggest loss on any given mission. Just before the fighters hit, Lt. Mendolson went back to use the relief tube. So, when I heard every gun firing, he knew we were being attacked, and there he was – right in the middle of 1,200 four-pound bombs. He tried to get back to the nose, but S/Sgt. White was busy firing and turning his top turret. Lt. Mendolson could not get through. So, finally, Lt. Mendolson caught White by the leg and drug him out of the turret so he could get by. It was the only way he could get White out of the turret.

The fight lasted for 45 minutes, and White did not have his oxygen mask on good, so he passed out for lack of oxygen. I saw him just in time and had Lt. Asper help him out. This mission scared me more than any before.
— *Lt. Ruben Neie, pilot*

July 28, 1943: Oschersleben, Germany

FROM: SNETTERTON FALCONS II, THE 96TH BOMB GROUP IN WWII EDITED BY ROBERT DOHERTY AND GEOFFREY D. WARD

The dark, leadened skies which shrouded Snetterton Heath at dawn were to portend tragedy. The group dispatched 21 Forts as early as 0545. The weather cursed climb-and-form-up procedures throughout the Wing. Everyone's timing was off. Briefing had planned the Wing as follows: the 388th would lead with the 100th low and the 96th high. But groups were late. Rendezvous points were missed. Emerging at last into the wild blue, the 96th found the Wing to be stretched to Kingdom Come. With as much speed as possible, the 96th struck out for the planned target, the Folke Wulf assembly plant some 80 miles from Berlin. Oschersleben would set a new distance record. It would set some other records, too.

Over the North Sea, the entire bomber stream displayed nonsensical altitudes, unsure elements, mixed groups and straggling planes. Trying to follow route-briefing instructions, the Wing made a feint at the Friesian Islands, tried to execute a 180-degree turn toward England, and then bank once more on the predetermined approach via Emden-Hamburg. To compound the situation, other bad circumstances began developing. The weather began closing in. Exceptionally strong north winds buffeted the Fortresses. Some drifted over the Luftwaffe Airfields and flak batteries of Heligoland. One B-17 received a direct hit from a 250-pound air-to-air rocket. These rockets were carried in launch tubes under the wings of FW-190's and ME-100's which fired their 21-pound warheads from beyond the Fortresses' range. All three aforementioned Forts went down amid attacking E/A from Heligoland and Jever. Starting some 25 miles from the north German coast in the area of Wilhelmshaven, 60 E/A of various types began pressing attacks – mainly from behind. Determined to maintain course and altitude, the Wing entered a deep, wide cloud bank. But when they emerged, they were even more stretched out. Many aircraft abandoned the mission at this point. Bombers started limping home.

By 1530, the raid was over. Surviving 96th crews had landed either at Snetterton or another British haven. Of 21 Fortresses dispatched by the 96th, only five bombed the target. Ten planes aborted, but not without impunity, because every one of them returned somewhat crippled. Even those aborts gave as well as they got. An analysis of Major Reynolds Benson's "Gunner's Claims" shows that even the ten aborting bombers accounted for six E/A destroyed, seven probable and another 11 damaged. But the group nightmare came with the realization that seven planes did not return. This loss of one-third of our attacking force sent shockwaves rippling out from the group to Wing to Division to High Wycombe itself.

In spite of the fact that Snetterton was a nest of distinguished visiting journalists at the time, none of them reported the loss. Wartime censorship intervened. Consequently, 8AF Public Relations tried to put the best foot forward by focusing on the only positive aspect of this "Battle Within the Clouds."

THE FOLLOWING IS THE PR RELEASE AUTHORIZED BY THE 8TH:

"A USAAF BOMBER FIELD, ENGLAND, July 28 – Five Fortresses of this group, separated from their wing by heavy cloud formations, and buffeted by countless fighter attacks, refused to return to their base until they released their bombs and incendiaries on Germany. All but one returned… Captain Francis Madsen… flying *Lucky Lady*, shoved his ship into the lead tallied by *Little Caesar*, piloted by First Lt. Cecil Walters, and *Gay Caballero*, piloted by First Lt. Charles T. Mooreland… Reaching the interior of Germany, Madsen led his tiny but determined formation until he saw another Fortresses formation a few miles ahead. 'We gave full throttle and pulled up to them,' Madsen related… A bombardier, Second Lt. Edward Quigley, who was on Walters' crew, dropped his bombs along with the rest, and then returned to his place on the guns. It was only while on the way back to England that Quigley reported that he had suffered a deep and painful wound in the back by a fragment of .20mm shell."

"The fifth ship," the PR release concludes – without having even identified the four – "was lost near the English coast…"

If that PR release did not read like a great victory, it surely did not even hint of disaster, which had struck the 96th.

That disaster really started about 0900 when the force approached the German coast. The 337th lead ship, *Liberty Bell,* came under attach. Flying with the pilot, Capt. M.C. "Steamboat" Fulton, was his squadron commander, Maj. Virgil Emerson. Critically hit, the plane was abandoned over the North Sea, but near the German coast.

Frank Cardaman witnessed the incident from *Tarfu's* ball turret.

"Maj. Emerson was on our left wing when the Germans hit us. Emerson leaned out the co-pilot's window and saluted just before the plane went into a dive."

Waist-gunner Al Neff watched *Liberty Bell's* struggle from his window position in Lt. Jim Sanders' *Rum Boogie.* Neff's best friend, Don Gordoni, was aboard the stricken Fort. A Chicago lad, Gordoni had been the radio voice of "Jack Armstrong, All-American Boy" during the early days of the program. When Gordoni's voice changed, he lost that job, but developed a great singing voice.

"He'd sing everybody in the hut to sleep on many nights or after missions," Neff remembers. "*Liberty Bell,* having fallen out of the lead, was on our left and a little behind, so I had a terrifying view of the whole scene… The right engine was on fire, and those who bailed out pulled their ripcords too fast…most chutes burned as they opened." After the war, Neff visited Don Gordoni's mother. "Watching your buddy die is an unforgettable experience," Al Neff writes 46 years later. "I am close to tears even today when I think about Don and the way he died."

Actually, only bombardier Lawrence Wolford survived the Fulton-Emerson crew. After liberation from prison camp, Wolford provided this testimony for squadron leader Virgil Emerson's mother: "We were flying at 19,000 feet near Heligoland when

"A Day in the Clouds" illustration by Joe Jones. Kiplings' Error III, 15th mission, Oschersleben, Germany. *(See page 122)*

St. Andrews Chapel, Quidenham, UK

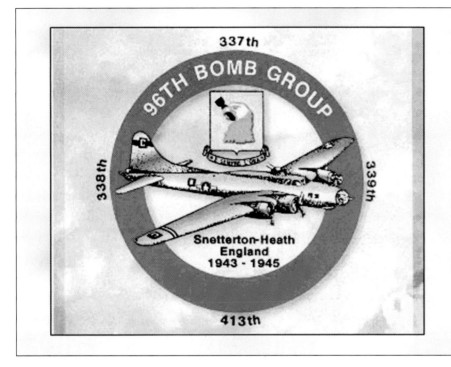

337th

96TH BOMB GROUP

338th

339th

Snetterton-Heath
England
1943 - 1945

413th

**96th bombardment
Group Emblem**

first attacked. For the same reason (being the lead crew) that we had Maj. Emerson as co-pilot, we had two navigators, Dean Howell and Dave Humke. Lt. Bob Anderson, our usual co-pilot, was flying as tail-gunner. German planes attacked before we were aware of their presence. Bob Anderson fired a few bursts, and then we were hit. This first attack by enemy planes killed Lt. Anderson and destroyed about half the plane's tail surface."

Wolford goes on to explain his belief that the same burst further destroyed every gunner and gun behind the bomb bay. Fulton and Emerson dove to 7,000 feet, hoping to lose the Germans, but Luftwaffe fighters hung on tenaciously. "Never have I seen such piloting as Maj. Emerson and Capt. Fulton did with that crippled bomber," Wolford wrote. "But it soon became apparent that we must abandon ship."

Unable to drop life-rafts, the men had to jump with faith in their "Mae Wests." The two navigators joined Wolford in parachuting from the nose hatch. While still descending, Wolford could see the two navigators parachuting below him, and he saw three men, two of whom he believed to be Emerson and Fulton, leave the plane before it struck the water. That was the last he saw of any of the crew. Larry Wolford was in the water for over eight hours before being rescued by a German air-sea plane. His captors treated him for shock, for he suffered from over-exposure and exhaustion. And they promised to continue the search for his crew. At this point, he lost consciousness until he came to hours later in a Friesian Island hospital. The body of Dave Humke was the only one recovered. It washed ashore on the German-Danish border a week later. The Germans provided full military honors.

After *Liberty Bell* was hit, Capt. Joe Bender tried to exercise his responsibility as Deputy Lead. But *Tarfu,* as Frank Cardaman explains, had already been hit by cannon fire,

**96th Memorial
Window,
St. Andrews
Chapel**

96th
Bombardment
Group Memorial

1990 Kipling's Error Reunion l-r Howard "Freddy" Breson, Leo Lakey, Steve Malinowski, Joe Kotlarz, Lloyd Mitchell, Ruben Neie

Lloyd Mitchell, sons and grandson at Snetterton Museum l-r David, Lloyd, Tyler (grandson), Mark, Brooks

Kipling's Error Under Heavy Fire (See pages 68-69)

leaving a hole in the right wing that "you could almost drive a car through. We, too, left the formation," Cardaman concludes, "when our number three caught fire." *Tarfu* would lose two more engines in the running battle homeward and would, at last, safely land on one engine.

With *Liberty Bell* shot down and *Tarfu* aborting, Lt. Bill Nance and Lt. Norville Gorse tried to take over the lead in the 337th's *Dallas Rebel*. Norville Gorse, although listed as co-pilot, was actually flying the Fortress. L/Lt. Bill Nance was an instructor pilot and had decided to sit in the right-hand seat this day – the better, he had thought, to keep tabs on the formation. But after the Group lost their lead and deputy lead, their formation came into heavy clouds just long enough to become separated from the Wing. It was severely attacked over the North Sea and the Friesian Islands, and *Dallas Rebel* took the brunt of the attack. There was a fire in the radio room and it spread from gas leaking from a bullet-shattered wing. Lt. Gorse put the plane into a dive, hoping to extinguish the flames. But the intercom wasn't working, and he couldn't warn anybody. When the dive began, most thought they were doomed, so much so that when Lt. Gorse leveled the aircraft, many began bailing out in spite of the advice of the tail-gunner, Sgt. Youngsters. Those who did bail out did not survive the North Sea.

Eventually, Gorse ditched the plane successfully and the surviving members crowded into a dinghy. This was not the first emergency situation for Lieutenants Norville Gorse and Joe Hudson, the co-pilot and navigator. They had their first "Geronimo!" that fateful day, May 13th, when Capt. Rogers was killed while the Group was attempting to assemble for its first mission.

The six survivors of *Dallas Rebel* spent three days and two nights in the small dinghy until help came. And when it came, irony of ironies, it came in the form of a German Dornier Flying Boat. Joe Hudson had previously been sent to a British Intelligence School where he had studied POW escape procedures and secret codes. Although he was never to escape himself, Hudson made great use of his training in Stalag Luft II and VIIA.

The battle still raged aloft. Even when the Luftwaffe's time-detonating rockets failed to down a Fortress, it did the next best thing – it caused the bombers to spread out. Fortresses lost their defensive fire power. B-17s turned for England in disarray. The Luftwaffe was having a turkey shoot. Many Americans were flying in their fourth mission in five days. They had been exhausted before they even took off this morning. Not so, the Germans. They were secure in their knowledge that they could always land, reload, refuel and continue the battle. Today's clash displayed remarkable Luftwaffe teamwork. Germans bounced out of the clouds on Lt. Steve Hettrick's 338th A/C 42-30401. The first pass reduced Hettrick's air speed just enough to isolate him for the second pass. The crew bailed out over the North Sea; there were still no known survivors. A similar fate awaited Lt. Hugh Moore's 413 crew in *Moore Fidite*. Then, the next crew to suffer casualties was that of Lt. Gene Wilcox in the 339th's 42-30351, *Alcohol Annie*.

Co-pilot Phil Stratton takes up the story right after *Alcohol Annie* had been hit. "Number three has a gaping .20mm hole on top. The manifold pressure drops to almost nothing. Hell – number four and one are out. It's time to go home. At 9,000 feet, we break into the open. No fighters in sight. We rip off the oxygen masks and breathe deeply. Jorgensen, the navigator, gives us a course for home."

But *Annie* is a long way from home, and she's riding heavy on one wing. And no wonder – the wing is on fire. And there is still plenty of gas in it to explode! Wilcox and Stratton order everyone into ditching positions. The tail-gunner does not respond. No way to check for him now – they are diving at 4,000 feet per minute in an attempt to ditch and escape before an explosion overtakes them.

Stratton continues: "We are down. I unfasten my safety belt, throw off my headset and pull the mike plug. My window is slightly ajar; I yank it open. Quick as I am, Wilcox is already climbing out of his window. The nose sinks rapidly. The water is up to my waist. I scramble through the opening and find the wing with my feet. I hear a great crackling and look round to see *Annie* breaking in half. Mercer, Wilcox and Jorgenson are above the radio hatch. Mercer and Wilcox are struggling with the life raft. Suddenly, Johnson's head appears in the opening. The plane is sinking rapidly. Wilcox, still struggling with the raft, is half under water. Finally, it comes free and begins to inflate. Johnson swims past me, heading west. I catch him, yank the cord inflating his Mae West, and head him back toward the rubber dinghy. Where are the others? Too late; *Annie's* gone, taking with her Calvert, Holton, Holcombe, O'Neill and Lewis. They are all gone – gone forever. I look at my watch; it's only 0945."

Much later, in fact – not until just before midnight – these five survivors were returned to base by British air-sea rescue.

By 0945, when Phil Stratton was treading water, the battle was still being waged within the clouds. Somewhere up there, the Germans found Lt. Deshotels trying to abort in his *Paper Doll*.

Then they attacked Lt. Clarence Covert's 339th 42-30394. Covert did his best to ditch. But because he had to execute the ditching under enemy fire, the result was exceptionally hard. Four gunners were pinned in the wreckage and drowned. Among those injured while engaged in the aerial battle was Sgt. Charles Differdoll. Those who survived the ditching were the four officers and Tech. Sgt. Don Colvin, the engineer. They all saw the injured Differdoll in the water. But he drifted away, in spite of their best efforts. It would take six hours before the Germans picked up the survivors. The Germans and Americans looked for Differdoll again, but to no avail.

By now, the few enduring 96th planes had tacked onto a bigger flight of the 94th Fortresses. This bastardized group was determined to hit the target. But together, the two bomb groups numbered only 28, and there was a rule which stipulated that if a target couldn't be bombed by 30 planes, then it should be abandoned. The order to abandon was on the lips of the 94th's Col. Castle, when someone passed the word that there were more planes coming up from behind. Their nationality, however, was not reported. At any rate, Col. Castle pushed on to Oschersleben.

The final 96th testimony comes from Ed Quigley, bombardier aboard Lt. Cecil Walters' *Little Caesar*. There was nothing left of the lead squadron by now. The lead and his deputy had been shot down. The others had aborted. Over in the low squadron, Hugh Moore had been shot down, and the others, heading for home, were running a terrible German gamut. At this juncture in the slaughter, Capt. Francis Madsen had taken over the 96th lead from his high squadron position. He didn't have much of a group behind him – just Walters, Bob Hodson and Charlie Mooreland (and perhaps that mysterious fifth plane mentioned in the official press release).

Bombardier Quigley finished the Oschersleben story from his perspective, just before the approach to the target: "Fighters were pressing home savage attacks. A Fort broke out in flames across all four engines. I saw five chutes open. A German fighter exploded – a ball of orange flames hanging in the air. Another Fort twisted out of control, an engine burning, its tail sheared off. In the nose of *Little Caesar*, empty shell casings were piling up. Jerry was coming in for the kill and was swarming all over our tiny four-ship element. I began firing from the right nose gun. A Yellow Nose dipped to go under. All of the guns on *Little Caesar* were firing now. I could hear the firing of the top-turret and the distinctive "chug-chug" of the Ball. Tracers were everywhere. I started to turn back to the nose guns when something smashed me in the back. I was thrown face-down upon the bomb site. I looked around. Sid Rosenberger, the navigator, was sprawled on his back, almost on the escape hatch; the unmanned guns were swinging wildly, and smoke was pouring through the shards of plexiglass. Then Sid and I both got up. Walt, the pilot, was calling on the interphone. Told him everything was okay and got back on the guns. About ten minutes later, when Germans gave us a breathing spell, I knew that I had been hit. I put my hand under my jacket in back and showed Sid the blood. He took a closer look and said he thought it wasn't too bad. I went back to the fighters again."

Lt. Quigley eventually put his bombs on target. "I guess there must have been flak," he writes, "but I don't remember. We turned on the I.P., the lead ship shot off its flares and I opened the bomb bay doors. I tried looking for the target, but it was too painful to bend over. The lead ship dropped and I let our bombs go, too, and closed the doors." On the way home, Quigley had time to think of his wounds for once. "When England appeared on the horizon," Quigley recalls, "I went into the radio room where I became scared for the first time. I started shaking and smoking my way through a pack of cigarettes. We came over the field, shot off a flare to tell the Sawbones to be ready with the Meat Wagon, and came in. Walt pulled off the runway, leaned out of the cockpit window and waved to me as I struggled between two medics. That was the last I ever saw of him."

The tragedy of the Oschersleben did not end that day. Quigley would be hospitalized for months, but the next day, as we shall see, the rest of the crew, except for Sid Rosenberger, would be lost. In November, when Ed Quigley returned to combat, the only person he recognized was fellow bombardier, Ray McKinnon. "Dear God, Ray," Quigley would ask, "Where is everybody?" McKinnon didn't have to answer. Inside the lonely Nissen, the two charter-member bombardiers embraced and wept.

Remember Lt. Shelton, who had to wrest control of his aircraft from an inflated life-raft on the 17th? Well, here he is again. He had lost the number-two engine during a concentrated enemy attack, and now number one was giving out. Exploiting whatever power he had left, Shelton dove and wrestled the controls for a leveling at only 200 feet. Here, while his crew fought off two successive attacks by 15 FWs, Shelton executed evasive actions. But the condition of their plane was deteriorating. The warning to ditch was given. All loose equipment was jettisoned. Lt. Frank Wiswall was flying his first mission as Shelton's bombardier and was ministering first-aid to Sgt. Knowles, the radio operator. Sgt. Knowles, although being doctored, was still radioing SOS signals. Eventually, Shelton managed to revive number one and to regain precious altitude. The alert to ditch was rescinded and Shelton's superb flying brought them home.

When the final toll was taken, it was revealed that seven aircraft failed to return to Snetterton. Listed as MIA were the crews of Lieutenants Deshotels, Covert, Wilcox, Moore, Hettrick and Nance, and Capt. Fulton. (Five of the Wilcox crew would be returned by Air-Sea Rescue.) Even so, by lights-out, there were 70 empty cots at Snetterton. In fact, the 96th had sustained the highest losses of both the 1st and 4th Bomb Wings.

Some of those empty cots motivated Bill Thorns' diary entry. "Clouds broke up formations, and enemy fighters accounted for a good many planes. Two crews I lived with went down. Sure is lonesome in this hut! A swell bunch of guys."

JULY 29, 1943

✠ Today, we went to Warnemunde and bombed a Focke-Wulf plant. The weather was good, and bombing results were good. There wasn't much flak, and only two fighters. We lost one plane from a collision with another. It happened near the English coast on return trip. Walter's crew. 15/30 or 1/2.
— *Lt. Lloyd Mitchell, navigator*

✠ Sixteenth Mission – flew 7-1/4 hours – Warnemunde, Germany.

Got up at 0100. Breakfast 0130. Briefed 0200. Clean guns and load ammunition. Weather clear. Only two ships from our squad went on this mission. Rest are out of commission. Dress up before take-off. Take-off was at 0515. Most of us tried to catch a few winks before hitting altitude. We started to climb about two hours after take-off. Hit altitude near Denmark. Visibility over Denmark was very good.

Flak over the target was heavy. We flew at 23,000 feet, dropping ten 500-pound bombs on an FW-190 factory. It looked like the bombs did their work. We saw two fighters a few minutes after leaving the target. They were about 1,500 yards away when we fired at them. They high-tailed it back into Germany. I fired about 25 rounds at them.

We flew back the same way we came in, only, this time, the flak on the coastline missed us by several hundred yards. The lead ship did some good dodging. We came down from altitude very fast in order to get out of the fighters' range in case any came up. But no more came up. About one mile from England, two 17s crashed, flying too close, and the strain on the pilots in the past week has been terrific – one ship from the 337th and one from some other group. One boy hit silk; rest went down. Land 1300. Interrogated, cleaned gun, showered and shaved, went to bed.

Our ship was the only one to go over the target. Lt. Tanner developed engine trouble 15 minutes before hitting Denmark. Saw the smoke coming up from the target a few minutes after making the turn. The smoke pots did not hinder the bombardiers.
— *Sgt. Leo Lakey, gunner*

✠ Mission #16 – Up again at 1:00 a.m. and listened to briefing. Target: Warnemunde, Germany, again! An FW Aircraft Corp. Carried ten 500-pounders. Took off at 5:11 a.m. and returned at 1:03 p.m. Encountered only two fighters and some inaccurate flak. Mission very successful. Two ships collided as we approached English coast. Shows how tired we all were, and went down into the sea. As we crossed the coast, two strange B-17s that we hadn't noticed turned and headed back for Germany. I reported via radio T-wing. Seems that every so often, strange ships, supposedly manned by Germans, have been seen. We couldn't see one soon enough – we'd shoot it down. At 5:00 p.m., our crew was given a 48-hour pass. Eddie and I went to movies and to the dance.

— *Sgt. Dick Haseltine, radio operator*

✠ Warnemunde, Germany – The mission was considered pretty easy. We only saw two fighters and got one of them. Lt. Walters collided in mid-air with a ship from the 288ᵗʰ Group. Both ships went down in the North Sea. But also good news: Lt. Wilcox, three officers and the radio man were picked up by Air Sea Rescue. They went down on the Oschersleben mission. Lt. Jergens, the navigator, is a friend of mine from Clifton, Texas.

— *Lt. Ruben Neie, pilot*

✠ Mission #16.

Woke up at 1:00 a.m. and briefed for mission to Warnemunde, Germany. Target: Focke-Wulf Aircraft Corporation. Bomb load: ten 500-pounders (demolition). Bombing altitude: 23,000 feet. Take-off was at 5:11 a.m. and came back at 1:03 p.m. Went in a wing of three groups (about 50 ships) over Denmark and into Germany. Flak was encountered and only two enemy fighters. The mission was a success, but as we came back on the English coast, two of the planes in the group collided and the two ships went down.

At 5:00 p.m., got word that our crew was on pass till Saturday at 6:00 p.m. Went out to North Hampton with Steve and had a swell time.

Resume of Mission #16:
First Wing: Kiel, Germany
Target: Deutsche Werke Shipbuilding Yards
Six groups: 112 B-17s dispatched; four B-17s lost
E/A claims: 35 – 2 – 29
Casualties: 2 – 8 – 41
Bombs on target: 596 500-pounders; 332 250-pounders; 348 100-pounders

Last-resort target (opportunity)
Three groups: 56 planes (B-17s); two lost
E/A claims: 13 – 4 – 4
Casualties: 20 missing
Bombs on target: 261 500-pounders; 336 250-pounders

Fourth Wing: Warnemunde, Germany
Target: Ernst Heinkel Aircraft Manufacturing Company
Six groups: 81 B-17s dispatched; four lost
Casualties: 40 missing
Bombs on target: 420 500-pounders; 192 250-pounders

— *Sgt. Joseph Kotlarz, gunner*

JULY 30, 1943

✠ Today, the boys bombed Kassel. Good results. Lots of fighter opposition. Shelton took our ship and brought it back in good shape. We lost two planes, *Pelusi* and *Miracle*. *Miracle's* crew was picked up, however. I guess they figured five raids in six days was enough for us.
— *Lt. Lloyd Mitchell, navigator*

✠ Resting – Kassel, Germany.

After making five missions out of the last five days, we were given a rest we badly needed. Our crew was the only crew to make all of these missions in the entire group. We didn't even hear Capt. Ford's crew get up, that's how tired we were. We slept 'til about 1000 this morn. Lt. Shelton's crew flew our ship. They took off about 0630. Landed 1200. Flew 22,000 feet. Dropped five 1,000-pounders. Did a darn good job of hitting the target. Flak and enemy fighters were thick. Visibility was good all the way into the target, over it, and back out. Our ship was hit by flak, putting it out of commission for two days. No one was hurt.

After they landed, we were all given a 48-hour pass, first one in six weeks.
— *Sgt. Leo Lakey, gunner*

✠   **Address:**
        July 30, 1943
        Miss Greta Curtis
        56 Gwyder Street Millroad
        Cambridge, England

Left for Cambridge with Steve. Steve went on to Leicester. Group had a mission today. Target: Kassel, Germany. Arrived in Cambridge and feeling fine. Met a Polish soldier.

        Address:
        L/Cpl. Banasiak, J.
        P-31 Polish Forces
        (to write to him later)
        Chesveley 231 (Cadet Officer)
        Podrazazy Swiecicki

Met Greta Curtis with two other girlfriends and had a swell time. Later, took Greta to the theater.
— *Sgt. Joseph Kotlarz, gunner*

JULY 30 TO AUGUST 3, 1943

✠ Pass after pulling five missions in six days – and don't think we didn't need this four-day pass! Naturally, went to London again. Lt. Mitchell and I visited St. Paul's Cathedral and Westminster Abbey of London. They are two of the most beautiful and historical churches I have ever seen.
— *Lt. Ruben Neie, pilot*

JULY 31, 1943

✤ Our crew came to London on Thursday night. We stayed at the Jules Club, which is the American Red Cross Club. I had a good time while I was there – too good, perhaps. I pulled two of the best (or worst) drunks I've been on for a long time. I met a girl I liked. Her name is Helen Taylor. She is rather cute, but she is too cynical and rather hard for a girl her age (19). I might go see her again. Mabs, Darling, I hope you understand. I'll ever be faithful to you, but this war is hell, and losing good friends like Joe, Dean, Dave, Hugh, Monroe and Mac doesn't help. Maybe God will have leniency on me.

— *Lt. Lloyd Mitchell, navigator*

✤ Loafed around town and talked with all the Polish Forces. Went out to Greta's house and met her sister and brother-in-law. Sure had a swell time. Went back to camp on the 4:03. Greta saw me off. At the station, met Dick and gave him an introduction. Came back to camp to find out that our pass was extended one more day.

— *Sgt. Joseph Kotlarz, gunner*

JULY 31-AUGUST 9, 1943

✤ After a very busy week, the entire Air Force (combat crews only) were given a two-day pass, and we needed that pass. Our crew went on five raids out of the six. We were all dog-tired when we were notified that we didn't have to fly the one going to Kassel, July 30th. We were willing to go, but we were all worn out. Most of all, not getting enough sleep. The pilot and co-pilot were the boys that were worn out.

After our pass, on which we had a chance to relax and try to forget what we went through, we were ready to go up again, but the weather has been lousy. Cloudy, cold and rain most of these days. Went to school several times, but in general, just laying around, taking things easy, waiting for some good, clear weather. Cleaned guns several times and loaded ammunition. Several more new crews in.

Heard that Lt. Morrison and three others were prisoners somewhere in Germany. They went down June 22nd over Huls, Germany.

— *Sgt. Leo Lakey, gunner*

AUGUST 1, 1943

✤ Went to 8:00 a.m. mass on the base. Just roamed around the villages today. Found out that the pass was extended till Monday, 10:00 p.m.

— *Sgt. Joseph Kotlarz, gunner*

AUGUST 2, 1943

✤ Slept till late. Left for Norwich, 30 miles away. Norwich is all protected by barrage balloons. First time I saw an American WAAC in Norwich at the American Red Cross Club.

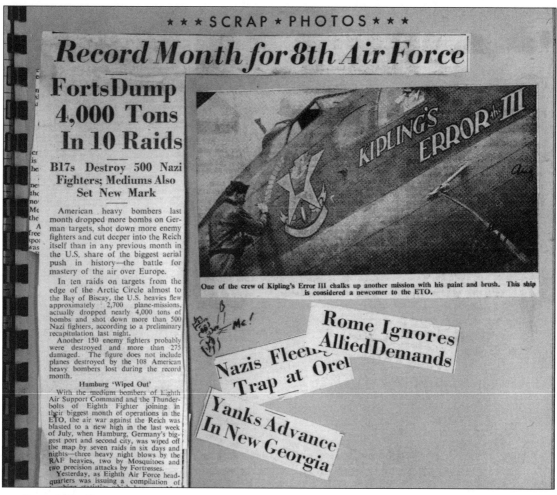

★ ★ ★ SCRAP ★ PHOTOS ★ ★ ★

Record Month for 8th Air Force

Forts Dump 4,000 Tons In 10 Raids

B17s Destroy 500 Nazi Fighters; Mediums Also Set New Mark

American heavy bombers last month dropped more bombs on German targets, shot down more enemy fighters and cut deeper into the Reich itself than in any previous month in the U.S. share of the biggest aerial push in history—the battle for mastery of the air over Europe.

In ten raids on targets from the edge of the Arctic Circle almost to the Bay of Biscay, the U.S. heavies flew approximately 2,700 plane-missions, actually dropped nearly 4,000 tons of bombs and shot down more than 500 Nazi fighters, according to a preliminary recapitulation last night.

Another 150 enemy fighters probably were destroyed and more than 275 damaged. The figure does not include planes destroyed by the 108 American heavy bombers lost during the record month.

Hamburg 'Wiped Out'

With the medium bombers of Eighth Air Support Command and the Thunderbolts of Eighth Fighter joining in their biggest month of operations in the ETO, the air war against the Reich was blasted to a new high in the last week of July, when Hamburg, Germany's biggest port and second city, was wiped off the map by seven raids in six days and nights—three heavy night blows by the RAF heavies, two by Mosquitoes and two precision attacks by Fortresses.

Yesterday, as Eighth Air Force headquarters was issuing a compilation of

One of the crew of Kipling's Error III chalks up another mission with his paint and brush. This ship is considered a newcomer to the ETO.

Rome Ignores Allied Demands

Nazis Fleeing Trap at Orel

Yanks Advance In New Georgia

Record Month with *Kipling's Error III* Photo

Met some girl at the Castle Bar and took her to the theater. She was okay and really had a pleasant time with her.

— *Sgt. Joseph Kotlarz, gunner*

AUGUST 3, 1943

✠ On the alert list today, but no mission on account of unsettled weather.

Norwich was bombarded a few times, and sure has a lot of wrecked sections in all parts of the city. So far, Cambridge has London and Norwich beat.

—*Sgt. Joseph Kotlarz, gunner*

✠ Awarded First Oak Leaf Charter today. Squadron party tonight. I took Sylvia Starling, a London girl who lives in Old Buckingham. Had a swell time. My partially finished

Honor Roll was exhibited at the party. Guys thought it was swell, but I can see a lot of errors.
— *Sgt. Dick Haseltine, radio operator*

AUGUST 4, 1943

✠ Big dance for the birthday of our squadron, the 413th. I had a date with Miss Betty Johnson. Also ferried plane to and from Watersham to home base.
— *Lt. Ruben Neie, pilot*

✠ No mission today on account of unsettled weather. Invited to a Polish dance a week from tomorrow at Diss. The Poles are giving this and want Steve and myself to come out there. Went out to North Lapham to a dance for benefit of prisoners of war and met half the Polish Army.
— *Sgt. Joseph Kotlarz, gunner*

AUGUST 5, 1943

✠ Slept 20 out of 24 hours. How is that for getting some rest?
— *Lt. Ruben Neie, pilot*

✠ No mission today on account of unsettled weather.

> **Address:**
> Capt. R.B. Ward
> S. Union Street
> T. Concord, North Carolina

Went to Norwich tonight and just messed around at American Red Cross Club, etc.
— *Sgt. Joseph Kotlarz, gunner*

AUGUST 6, 1943

✠ No mission today on account of unsettled weather. Went to confession and communion for 5:30 p.m. mass.
— *Sgt. Joseph Kotlarz, gunner*

AUGUST 7, 1943

✠ Today I received a telegram reading: "James Brooks. 8 lbs., 12 oz. 10:40 p.m." I was very happy and pleased indeed.
— *Lt. Lloyd Mitchell, navigator*

AUGUST 7, 1943

✠ Bad weather here today. Had fresh eggs for breakfast today. Gunnery class conducted by Capt. Deppon.
— *Sgt. Joseph Kotlarz, gunner*

AUGUST 8, 1943

✠ Rainy and foggy here. Went to mass on the base. Had an evening pass tonight.
— *Sgt. Joseph Kotlarz, gunner*

AUGUST 9, 1943

✠ Bad weather today.
— *Sgt. Joseph Kotlarz, gunner*

AUGUST 10, 1943

✠ Woke up at 4:00 a.m. and briefed for our mission to Germany. Take-off was at 7:20 a.m. and immediately after take-off, the mission was canceled on account of bad weather.
— *Sgt. Joseph Kotlarz, gunner*

✠ Secret mission scheduled, but was scrubbed. So I will write it up when we try it again.
— *Lt. Ruben Neie, pilot*

✠ Dry run – flew three hours – Germany.

Got up 0400. Breakfast 0430. Briefed 0500. Cold and slightly cloudy. Cleaned guns. Take off at 0745. Put on heavy underwear and socks before take-off. We were Tail-End Charlie of our group. About a half-hour after take-off, orders came through to scrub the mission to Germany and go on a practice mission. We were loaded with five 1,000-pounders bound for Schweinfurt, Germany, a big ball-bearing and vital plane parts plant.

We flew around England for several hours in formation. Lt. Asper, our co-pilot, did most of the flying. Landed at 1045. Security lecture in briefing room. Had dinner. Will go out and clean my gun after a short nap. Saw quite a few gliders on several English fields. Number 3 engine was bad. Put in new engine.
— *Sgt. Leo Lakey, gunner*

AUGUST 11, 1943

✠ Ground school all day.
— *Lt. Ruben Neie, pilot*

✠ Ship in commission again, 2100. All combat crews restricted until further notice. Sent home picture of our ship.
— *Sgt. Leo Lakey, gunner*

AUGUST 12, 1943

✠ Mission #17.

Woke up at 1:30 a.m. and briefed for mission to Wesseling, Germany (five miles south of Kabou, Germany). Target: gas refineries. Secondary target: Bonn, Germany. Bomb load: 16 150-pound English incendiary bombs. Altitude: 24,000 feet (temperature: 30 degrees). Take-off was 6:00 a.m. and came in at 11:15 a.m. We were fill-ins today and filled in just before we hit the Germany coast. There were six abortions out of 413th squadron. We were the only ship that went through the mission. Saw about 25 fighters and attacked three or four times. I got in only one burst on four fighters. We got a .20mm right through the center of the glass nose, which left a big dent in the armor plate. Whether the target was hit or not, I don't know. We'll know today later. Lt. Mendolson and Lt. Mitchell were really lucky, having that armor plate. Another shell went through the ceiling and through the exhaust (Number 3 engine). We really were lucky. All enemy fighters were black (night fighters).

> **Resume of Mission #17:**
> First wing: Bochum-Gelsenkirchen and Recklinghausen in Germany
> Target: Steel works, synthetic oil plants and factories
> Nine groups: 183 B-17s dispatched; 23 B-17s lost
> E/A claims: 25 – 5 – 11
> Casualties: 5 – 49 – 232
> Bombs on target: 836 500-pounders; 784 250-pounders
>
> Fourth wing: Bonn, Germany
> Targets: of opportunity in Bonn
> Seven groups: 147 B-17s dispatched; two lost
> E/A claims: 4 – 2 – 2
> Casualties: 1 – 7 – 21
> Bombs on targets: Two 2,000-pounders; 703 500-pounders;
> 523 250-pounders

— *Sgt. Joseph Kotlarz, gunner*

✠ Bonn, Germany: American incendiary bombs, and don't think we didn't burn the hell out of a river, in which most of our bombs fell. The target was missed. I led a three-ship formation all over England and to the Germany coast before we saw a ship abort, so we could fill in and made the mission. My two wingmen also found a place to fly due to abortions. My three ships were fill-in ships. We finally flew on the wing of Lt. Bacon and Capt. Goode, and I have never seen any worse formation flying as they did. An Me-109 fighter flew within five feet of my left wing, knocking out the nose of my ship and Number 2 engine. He scared the hell out of all of us.

T/Sgt. Haseltine received word late last night that his sister was dead, but he flew the mission this morning. I asked him if he would rather stay at home, but he preferred to go.
— *Lt. Ruben Neie, pilot*

AUGUST 12, 1943

✠ Lt. Mitchell (a daddy very recently), Steve Nelson and myself took the bet. This is one bet we were hoping to lose (which we did). His orders were to follow the group for only five minutes off the English coast. But we know our pilot and we were thinking the same thing. Follow them until three dropped out, which is just what happened. When we got into formation, we were a few minutes over Germany. While the group was circling over England and gaining altitude, we flew several hundred yards behind it. We put on our oxygen masks about one hour after take-off. Take-off was at 0600. We got to our bombing altitude over England, which was 24,000 feet. It was very cold and miserable – almost froze our feet, Nelson and myself. We saw ten other groups just before we left England – a very pretty sight to see. After we got into formation, our position being Tail-End Charlie again, we saw our P-47 escort several thousand feet above us. A very good morale-builder, those P-47s up there. They stayed with us 30 minutes, not quite halfway to the target. After they left us, the flak came up. In spots, it was very thick, but not too accurate. A piece of flak hit our Number 2 exhaust pipe, putting quite a hole in it, but not enough to put it out of commission. Enough damage was made that it will take about six hours to repair.

A few Me-109s made a pass at us about ten minutes before hitting the target. They came in out of the sun, which was directly in front of us. One .20mm shell hit the nose square on the button, shattering the entire nose. The armor plate stopped the shell, because if it hadn't been there, our bombardier would have gotten it in the chest, and he wouldn't be alive at the present time. As it was, the force of the shell hitting the plastic nose and stopping in the armor plate knocked him over backwards. Luckily, he wasn't even scratched. And the ship that shot at us went by my window so fast, I just saw a silver streak. The second one came through just as fast. Both were within 100 yards. They were going so damn fast, I didn't get to shoot at either one. Those were the only ones to give us any trouble. We saw 14 of them at the 9 o'clock position, too far out and going in the opposite direction. I poured in about 25 rounds just to let them know we were around.

After this little brush with these fighters, we ran into some heavy flak, not very accurate. Bomb bay doors were opened by the entire group. A few minutes later, that most welcome "Bombs away" came over the interphone. We dropped 15 250-pounders. All were the English incendiary type. Our target was a few miles from being covered over by clouds. It was a big synthetic gas and oil factory.
— *Sgt. Leo Lakey, gunner*

✠ Seventeenth Mission – flew 5-1/2 hours – Bonn, Germany.

Five miles south of Cologne – Bonn, Germany. The factory was hit because we saw big columns of black, dense smoke after we made the turn and 15 to 20 minutes after leaving the target.

On the way back, we ran into more flak – thick, but not doing any damage. The clouds were getting thicker, staying at a level of about 15,000 feet above the clouds. Visibility was very good and the sun was very bright.

15 to 20 minutes from the German coastline, our Spitfire escort picked us up. They were flying at about 30,000, leaving a fine vapor behind them. They flew past us deeper into Germany, looking for damaged 17s in need of help. None were sighted, so they flew with us – part of them with several other groups back to England. We also saw a bunch of B-26s and their escorts raising Cain along the coastline.

We started down as soon as we left the German coastline. The cold air coming through the shot-up nose really chilled off Mitch and Mendy. They got as cold as Nelson and myself. Over England, it was cloudy and rather chilly.

We were the last to land. 1130. All the sandwiches were gone; also the hot cocoa. After interrogation, we went out and cleaned our guns. The ground crew was already at work fixing up and taking the nose apart. We hope to have it fixed up for tomorrow. At the present, it is out of commission. Now for a hot shower, some chow and a good night's sleep. On oxygen 3-1/2 hours.
— *Sgt. Leo Lakey, gunner*

✠ Mission #17 – Briefed at 1:30 for mission to Bonn, Germany. Loaded with 15 250-pound British incendiary bombs and took off at 6:00 a.m. We were to stand by to fill in abortions. We were supposed to turn back shortly after passing English coast, but we decided to stay with formation for a few more minutes. Just as we were to turn back, three ships aborted and we filled in. Six ships of the 413th aborted. We were the only ship to go in over the target and out of this squadron. We were attacked by 25 night fighters that came out of the sun. A .20mm hit the nose squarely, making a dent in the armor plate. If it hadn't been for that plate, Mendolson and Mitch would have been hit for sure. Nose was shattered badly. Another went through the cowling and exhaust of Number 3 engine. Our luck is still holding.
— *Sgt. Dick Haseltine, radio operator*

✠ That one time when the flak penetrated the nose, I was bent over working on my maps, trying to figure out where we were and how to get home, and this piece of aircraft came through the hull of the plane. It came right across where I was sitting – above me – and dropped. The velocity of it was pretty much spent at that time. I doubt if it would have killed me if it had hit me, but I am sure it wouldn't have been any fun. I kept that piece of flak for years and years…
— *Lt. Lloyd Mitchell, navigator*

AUGUST 13, 1943

✠ Unsettled weather today. Slept rather late.
— *Sgt. Joseph Kotlarz, gunner*

AUGUST 15, 1943

✠ Birthday – 26 years old, and celebrated it by going on my 18th mission. We hit airports at Merville, France and Lille, France. My gift was a .20mm shell in the back of my head. An Me-109 attacked directly out of the sun, which made it impossible for us to see him come in. I knew he was out there, because I saw him go into the sun. But we had to stay in formation and could do nothing about it. The .20mm missed my shoulder by six inches and exploded against the armor plate just behind my head. Three small fragments hit me, causing a small wound and bleeding. I stopped the bleeding with my handkerchief stuffed under my headset. X-rays showed the fragments to be small and would be better to leave in than attempt to dig them out. So, from now on, I will have a little steel dust in my head. I will be awarded the Purple Heart for being wounded in action. My tail-gunner, S/Sgt. Kotlarz got the boy who got me, but he won't be back and I will.

Last night I celebrated my birthday by going to a 96th Group dance, and the mess hall boys baked me a large cake. So, about the only thing I missed this time was being home with my folks.
— Lt. Ruben Neie, pilot

✠ Mission #18.

Briefed at 3:00 p.m. for mission to Merville and Lille, France. Target: airfields and dispersal areas. Bomb load: 24 100-pounders. Bombing altitude: 20,000 feet. One enemy fighter intercepted, but saw three total. Take-off was 4:45 p.m. and came in at 9:30 p.m. Had a few holes through vertical stabilizer and one through the cockpit and Tokyo tanks. Lt. Neie got a cut on his head from the shell that came in through the cockpit window. This will be the first Purple Heart in our crew. Took along a new gunner as observer.

> **Resume of Mission #18:**
> First wing: Flushing, Vlissengin Amiens, Glissy and Paix, France
> Targets: airfields above towns
> No enemy aircraft encountered; no planes lost.
> Nine groups: 180 B-17s dispatched
> Three wounded casualties to flak.
> Bombs on target: 807 100-pounders; 143 300-pounders; 478 120-pounders
>
> Fourth wing: Merville, Lille and Vendeville, France
> Targets: airfields above towns
> Seven groups: 147 B-17s dispatched; two lost
> E/A claims: 9 – 0 – 1
> Casualties: 1 – 3 – 20
> Bombs on targets: 926 100-pounders on Merville and
> 1,036 100-pounders on Lille and Vendeville

— Sgt. Joseph Kotlarz, gunner

✠ 18th Mission – flew 4-1/2 hours – Merville and Lille, France.

Briefing at 1400. Clean gun. Put on warm clothes before take-off. Take-off was 1700. Rather cloudy over England. We were Tail-End Charlie again. Put on oxygen mask half-hour after taking off. A new man flew with us. This was his first mission. We reached our bombing altitude over England a few minutes before we left England. We flew at 20,000 feet. Flak was light. We carried four 100-pound demolition bombs.

Dropping 12 on the airfield in Merville, France. The other 12 were dropped on an airfield in Lille, France. Doing a good job on both.

I saw a big gas tank explode a few minutes after leaving the last target. Saw five batteries of ack-ack guns in and around Lille.

Five minutes after leaving the target, one lone fighter came in out of the sun, hitting our plane. A .20mm came through, hitting the armor plate behind Lt. Neie's head, missing him by inches. When it exploded behind his head, as it hit the armor plate, a few pieces hit Lt. Neie in the back of the head. It bled for a while, but not for long. After we landed, he went to the hospital to make sure he isn't hit worse than we think.

A .20mm also hit over vertical stabilizer. Only one fighter came through. I fired 100 rounds. The fighter escort picked us up over the coast of France. We landed in the dark, about 2130. Take clothes to drying room. Interrogated. Had supper. We had our first orange since leaving the good old U.S.A. Went to bed around 2245. Used 125 rounds.
— *Sgt. Leo Lakey, gunner*

✠ Mission #18 – Late briefing at 3:00 p.m. for mission to Merville and Lille, France to get airdromes and dispersal area using 24 100-pounders. One fighter came unexpectedly out of the sun and put a .20mm through the window about five inches back of Lt. Neie's head. It exploded, and one piece struck his head, and later examination showed that a small piece plowed in under the skin from the back of his head to just above his forehead. Another minute piece went down into the outer surface of his neck. They are going to let these pieces work out themselves. He's still on flying status. His is the first wound received on this crew. Thank God it wasn't worse. Took an observer along today – his first mission. Saw only three fighters and light flak that hit our ship.
— *Sgt. Dick Haseltine, radio operator*

✠ Ship out of commission.

Got up about 0930. Went out and cleaned my gun. A .30 caliber explosive hit our right wing a few inches to the left of the landing light inside of the wing. It exploded, ruining a few wires and gas lines. So, the right half of the wing is being taken off to repair the damage of that little bullet. It will take about two days to put our ship into commission again.

Saw Lt. Neie this noon. He has a little patch on the back of his head. He is okay, ready to fly.
— *Sgt. Leo Lakey, gunner*

AUGUST 16, 1943

✠ Another mission today. LaPaix and Abbeyville, France. But I had to stay home with a sore head.
— *Lt. Ruben Neie, pilot*

AUGUST 16, 1943

✠ Mission for the group today. Lt. Mendolson, Lt. Mitchell, Sgt. White and Malinowski were scheduled for this one. So now Lt. Mitchell is even with us, and Lt. Mendolson, White and Malinowski are one ahead.
— *Sgt. Joseph Kotlarz, gunner*

✠ Ship out of commission.

Boys got up at 0230. Breakfast 0300. Briefed 0330. Work on their guns and plane. Take-off 0700. Altitude 20,000 feet. Not too cold. Bomb two airfields in France. Twelve 100-pound demolition bombs on Abbeyville and 12 100-pound demolition bombs on LaPaix. Lt. Mitchell our navigator, Lt. Mendolson our bombardier, S/Sgt. C.E. White our A.E. and top-turret and Sgt. S. Malinowski A.R. and ball-turret flew with Lt. Baker making his first mission. Part of our crew flew with him because two are sick and two are in school. The rest of our crew did not fly.

The flak was heavy over Abbeyville and light over LaPaix. No fighters were seen. Six planes came back with one engine knocked out. Every ship had at least ten flak holes in it. They landed 1100. Both targets were hit.
— *Sgt. Leo Lakey, gunner*

AUGUST 17, 1943

✠ Nineteenth Mission – Regensburg, Germany.

Got up at 0100. Breakfast 0130. Fresh eggs. Briefed 0200. Flying a ship from the 339th. Ours still out of commission. Clean gun. Load ammunition. Take along our mess gear, canteen, one blanket, shaving equipment, shorts and socks. This is to be our first shuttle mission to North Africa. Take-off time was delayed one hour. We took off at 0700, our position being Tail-End Charlie again. We flew around England for almost two hours, picking up other groups. We put our oxygen masks on one hour after take-off and reached our bombing altitude while still over England – 19,000 feet. Several squadrons of P-47s flew with us 50 miles into enemy territory. A minute or so after they left us, the enemy fighters hit us. About 25 of them made a pass or two at our group, then hit the groups behind us. Our group led the entire two wings over the target. We had fighters and flak all the way to the target. The flak was thick, but did no harm. Our leader used plenty of evasive action to miss most of it. The groups behind us caught most of the fighters. The 100th lost 12 planes in this raid. Visibility over and around the target was very good. No fighters or flak while over the target. We dropped ten 500-pound bombs right on the target. Nelson and I saw the bombs hit. I took several pictures of the hits with the GI camera they gave me. We saw one hospital with a big red cross on its roof. The bombs came nowhere near it. The target itself was destroyed. It was an aircraft plant making Me-109s. None of the buildings were guarded and no A.A. guns around it. I guess the Germans figured they were safe here.

After we hit the target, we headed south toward the western part of Italy, crossing the Alps. They were really pretty. Snow covered several of the higher ones. We flew over the western part of Italy. We met no flak or fighters in the little time we were in Italy or on the coast line. Just after we left the shores of Italy, we started to go down from our 19,000 feet. The Mediterranean Sea was calm and looked good enough to swim in. For an hour or so, we flew about 50 feet above the sea. We saw several sharks, which we shot at. A few B-17s ditched in the Mediterranean Sea due to gas running out.

I saw two B-17s go down over Germany, about 45 minutes before we hit the target. Seven boys hit the silk out of one, and six boys out of the other one. I also saw three German fighters go down in flames. Fired 150 rounds.

— Sgt. Leo Lakey, gunner

✠ One of the other missions I remember particularly was the Germans had concentrated their ball-bearing manufacturing around a town named Schweinfurt. And it was odd to me that they would do this, you know, because ball bearings are such an essential thing, such an integral part of the war effort – they were used in so many different things – all kinds of vehicles and things. But they did, and so we were, the 8th Air Force, going after the ball-bearing works. We sent out 300 planes that day. They went in two wings. A wing was made up of several bombardment groups. One wing went into Schweinfurt, and our group was with the second wing and we went to Regensburg, where they manufactured Messerschmitts and Focke-Wulfs. Messerschmitts and Focke-Wulfs were two of their better fighter planes. And so, we were going down to bomb the fighter manufacturer.

That was one of the toughest raids of that year. We lost 60 out of 300. We lost 20%. Two-thousand men on that one raid. We went, and after we hit Regensburg, we crossed the Mediterranean and went into North Africa. That was the first shuttle-type – they called it a shuttle raid, and that was the first shuttle raid. We spent about two weeks in North Africa, and loaded up and hit some sub pens on the French coast, and then on back into England. But that was a very, very tough raid. The United States was beginning to be doubtful if they could continue daylight bombing after that raid. They started putting flame dampeners on their planes, so when we flew at night, our planes wouldn't be too visible with flame dampeners. We knew then something was happening when they went that far – thinking that we were going to have to start night bombing, like the British, but we didn't. You see, the RAF bombed at night, and we bombed at day – the RAF didn't do daylight bombing. The British didn't make an attempt to target-bomb. They saturated. They'd just pick out a city with military targets and they'd just drop them on there. Later I heard – there was a lot of discussion and debate going on among the high echelon: "Could the United States afford to keep up daylight bombing, afford these kinds of losses?" And they decided that they could. So, they did continue daylight bombing.

There were a lot of tough raids. We were – our squadron – was very fortunate. I don't know how it happened. But two or three years ago, I talked with a squadron C.O. at one of our reunions, and we took over 12 air crews, and we lost only one. The rest of them made their 25. But then, later on, during the war, the 96th took a heavy, heavy beating. I was reading somewhere that there were 45 heavy bombardment groups, and out of the 45, we took the second heaviest loss, our group did. We were fortunate.

— Lt. Lloyd Mitchell, navigator

Fire at a Bend of the Blue Danube

U.S. Army Air Force Photo

Smoke, dust and debris blossom across the huge Messerschmitt factory at Regensburg, on the banks of the Danube, as Eighth Air Force Fortresses, their devastation done, head for the Alps and Africa on the first USAAF shuttle raid, which crippled one-third of Germany's day fighter production.

Regensburg Bombing

AUGUST 17, 1943

✠ Nineteenth Mission – flew 11 hours – Regensburg, Germany.

As we hit the African coastline, quite a few of the boys landed on the airfield just at the coastline. They were almost out of gas. The rest of us flew on, 75 miles inland, to the base we were scheduled for. The part of Africa we were in was hot and dusty, over 100 degrees in the shade every day. We landed in Telergma, North Africa. Dirt runways, big airfield, Italian prisoners all over the place doing KP – cooking and general duty. They were in high spirits, asking us where we bombed. When we told them it was Germany, they were very happy.

We landed in Africa 1800 our time, 1900 Africa time. After we landed, we were interrogated, had supper, then went to sleep under our own plane, making a bed out of our flying clothes and one blanket.

— *Sgt. Leo Lakey, gunner*

✠ Mission #19.

Woke up at 1:30 a.m. and briefed for bombing mission to Regensburg, Germany. Target: Messerschmitts Aircraft Manufacturing. Bombing altitude: 19,000 feet. Bomb load: ten 500-pound demolition bombs. Take-off was at 7:00 a.m. Rendezvous at coast of England with seven other groups (21 planes to a group). Three groups to attack Schweinfurt (ball-bearing factory) and eight the Messerschmitt plant. We cut in through Belgium and a small portion of Holland, then Germany, Italy and North Africa. Our wing only saw and was attacked by 75 fighters through Germany and enemy territory. Thunderbolts (P-47s) escorted us through Belgium and Holland about 50 miles in Germany. The wing behind us was attacked by as many as 150 FWs. They lost quite a few. I saw one 17 go down from our wing, and two go down in flames from the one behind us. The one in our wing had his Number 2 engine catch on fire. Saw one man parachute out, and the rest were blown to pieces. Also saw two fighters go down. Flak (AA) was light throughout the entire trip.

No opposition through Italy and no flak. The Alps really are rugged mountains where we passed over the Germany-Italy boundary. At Spezia, Italy, we rendezvoused with the six groups and cut across the Mediterranean Sea, and hit the coast of Africa at 5:00 p.m., and arrived at Telergma, North Africa at 5:30 p.m.

Thirty-six Fortresses were lost on the Schweinfurt mission. The losses on the Regensburg mission are not known as yet, although seven planes were supposed to have ditched in the Mediterranean Sea.

> **Air Task Force:**
> Target: Schweinfurt, Germany; ball-bearing machine works
> Nine groups dispatched: 230 B-17s total dispatched (36 B-17s lost)
> 147 enemy aircraft shot down
> 150 to 300 E/A encountered
> 3 casualties; 15 wounded; 371 missing
>
> **Air Task Force:**
> Target: Regensburg, Germany; Messerschmitt-109 factory
> Seven groups dispatched: 147 B-17s total dispatched (23 B-17s lost)

— *Sgt. Joseph Kotlarz, gunner*

AUGUST 19, 1943

✠ Telergma is situated 46 miles from Constantine in northern Algeria. It's an American base and formerly was a B-17 and B-26 base. It's almost like Pyote, Texas. Yesterday was the first time I ever took a bath in a natural hot spring at Qued Athmenia, 25 miles away. All Arabs around here – and are they dirty and full of sores and filth. Camels are plentiful around here, but most of the Arabs use burros and jackasses, riding them on the extreme end of the animal.

A lot of Italian prisoners here. They are really agreeable and do all of the KP and cooking here. They are not guarded. There are quite a few of Algerian troops stationed here, too. Sure a variety of planes here: B-26, B-25, P-38, P-51, C-47, A-20 and P-40.

— *Sgt. Joseph Kotlarz, gunner*

Lt. Mendolson

AUGUST 20-21, 1943

✤ Checked up on our ship and had it loaded with ten 500-pound bombs for the return trip. Went out with Leo Lakey and visited the graveyard (wrecked planes) and selected souvenirs. Took some plane snapshots with Dick's camera and the K-3 camera. Told we would get to visit Constantine, Algeria this p.m. Lt. Mendolson left for Constantine. Nelson (engineer) got sick and did not go.

Left with the rest of the crew in a truck for Constantine. Ate ice cream (banana flavor) and went out souvenir-hunting. Constantine is situated on the side of a mountain. It's the most modernistic city I've ever seen. All the buildings have balconies. Sanitation is awful. Ate at the Red Cross. We sure are a shabby lot. None of the fellows were dressed. The Arabs around the city sure are filthy. The Arabian women still wear the veils over their faces. There is a narrow gorge in the heart of the city, with a high suspension bridge over it. Sure a picturesque sight. Electric motor buses are common in Constantine.

We (the crew) came in around midnight last night, all set for an early take-off. The mission was scrubbed later on, so we got a good night's sleep. Went out today and had a good hot bath at the hot springs (Qued Athmenia). We have iced tea and other cold drinks here. Cold beer and wine is available nights at the Foyer Militaire (Officers' Club).

— *Sgt. Joseph Kotlarz, gunner*

Capt. Rube Neie (Note the damage to place compared to previous photograph)

AUGUST 22-23, 1943

✠ Loafed around here on account of weather for the next 48 hours. Went to 9:00 a.m. mass here on the base. Lakey and I are out to get a tan here, so we usually are walking around in our shorts. The airport here is just like a busy commercial airport here in the States, with transport (C-47) and other planes landing at all times. All types of soldiers and nationalities pass through here on the Mediterranean Air Transport Liners (generals, privates and all others; French, English and all types). There are machine gun and AA units all around the field, always on alert. Saw quite a bit of scenery today. Went on a trip this afternoon to visit some ruins that were supposed to have been built by the Romans. Did not get there on account of the place was farther than we expected. Passed through Batna, Algeria en route (French garrison). Visited a church here and made a wish for our intention [engagement] (BCH and JFK). Services in French were being held while I was there. The French soldiers and Algerian blacks wear a sort of pajama outfit. Eggs and melons and fruit are plentiful around here, and we sure take advantage of the eggs. Tonight, each of us ate six eggs and a melon apiece.

Well, tomorrow is the day when we leave for England. Bordeaux, France to be the target.

— *Sgt. Joseph Kotlarz, gunner*

AUGUST 20, 1943

✠ Mission #19 – Shook awake and heard the words, "Bring toilet articles, mess gear, blanket and extra suit of underwear" at 1:30 a.m. We knew at once that this was a big day. We were going all through Germany to Africa. Guess everyone had his own misgivings as we took off at 2:00 a.m. loaded with ten 500-pound demolition bombs and plenty of ammunition. We rendezvoused at coast of England with seven other groups. We led our wing and were to bomb Regensburg, a Messerschmitt plant, and one of the most important targets of the war. Another wing was hit at Schweinfurt, just a few miles from our target and returned to England. Encountered series of heavy ack-ack, and we made our way through Holland and through Germany, and were attacked by about 75 fighters. We were fortunate in being the lead group, as other groups encountered from 300 to 500 fighters and suffered heavy losses. But we took quite a toll of enemy ships, too. I saw three B-17s go down out of our wing – only one parachute got out. The course was very well-planned, and we were just a bit out of range of all anti-aircraft fire until we were over the target. Bombs away, and I started my camera and I took 20 pictures of the results. We laid bombs precisely on the target for excellent results. Over the rugged, snow-capped Alps – encountered no opposition over Italy, rendezvoused with rest of groups, and headed out over the Mediterranean Sea at the same time, letting down to approximately 8,000 feet. Crossed coast of Africa at 5:00 p.m. to arrive at Telergma at 4:30 [local time]. Africa from the air looks like a tough, dirty brown elephant's hide. Many planes were shot down, and quite a few ran out of gas and had to ditch into the sea.

Telergma is 40 miles from Constantine in North Africa and reminded us of Pyote, Texas. The boys there were on the ball and all out to help us. A few native Arabians lived in their thatched mud huts on the base, and we had fun talking to a few of the kids. Pretty smart little fellows.

The next few days included sitting or lying beneath the wing of the plane in the shade out of the hot sun, reading in the so-called "library," and eating regularly in small 10x10 mess hall. Cooks and KP are Italian prisoners. Go into mess hall, get food, mostly canned goods and ice cold drinks, go out other side and eat out of doors in company with some of the millions of flies there. We bathed in natural hot springs that were enclosed in an old, old building that was built around the spring to form pools. Saw quite a few camels, but most Arabs ride a jackass or burro. Sure looks funny to see them riding – feet dragging in the dust, and the little burro treading along.

We saw Constantine one day there – riding in a truck. A beautiful city, but bit by bit, very dirty. It's built around a huge gorge – narrow streets, small Arabian shops. Bought some ice cream there, though. First we've had for some time.

We went to chapel services – good sermons. We're all after tans, so the majority of us just go around in our shorts.

C-47s (transports) are continually coming in and going out. P-38s, Mustangs, B-26s, P-47s – a real variety of aircraft here.

Slept on the ship every night, and nearly every night when it was cooled off, we'd build a campfire and cook eggs that Nelson bought from an Arab for a few packages of cigarettes.

Visited Telergma on Market Day (Sunday). They butcher sheep as they're bought, and there were heads all over the place. One Arab had opened a delicatessen counter and was selling choice bits of guts that they ate like we would eat candy.

— *Sgt. Dick Haseltine, radio operator*

AUGUST 17-24, 1943

✠ August 17, 1943: Regensburg, Germany – my 19th mission. We completely knocked out 30% of the German aircraft output by hitting an FW-190 factory.

We were gotten out of bed at 2:00 and were told to pack the following articles for a few days in North Africa: one blanket, one set of underclothes; shaving set; canteen and cup; and one towel. So we did, and went as planned. We flew straight through Germany, hitting the target, then through Switzerland, Italy and the Mediterranean Sea and, finally, after flying for 11 hours and 15 minutes, we landed at Telergma, Africa.

Our group led the formation and did not lose a ship or man. But out of the two wings (378 planes), we lost 64 B-17s. The fighters and flak were accurate and very angry with us, so they gave us holy hell. Six B-17s ditched in the Mediterranean Sea because of gas shortage. The crews were all rescued. I saw one plane get his Number 2 engine completely shot off by a flak shell, but he still made the trip.

When we landed on the desert sandy field, the dust got so bad, a couple of ships ran together. It was much worse than any West Texas sandstorm I have ever seen. The sun was beaming down and it was plenty hot and dry. It was a great change from England, where we always wear a leather jacket. But here, all the soldiers wore khaki shorts. They were all just about as brown, or, should I say, black, as the native Arabs were. After being interrogated, it was almost sundown, and we all ate some supper – K-rations – got our blanket and went to sleep on the ground. The ground was as hard as hell, the ants were thick, and the night got cold as hell, but we were all so tired, we slept like hell also. I even dreamt about a beautiful blonde I know and didn't wake up until the sun was a couple of hours high and it got too hot to sleep.

The next day, we were told that we would reload with gas and bombs, and run another mission on the way home. So, we got all set, but had weather set in over the target area. So it was postponed. But we would go when it was cleared up again. Well, we stayed there until August 24th before that happened.

In the meantime, we got sunburned, and about half of the boys got sick with the GIs from the water and the heat. Telergma was only 30 miles from Constantine, which I visited twice. It was one of Africa's most modern cities. It does have a few modern buildings, but it still has those nasty Arabs and black French people to clutter up its beauty. The town is built on top of a high hill, which is divided by a deep canyon. Horse, donkey and oxen draw carts as common as cars in a modern U.S. city. No one speaks English except the American troops.

We also enjoyed speaking to the Italian P.O.W.s, who were captured when the Germans were driven out of Algeria. They love Americans, and no guard is necessary. They hate Germany and do a hell of a lot more work to win the war for us than the American GI soldier. They would have to be forced to return to Italy before the Germans are driven out. They also have to be forced not to work.

We bought ten hen eggs from the Arabs for three packages of cigarettes. The cigarettes cost us about eight cents a pack. We built a fire by our plane and had all the fresh eggs to eat we liked. And they tasted really good, after eating powdered eggs for so long in England.

Every day, a truck would take us to the hot springs (20 miles) for a bath. The water came out of a mountain and was real clean and hot. And you don't need bathing suits in Africa. I even went one whole day all over Telergma with only my shorts on.

We were there on a Sunday, so I went to church, which didn't hurt me a bit. In fact, it made me much better. I tried to send a wire home to let my folks know I was still alive, but no blanks were available.

Finally, on August 24th, we took off for England and to bomb Bordeaux, France. We took off at six in the morning, and landed at six that night. Twelve hours behind the controls of a bomber in formation is a long, tiresome drag. The trip was much better than the one down, because we hit our target easy, saw only a few fighters and little flak, and lost no ships.

Capt. Hand and Lt. Shelton had to stay in Africa until their ships could be repaired from the previous mission. They will return to England by the route around Spain, out of the range of fighters. When I landed, Gen. Anderson, Col. Wilson, Col. Old and three other big shots came out to meet us and congratulate us on our return. Our picture was taken as we were talking, which I have one, and one is pasted on our officers' bulletin board.

— *Lt. Ruben Neie, pilot*

AUGUST 17-24, 1943

 Telergma, North Africa.

Our first day in Africa was spent looking the country over, and the Arabs. The Arabs are a dirty, filthy race that live around here. The week we were here, we saw two Arab women from a distance.

What we liked were the little burros these people have. They carry tremendous loads on their backs. They are very tame. We also saw several camel caravans going across the desert. These Arabs don't seem to do much besides watching their herds of cattle, sheep, goats and horses grazing in dried-up pastures. We saw them threshing wheat several times by the old method, using horses to stomp on it, going around in a circle – a very slow process of threshing wheat.

The Arabs came around to our planes trading and selling eggs. We bought eggs by trading three packs of cigarettes for one dozen eggs. We had fresh fried eggs every night before going to bed underneath our own planes.

Asking the Arabs what they thought of the Germans, Italian, English and French, they all said 'No @#$& good!' They really like the Yanks. Maybe because we treat them so nice and buy their goods.

They have quite a few Italian prisoners on this base. They are not guarded. They have their own barracks. They do general duty, KP, even cook in the enlisted men's mess hall. We really had some good meals there. Ice cold drinks every meal. Plenty of food.

The weather was hot and dusty, near 120 degrees every day. We took baths in some hot springs 25 miles from the base almost every day.

We went to the town of Constantine for several hours. Had some ice cream and cold beer. Bought knife and French money.

We visited the AA gun crews stationed 100 feet from our airplane. They are a swell bunch of boys, all wanting to go back to the U.S.A. – and who doesn't! Troop trains and truck convoys fully loaded, going through camp all day and night, all week long.

One crew from our outfit brought back a burro with him – a cute little devil. We saw an Arab burial in the country behind our mess hall.

— *Sgt. Leo Lakey, gunner*

AUGUST 17, 1943: REGENSBURG, GERMANY (NORTH AFRICAN SHUTTLE)

FROM: SNETTERTON FALCONS II, THE 96TH BOMB GROUP IN WWII EDITED BY ROBERT DOHERTY AND GEOFFREY D. WARD

The 4BW won the shuttle to North Africa because it had been equipped with long-range Tokyo tanks. So far, the Americans' farthest target had been Kassel, 200 miles from the East Anglian bases. Regensburg was 525 miles away.

If this plan for the 96th to bomb Regensburg seems rather straightforward, it wasn't. The original concept was for the entire 8th to bomb Schweinfurt. To this end, group bombardiers had studied the target plans for that city.

Lt. Ray McKinnon, bombardier for Lt. Harman's crew, tells it best: "For weeks, bombardiers and navigators were shown a photo of a town on a river, and three essential targets were pointed out. We were even asked to draw a diagram of the town and show the relationship of the three buildings to natural landmarks so we could pick them out easily on the bomb run. But we were not told the name of the town or which country it was in, or what those factories produced. Whatever it was, it seemed big, and though I was dreading that target coming up in the near future, when it did come, we'd be ready."

When early morning briefing was called and the cover was yanked off the wall map, crews were amazed to find that they were *not* being sent to the target they had studied so minutely! This flash of confusion was immediately replaced by the excitement of the long flight to North Africa and the possibility of fooling the Luftwaffe.

But most of all, it was replaced by a sense of pride. The 96th had been chosen to lead the entire 4BW. And the stern 4BW commander, Col. Curtis LeMay, would lead the way in Capt. Tom Kenny's *Fertile Myrtle III*! In 26 missions, the 96th had flown lead now and then, but never on such an important mission. The group was about to distinguish itself in the annals of the 8th. Archie Old's insistence on tight formation and

Shuttle Raid: Flying over the Alps to North Africa

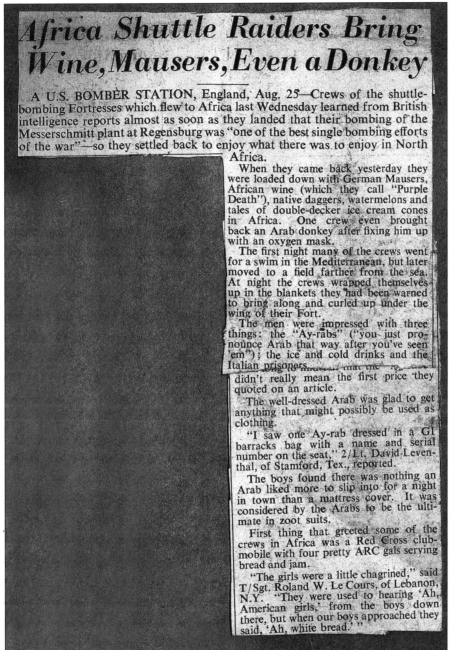

Africa Shuttle Raiders Bring Wine, Mausers, Even a Donkey

A U.S. BOMBER STATION, England, Aug. 25—Crews of the shuttle-bombing Fortresses which flew to Africa last Wednesday learned from British intelligence reports almost as soon as they landed that their bombing of the Messerschmitt plant at Regensburg was "one of the best single bombing efforts of the war"—so they settled back to enjoy what there was to enjoy in North Africa.

When they came back yesterday they were loaded down with German Mausers, African wine (which they call "Purple Death"), native daggers, watermelons and tales of double-decker ice cream cones in Africa. One crew even brought back an Arab donkey after fixing him up with an oxygen mask.

The first night many of the crews went for a swim in the Mediterranean, but later moved to a field farther from the sea. At night the crews wrapped themselves up in the blankets they had been warned to bring along and curled up under the wing of their Fort.

The men were impressed with three things: the "Ay-rabs" ("you just pronounce Arab that way after you've seen 'em"); the ice and cold drinks and the Italian prisoners.... that the didn't really mean the first price they quoted on an article.

The well-dressed Arab was glad to get anything that might possibly be used as clothing.

"I saw one Ay-rab dressed in a GI barracks bag with a name and serial number on the seat," 2/Lt. David Leventhal, of Stamford, Tex., reported.

The boys found there was nothing an Arab liked more to slip into for a night in town than a mattress cover. It was considered by the Arabs to be the ultimate in zoot suits.

First thing that greeted some of the crews in Africa was a Red Cross club-mobile with four pretty ARC gals serving bread and jam.

"The girls were a little chagrined," said T/Sgt. Roland W. Le Cours, of Lebanon, N.Y. "They were used to hearing 'Ah, American girls,' from the boys down there, but when our boys approached they said, 'Ah, white bread.'"

African Shuttle Raiders

instrument flying had paid off. And, being the spirited commander that he was, he was determined to go along.

The teleprinter plan was for the Regensburg force of 146 planes to have its leading element, the 96th, cross the coast of Holland at 0830. The Regensburg force would attract fighter opposition, but would soon fool them by continuing to Africa. Original timing called for almost simultaneous bombing. The 1BW was expected to have a tough time coming home. As the briefing officers anticipated things, the Regensburg people would have to fight their way in, and the Schweinfurt people would have to fight their way out.

For those who care to examine this famous two-target mission in detail, we have listed the most authoritative books in our bibliography. For now, however, we must keep faith with the 96th's role in the Regensburg raid. Simply, we know that when the 0530 take-off time arrived, British weather was at its worst. The take-offs were delayed, more so for the Schweinfurt force. It was to prove tragic for them, indeed.

Meanwhile, back at Snetterton, bombs had been loaded, and Tokyo tanks had been topped off. The ceiling was only some 1,000 feet. A half-hour had passed. Take-off could not be delayed any more for the 4BW…not if it was to get to North Africa while there was still daylight. At 0600, they began taking off.

The 1BW was still held back, because Col. LeMay, as wing commander, had insisted that his 4BW pilots practice until they became proficient at bad weather (instrument) take-offs. The 4BW had been released to orbit in the swirling mists. A little earlier, Col. Old had been about to board *Fertile Myrtle III*, when a staff car had arrived from Elvedon Hall. There was LeMay, in full gear, ready to fly the lead plane. Old, realizing that he would have to defer to rank, resorted to his colorful pattern of speech and fumed off to commandeer the pilot's seat in Capt. Vern Iverson's deputy lead plane, *Mischief Maker*. Col. Old's troubles were not over.

Capt. Vern Iverson recalls how *Mischief Maker's* mischief got him on the colonel's black list for a while: "It seems that a tech-order revision had come out that had something to do with the hydraulic controls on the props. So, our engineering officer, Lt. Swanson, was going to do me a favor and fix my plane first. (I didn't find out about this until after the mission.) Anyway, just at the Dutch coast, one of my props ran away. I simply could not get it to operate correctly, but I did get it to feather. I then called my wingman and peeled out of formation for home. Naturally," Iverson recalls with a twinkle, "Archie had a full-fledged case of apoplexy because I didn't consult him. The next morning, he called me into his office and gave me a royal chewing. Before he was done, I had become madder than a hornet, and when he finally stopped for air, I said, 'Sir, if I had to do it all over again, I would do exactly the same thing.' Then I saluted and walked out. That was the last I ever heard about that situation from him."

Vern Iverson led his men on a complete tour of duty. As luck would have it, this turned out to be his only aborted mission. Yet, if they had tried to press on to Regensburg, there is little doubt that the 8th would have lost one of its outstanding commanders.

The mix-up in timing had a bad effect on the fighter escort, too. They ran out of fuel early because they had been circling around, waiting for bombers. From the Dutch coast on, enemy fighters began their attacks. They had seen our escorts turn back over Eupen. The bombers were on their own. This became more evident beyond Eupen when the Luftwaffe really began to show their nerve. Although the 96th was doing well, along with the 388th, in leading the combat wing, gunners from both of these groups were calling out a steady stream of casualties and dropouts within the formation behind. (Debriefing records show that Capt. Jack Ford, who led the low squadron, witnessed the downing of six B-17s and three fighters. Bill Hartman testified to two

B-17 downings, and Dick Jerger recorded four more. It is most possible that some of these were duplicate sightings.) Although E/A concentrated elsewhere in the bomber stream, some of them did damage to the 96th.

Doc Hartman, 337th Flight Surgeon, was making his record of five missions this day as an observer aboard Lt. Snyder's Fortress. "As an observer," Sam Hartman writes, "my main problem was to stay out of the way of the navigator, Larry Godley, and bombardier, John O'Brien.... I'll never forget the sensation when we came under fighter attack. The whole ship would shake and shudder. When you get ten .50 calibers going at once – well, you can't imagine the noise, confusion and terror... I remember slipping and sliding all over the place on shell casings... Believe me, I learned plenty about stress! Our top turret-gunner, Bob Padbury, vaporized an Me-109 while it was attacking from 11 o'clock high."

By relative measure, the 96th planes were not damaged. One exception, of course, just had to be Capt. Joe Bender's last chalked-up *Tarfu*. Although a 100-mph tailwind at their 10,000-foot altitude made it difficult for E/A to attack the 96th, some managed to home in on *Tarfu's* magnetism for rip-roaring combat. "We had our elevator control cables for the right side of the ship shot away," co-pilot Lew Feldstein writes, "and also, our rudder control cable and the oxygen system from the pilots' compartments to the tail."

Pilot Jim Sanders' engineer aboard *Rum Boogie*, T/A Ellis Savoie, takes up the tale. "Finally, at 12:10, we sight the target. That's funny; very little flak. Maybe they don't expect us this far in. Bomb-bay doors coming open. There they go! Oh, baby! We parted their hair that time! There she goes – the whole damn works! A beautiful hit. A smackeroo! On our way out now. At the Alps, we make a 360 so the back formation can catch up..."

Capt. John Latham was the lead bombardier, and he placed the first bombs smack on the leading edge of the target area and the main assembly buildings, much to the delight of Col. LeMay.

The potential danger from the German and Italian fighters haunted the African-bound task force. Unknown to them, the Luftwaffe had been and was still chewing the 1BW Schweinfurt attackers. Leaving Regensburg in ruins, LeMay's division began to sweat out other factors on this long flight.

Aboard Lt. Snyder's plane, Joe Hartman (like everybody else) relaxes just a tad to enjoy the last leg of the journey. "After the target," Hartman writes, "I was able to enjoy the scenery. Lake Como in Italy was a deep indigo, and, being hot and sweaty, I felt like diving in... The Alps were spectacular, even though we slid through rather than over them. I loosened my equipment a bit and sunbathed and drowsed in the nose as we passed serenely over the Mediterranean." (Much later, the British artist, Frank Beresford, would immortalize the 96th's passage through the Alps.)

But up in the lead plane, while LeMay and Tom Kenny expressed satisfaction with the strike, lead radio-operator Tech. Sgt. Otis Haslop was having problems. "The radio-operators had been supplied with identification and communication codes," Haslop writes. "But it turned out that these were applicable to the home territory – meaning

England. Consequently, all the direction-finding stations which we were now trying to contact refused to acknowledge us."

Eventually, LeMay gave the order to abridge security regulations. Haslop explained the task-force predicament to the D/F stations without code, and the planes were serviced immediately. Errors like this always highlighted the need for detailed planning. If such an oversight impaired one mission, at least the participants of some future mission would benefit. That's what common sense would say. But when the 4BW headed back for England in a few days, radio ops would be given "overseas" codes, and the whole embarrassing procedure would have to be repeated.

It took another five hours to fly from the target to their destination. They continued over Lake Como, on down to Italy, and then over to the Med to the west of Sardinia and Corsica before landing at Telergma near Constantine. Some didn't make it. But no 96ers ditched in the Med or were lost – except a few that had to land elsewhere in Africa for gas. Jim Sanders' *Rum Boogie* had to do that. It then caught up with other 96ers at Telergma's Bone Air Base.

The conditions here were far from ideal. Another snafu had plagued the planning. Even though LeMay had scouted the airfield some time ago, when the shuttle was first conceived, they soon realized a lot of water had gone under the bridge in the meantime. Here he was coming into a strange airbase with a riddled and crippled Task Force, only to find, like Mother Hubbard, that the cupboard was bare. Since his long-ago visit, war conditions in North Africa had improved for the Allies, to the point that repair depot facilities here had been removed! No one thought to alert him. Now, where was he to get spare parts! Or fuel? Or bombs, for that matter? That was some of the bad news. The good news, apparent right after landing, was that the 96th had taken no casualties. Doc Hartman's diary records the fact that on the 19th, pilots Flagg, McGibney, Bender and Gary Shelton had to fly to Marrakech in Morocco for repairs. Otherwise, everyone was okay. But the week at Bone really called for roughing it. Crews slept beneath the wings of their planes out in the desert.

Ray McKinnon remembers: "One day, I finally got a helmet full of water. First, I mixed some with my K-Ration. Then, I managed soup and instant coffee. Then, I shaved, and the rest was my bath water. All this was done in the sand by the plane."

While the frustrated Col. LeMay was scrounging up facilities, 96ers made the best of their situation. "There was a camp of Italian prisoners nearby," Ray McKinnon recalls. "Their perimeter fence was only chicken wire, but they had no desire to escape. Consequently, some were very willing to be pressed into service. They helped us man the hand-pumps for refueling. There were no bowsers, and all the fuel had to be pumped by hand from the barrels."

Help from Italian POWs was not so much appreciated by Staff Sgt. LeRoy Bradrick. This gunner's presence amid a bomber task force in North Africa was nothing short of amazing. From the day after Pearl Harbor, when he first tried to enlist in the service, "Brad" had been rejected for bad eyesight by the Army, Navy, Marines and Coast Guard. He was eventually drafted after he convinced a doctor to let him join on a limited service basis. The doctor prescribed glasses which would catch up with the new recruit at his first station. They never did. Meanwhile, Bradrick graduated with the second class of armorers from Buckley Field in Colorado, and was whisked through

Salt Lake to the 96th at Rapid City. He made corporal at Pyote, and rode as a guard on 16 boxcars of equipment from that dusty Texas base to Camp Kilmer. In all that time, he had never been given another physical, and he certainly didn't volunteer information about his restricted capacity. When Norm Tanner's BTG, Joe Tony, got wounded, Bradrick, who had been servicing Tanner's plane, volunteered to take Joe's place. The group was hard up for replacements, and Brad was accepted. When Tony came back from the hospital, Brad was a blooded veteran, and became Ralph Ward's BTG aboard *Shack Rabbit III.*

Now, here in Africa, the former armorer watched Italian POWs load his plane. "I looked them over," Bradrick remembers, "and discovered that the second bomb in the right bay had a shackle-release missing." With the help of Capt. Ward and the bombardier, the trio righted the situation. "We very well might have rolled a bomb right through the side of the ship."

Sgt. LeRoy Bradrick, rejected by every branch of the service, and without aerial gunnery training, would complete his tour of duty and be credited with four enemy planes, including an ME-262 jet!

The North African shuttle was a pleasant experience for most 96th men. Some, like Doc Hartman, didn't have to sleep under the wings every night. Doc visited the 57th Station Hospital and was delighted to find out that he had served with one of the doctors at Charity Hospital in New Orleans, and had graduated from the same high school as the chief physician. Other crew men visited the city of Constantine. At every step, they were besieged by begging Arabs. By local cultural standards, a mattress cover made a fine article of clothing.

The *Miracle Tribe* would return to England symbolizing all that was wonderful, wild and adventurous about the mission. They had decided to bring back a mascot that gunner Louis Klimchak said was too ordinary. "Coots" Matthews considered a baby camel, but not for long. Andy Miracle considered an Arab maiden, but was afraid of a kidnapping charge. Then, an Arabian boy said his family might have a donkey for sale. That certainly qualified for an unusual mascot, so Klimchak and co-pilot Jim Harris went off to make the deal. The little donkey, half-starved, was a sorry sight. She was hardly two feet tall, but she captured the hearts of the *Tribesmen*. An $80 deal was struck. The *Miracle Tribesmen* had no idea that they were bringing home a legend. This skinny, sloe-eyed donkey, which had been starving in a filthy section of an Algerian slum, was about to make a flight to England where she would become Queen of the Heath.

August 17, 1943

Regensburg, Germany (North African Shuttle)
from: The Saturday Evening Post
by Bernie Lay
(Appeared in issue dated November 6, 1943)

In the briefing room, the intelligence officer of the bombardment group pulled a cloth screen away from a huge wall map. Each of the 240 sleepy-eyed combat crew members in the crowded room leaned forward. There were low whistles. I felt a sting of anticipation as I stared at the red string on the map that stretched from our base in

England to a pinpoint deep in southern Germany, then south across the Alps, through the Grenner Pass to the coast of Italy, then past Corsica and Sardinia, and south over the Mediterranean to a desert airdrome in North Africa. You could have heard an oxygen mask drop.

"Your primary," said the intelligence officer, "is Regensburg. Your aiming point is the center of the Messerschmitt 109G aircraft and engine assembly shops. This is the most vital target we've ever gone after. If you destroy it, you destroy 30 percent of the Luftwaffe's single-engine fighter production. You fellows know what that means to you personally."

There were a few hollow laughs.

After the briefing, I climbed aboard a jeep bound for the operations office to check up on my Fortress assignment. The stars were dimly visible through the chilly mist that covered our blacked-out bomber station, but the weather forecast for a deep penetration over the Continent was good. In the office, I looked at the crew sheet where the line-up of the lead, low and high squadrons of the group, is plotted for each mission. I was listed for a co-pilot's seat. While I stood there, and on the chance suggestion of one of the squadron commanders who was looking over the list, the operations officer erased my name and shifted me to the high squadron as co-pilot in the crew of a steady Irishman named Lt. Murphy, with whom I had flown before. Neither of us knew it, but that operations officer saved my life right there with a piece of rubber on the end of a pencil.

At 5:30 a.m., 15 minutes before taxi time, a jeep drove around the five-mile perimeter track in the semi-darkness, pausing at each dispersal point long enough to notify the waiting crews that poor local visibility would postpone the take-off for an hour and a half. I was sitting with Murphy and the rest of our crew near the *Piccadilly Lily*. She looked sinister and complacent, squatting on her fat tires, with scarcely a hole in her skin to show for the 12 raids behind her. The postponement tightened, rather than relaxed, the tension. Once more, I checked over my life vest, oxygen mask and parachute, not perfunctorily, but the way you check something you know you're going to have to use. I made sure my escape kit was pinned securely in the knee-pocket of my flight suit where it couldn't fall out in a scramble to abandon ship. I slid the hunting knife between my shoe and flying boot as I looked again through my extra equipment for this mission: water canteen, mess kit, blankets, and English pounds for use in the Algerian desert, where we would sleep on the ground and might be on our own from a forced landing.

Murphy restlessly gave the *Piccadilly Lily* another once-over, inspecting ammunition belts, bomb bay, tires and oxygen pressure at each crew station, especially the oxygen. It's human fuel, as important as gasoline, up where we operate. Gunners field-stripped their .50-calibers again and oiled the bolts. Our top turret-gunner lay in the grass with his head on his parachute, feigning sleep, sweating out his 13th start.

We shared a common knowledge, which grimly enhanced the normal excitement before a mission. Of the approximately 150 Fortresses who were hitting Regensburg, our group was the last and lowest, a base altitude of 17,000 feet. That's well within the range of accuracy for heavy flak. Our course would take us over plenty of it. It was a cinch, also, that our group would be the softest touch for the enemy fighters, being last man through the gauntlet. Furthermore, the *Piccadilly Lily* was leading the last three ships of the high squadron – the tip of the tail-end of the whole shebang. We didn't relish it much. Who wants a Purple Heart?

The minute-hand of my wristwatch dragged. I caught myself thinking about the day, exactly one year ago, on August 17, 1942, when I watched a pitifully small force of B-17s take off on the first raid of the 8th Air Force to make a shallow penetration against Rouen, France. On that day, it was our maximum effort. Today, on our first anniversary, we were putting 30 times that number of heavies into the air – half the Force on Regensburg, and half the Force on Schweinfurt, both situations inside the interior of the German Reich. For a year and a half, as staff officer, I had watched the 8th Air Force grow under Maj. Gen. Ira C. Eaker. That's a long time to watch from behind a desk. Only ten days ago, I had asked for and received orders for combat duty. Those ten days had been full of swift action of participating in four combat missions, and checking out for the first time as a four-engine pilot.

Now I knew that it can be easier to be shot at than telephoned at, that staff officers at an Air Force headquarters are the unsung heroes of this war. And yet, I found myself reminiscing just a little affectionately about that desk, wondering if there wasn't a touch of suicide in store for our group. One thing was for sure: Headquarters had dreamed up the biggest air operation to date to celebrate its birthday, in the biggest league of aerial warfare.

At 7:30, we broke out of the cloud tops into the glare of the rising sun. Beneath our B-17 lay English fields, still blanketed in the thick mist from which we had just emerged. We continued to climb slowly, our broad wings shouldering a heavy load of incendiary bombs in the belly, and a burden of fuel in the main and wing-tip Tokyo tanks that would keep the Fortress afloat in the thin upper altitudes for 11 hours.

From my co-pilot's seat on the right-hand side, I watched the white surface of the overcast, where the B-17s, in clusters of six to the squadron, were puncturing the cloud deck all about us, rising clear of the mist with their glass noses slanted upward for the long climb to the base altitude. We tacked onto one of these clutches of six. Now the sky over England was heavy with the weight of thousands of tons of bombs, fuel and men being lifted four miles straight up on a giant aerial hoist to the western terminus of a 20,000-foot elevated highway that led east to Regensburg. At intervals, I saw the arc of a sputtering red, green or yellow flare being fired from the cabin roof of a group leader's airplane to identify the lead squadron to the high and low squadrons of each group. Assembly takes longer when you come up through an overcast.

For nearly an hour, still over southern England, we climbed, nursing the straining Cyclone engines in a 300-foot-per-minute ascent, forming three squadrons gradually into compact group-stagger formations – low squadron down to the left, and high squadron up to the right of the lead squadron – groups assembling into looser combat wings of two to three groups each, along the combat wing assembly line, homing over predetermined points with radio compass, and finally cruising along the air-division assembly line to allow the combat wings to fall into place in trail behind Col. Curtis E. LeMay in the lead group of the air division.

Formed at last, each flanking group in position 1,000 feet above or below its lead group, our 15-mile parade moved east toward Lowestoft, point of departure from the friendly coast, unwieldy, but dangerous to fool with. From my perch in the high squadron in the last element of the whole procession, the air division looked like huge anvil-shaped swarms of locusts – not on dress parade, like the bombers of the Luftwaffe that died like flies over Britain in 1940, but deployed to uncover every gun, and permit maneuverability. Our formation was basically worked out for the Air Corps by Brig. Gen. Hugh Knerr 20 years ago with 85-mile-an-hour bombers, plus refinements devised by Col. LeMay from experience in the European Theater.

The English Channel and the North Sea glittered bright in the clear visibility as we left the bulge of East Anglia behind us. Up ahead, we knew that we were already registering on the German RDF screen, and that the sector controllers of the Luftwaffe's fighter belt in Western Europe were busy alerting their *Staffein* of Focke-Wulfs and Messerschmitts. I stole a last look back at cloud-covered England, where I could see a dozen spare B-17s who had accompanied us to fill in for any abortives from mechanical failure in the hard climb, gliding disappointedly home to base.

I fastened my oxygen mask a little tighter and looked at the little ball in a glass tube on the instrument panel that indicates proper oxygen flow. It was moving up and down like a visual heartbeat as I breathed, registering normal.

Already, the gunners were searching. Occasionally, the ship shivered as guns were tested with short bursts. I could see puffs of blue smoke from the group close ahead and 1,000 feet above us, as each gunner satisfied himself that he had lead poisoning at his trigger tips. The coast of Holland appeared in sharp, black outline. I drew in a deep breath of oxygen.

A few miles in front of us were German boys in single-seaters who were probably going to react to us in the same way our boys would react – emotionally, if German bombers were heading for the Pratt & Whitney engine factory at Hartford, or the Liberator plant at Willow Run. In the making was a death struggle between the unstoppable objects and the immovable defense – every possible defense at the disposal of the Reich, for this was a deadly penetration to a hitherto inaccessible and critically important arsenal of the *Vaterland*.

At 10:08, we crossed the coast of Holland south of The Hague, with our group of Fortresses tucked in tightly and within handy supporting distance of the group above us at 18,000 feet. But our long, loose-linked column looked too long, and the gaps between combat wings too wide. As I squinted into the sun, gauging the distance to the barely-visible specs of the lead group, I had a recurrence of that sinking feeling before take-off – the lonesome foreboding that might come to the last man about to run a gauntlet line with spiked clubs. The premonition was well-founded.

At 10:17, near Woendrecht, I saw the first flak blossom out in our vicinity, light and inaccurate. A few minutes later, at approximately 10:25, a gunner called, "Fighters at two o'clock and low." I saw them climbing above the horizon ahead of us to the right – a pair of them. For a moment, I hoped they were P-47 Thunderbolts from the fighter escort that was supposed to be in our vicinity, but I didn't hope long. The two FW-190s turned and whizzed through the formation ahead of us in a frontal attack, nicking two B-17s in the wings, and breaking away in half-rolls right over our group. By craning my neck up and back, I glimpsed one of them through the glass roof in the cabin, flashing past at a 600-mile-an-hour rate of closure, his yellow nose smoking, and small pieces flying off near the wing root. The guns of our group were in action. The pungent smell of burnt cordite filled the cockpit, and the B-17 trembled to the recoil of nose and ball-turret guns. Smoke immediately trailed from the hit B-17s, but they held their stations.

Here was early fighter reaction. The members of the crew sensed trouble. There was something desperate about the way those two fighters came in fast, right out of their climb, without any preliminaries. Apparently, our own fighters were busy somewhere farther up the procession. The interphone was active for a few seconds with brief admonitions: "Lead 'em more"... "Short bursts"... "Don't throw rounds away"... "Bombardier to the left waist-gunner"... "Don't yell – talk slow."

Three minutes later, the gunners reported fighters climbing up from all around the clock, singly and in pairs, both FW-190s and Me-109-Gs. The fighters I could see on my side looked like too many for sound health. No friendly Thunderbolts were visible. From now on, we were in mortal danger. My mouth dried up and my buttocks pulled together. A coordinated attack began, with the head-on fighters coming from slightly above, the nine- and three o'clock attackers approaching from about level, and the rear attackers from slightly below. The guns from every B-17 in our group and the group ahead were firing simultaneously, lashing the sky with ropes of orange tracers to match the chain-puss bursts squirting form the .20mm cannon muzzles in the wings of the Jerry single-seaters.

I noted with alarm that a lot of our fire was falling astern of the target, particularly from our hand-held nose and waist guns. Nevertheless, both sides got hurt in this clash, with the entire second element of three B-17s from our low squadron and one B-17 from the group ahead falling out of formation and on fire, with crews bailing out, and several fighters heading for the deck in flames or with their pilots lingering behind under the dirty yellow canopies that distinguished some of their parachutes from ours. Our 24-year-old group leader, flying only his third combat mission, pulled us up even closer to the preceding group for mutual support.

As we swung slightly outside with our squadron in mild evasive action, I got a good look at that gap in the low squadron where three B-17s had been. Suddenly, I bit my lip hard. The lead ship of that element had pulled out on fire and exploded before anyone bailed out. It was the ship to which I had been originally assigned.

I glanced over at Murphy. It was cold in the cockpit, but sweat was running from his forehead and over his oxygen mask from the exertion of holding his element in tight formation, and the strain of the warnings that hummed over the interphone, and what he could see out of the corners of his eyes. He caught my glance and turned the controls over to me for a while. It was an enormous relief to concentrate on flying instead of sitting there watching fighters aiming between your eyes. Somehow, the attacks from the rear, although I could see them through my ears via the interphone, didn't bother me. I guess it's because there was a slab of armor plate behind my back and I couldn't watch them anyway.

I knew that we were in a lively fight. Every alarm bell in my brain was ringing a high-pitched warning. But my nerves were steady and my brain working. The fear was unpleasant, but it was bearable. I knew that I was going to die, and so were a lot of others. What I didn't know was that the real fight, the *Anschluss* of Luftwaffe .20mm cannon shells, hadn't really begun. The largest and most savage fighter resistance of any war in history was rising to stop us at any cost, and our group was the most vulnerable target.

A few minutes later, we absorbed the first wave of a hailstorm of individual fighter attacks that were to engulf us, clear to the target, in such a blizzard of bullets and shells that a chronological account is difficult. It was at 10:41, over Eupen, that I looked out the window after a minute's lull and saw two whole squadrons – 12 Me-109s and 11 FW-190s – climbing parallel to us as though they were on a steep escalator. The first squadron had reached our level and was pulling ahead to turn into us. The second was not far behind. Several thousand feet below us were many more fighters, their noses cocked up in a maximum climb. Over the interphone came reports of an equal number of enemy aircraft deploying on the other side of the formation.

For the first time, I noticed an Me-110 sitting out of range on our level out to the right. He was to stay with us all the way to the target, apparently radioing our position and weak spots to fresh *Staffein* waiting farther down the road.

At the sight of all these fighters, I had the distinct feeling of being trapped – that the Hun had been tipped off, or, at least had guessed our destination, and was set for us. We were already through the German fighter belt. Obviously, they had moved a lot of squadrons back in a fluid defense in-depth, and they must have been saving up some outfits for the inner defense that we didn't know about. The life expectancy of our group seemed definitely limited, since it had already appeared that the fighters, instead of wasting fuel trying to overhaul the preceding groups, were glad to take a cut at us.

Swinging their yellow noses around in a wide U-turn, the 12-ship squadron of Me-109s came on from 12 to two o'clock in pairs. The main event was on. I fought an impulse to close my eyes, and overcame it.

A shining silver rectangle of metal sailed past over our right wing. I recognized it as a main exit-door. Seconds later, a black lump came hurtling through the formation, barely missing several propellers. It was a man, clasping his knees to his head, revolving like a diver in a triple somersault, shooting by us so close that I saw a piece of paper blow out of his leather jacket. He was evidently making some delayed jump, for I didn't see his parachute open.

A B-17 turned gradually out of formation to the right, maintaining altitude. In a split second, it completely vanished in a brilliant explosion, from which the only remains were four balls of fire – the fuel tanks – which were quickly consumed as they fell earthward.

I saw blue, red, yellow and aluminum-colored fighters. Their tactics were running fairly to form, with frontal attacks hitting the low squadron, and rear attackers going for the lead and high squadrons. Some of the Jerries shot at us with rockets, and an attempt at air-to-air bombing was made with little black time-fuse sticks, dropped from above, which exploded in small gray puffs off to one side of the formation. Several of the FWs did some nice deflection-shooting on side attacks from 500 yards at the high group, then raked the low group on the breakaway at closer range, with their noses cocked in a side-slip, to keep the formation in their sights longer in the turn. External fuel tanks were visible under the bellies or wings of at least two squadrons, shedding uncomfortable light on the mystery of their ability to tail us so far from their bases.

The manner of the assaults indicated that the pilots knew where we were going and were inspired with a fanatical determination to stop up before we got there. Many pressed attacks home to 250 yards or less, or bolted right through the formation wide out, firing long 20-second bursts, often presenting point-blank targets on the break-away. Some committed the fatal error of pulling up instead of going down and out. More experienced pilots came in on frontal attacks with a noticeably slower rate of closure, apparently throttled back, obtaining greater accuracy. But no tactics could halt the close-knit juggernauts of our Fortresses, nor save the single-seaters from paying a terrible price.

Our airplane was endangered by various debris. Emergency hatches, exit doors, prematurely opened parachutes, bodies, and assorted fragments of B-17s and Hun fighters breezed past us in the slipstream.

I watched two fighters explode not far beneath, disappearing in sheets of orange flame; B-17s dropped out in every stage of distress, from engines on fire to controls shot away; friendly and enemy parachutes floated down, and, on the green carpet far below us, funeral pyres of smoke from fallen fighters marked our trail.

On we flew, through the cluttered wake of a desperate air battle, where disintegrating aircraft were commonplace, and the white dots of 60 parachutes in the air at one time were hardly worth a second look. The spectacle registering on my eyes became so fantastic that my brain turned numb to the actuality of the death and destruction all around us. Had it not been for the squeezing in my stomach, which was trying to purge, I might easily have been watching an animated cartoon in a movie theater.

The minutes dragged on into an hour. And still, the fighters came. Our gunners called coolly and briefly to one another, diving up their targets, fighting for their lives with every round of ammunition – and our lives, at the formation. The tail-gunner called that he was out of ammunition. We sent another belt back to him. Here was a new hazard. We might run out of the .50-caliber slugs before we reached the target.

I looked to both sides of us. Our two wingmen were gone. So was the element in front of us – all three ships. We moved up into position behind the lead element of the high squadron. I looked out again on my side and saw a cripple, with one prop feathered, struggle up behind our right wing with his bad engine funneling smoke into the slipstream. He dropped back. Now our tail-gunner had a clear view. There were no more B-17s behind us. We were last man.

I took the controls for a while. The first thing I saw when Murphy resumed flying was a B-17 turning slowly out to the right, its cockpit a mass of flames. The co-pilot crawled out of his window, held on with one hand, reached back for his parachute, buckled it on, let go, and was whisked back into the horizontal stabilizer of the tail. I believe the impact killed him. His parachute didn't open.

I looked forward and almost ducked as I watched the tail-gunner of a B-17 ahead of us take a bead right on our windshield, and cut loose with a stream of tracers that missed us by a few feet as he fired on a fighter attacking us from six o'clock low. I almost ducked again when our own top turret-gunner's twin muzzles pounded away a foot above my head in the full-forward position, giving a realistic imitation of cannon shells exploding in the cockpit, while I gave an even better imitation of a man jumping six inches out of his seat.

Still no let-up. The fighters queued up like a bread line and let us have it. Each second of time had a cannon shell in it. The strain of being a clay duck in the wrong end of that aerial shooting gallery almost became intolerable. Our *Piccadilly Lily* shook steadily with the fire of its .50s, and the air inside was whispy with smoke. I checked the engine instruments for the thousandth time. Normal. No injured crew members yet. Maybe we'd get to that target, even with our reduced firepower. Seven Fortresses from our group had already gone down, and many of the rest of us were badly shot up and shorthanded because of wounded crew members.

Almost disinterestedly, I observed a B-17 pull out from the group preceding us, and drop back to a position about 200 feet from our right wingtip. His right Tokyo tanks were on fire, and had been for a half-hour. Now the smoke was thicker. Flames were licking through the blackened skin of the wing. While the pilot held her steady, I saw four crew members drop out the bomb bay and execute delayed jumps. Another bailed from the nose, opened his parachute prematurely, and nearly fouled the tail. Another went out the left waist-gun opening, delaying his opening for a safe interval. The tail-gunner dropped out of his hatch, pulling the ripcord before he was clear of the ship. His parachute opened instantaneously, barely missing the tail, and jerked him so hard that both his shoes came off. He hung limp in the harness, whereas the others had shown immediate signs of life, shifting around in their harnesses. The Fortress then dropped back in a medium spiral, and I did not see the pilots leave. I saw the ship, though, just before it trailed from view, belly to the sky, its wing a solid sheet of yellow flame.

Now that we had been under constant attack for more than an hour, it appeared certain that our group was faced with extinction. The sky was still mottled with rising fighters. Target time was 35 minutes away. I doubt if a man in the group visualized the possibility of our getting much farther without 100% loss. Gunners were becoming exhausted and nerve-tortured from the nagging strain – the strain that sends gunners and pilots to the rest home. We had been the aiming point for what had looked like most of the Luftwaffe. It looked as though we might find the rest of it primed for us at the target.

At this hopeless point, a young squadron commander down in the low squadron was living through his finest hour. His squadron had lost its second element of three ships early in the fight, south of Antwerp, yet he had consistently maintained his vulnerable and exposed position in the formation rigidly, in order to keep the guns of his three remaining ships well uncovered to protect the belly of the formation. Now, nearing the target, battle damage was catching up with him fast. A .20mm cannon shell penetrated the right side of his airplane and exploded beneath him, damaging the electrical system and cutting the top turret-gunner in the leg. A second .20mm entered the radio compartment, killing the radio operator, who bled to death with his legs severed above the knees. A third .20mm shell entered the left side of the nose, tearing out a section about two feet square, tore away the right-hand nose-gun installations and injured the bombardier in the head and shoulder. A fourth .20mm shell penetrated the right wing into the fuselage and shattered the hydraulic system, releasing fluid all over the cockpit. A fifth .20mm shell punctured the cabin roof and severed the rudder cables to one side of the rudder. A sixth .20mm shell exploded in the number three engine, destroying all controls to the engine. The engine caught fire and lost its power, but eventually I saw the fire go out.

Confronted with structural damage, partial loss of control, fire in the air and serious injuries to personnel, and faced with fresh waves of fighters still rising to the attack, this commander was justified in abandoning ship. His crew, some of them comparatively inexperienced youngsters, were preparing to bail out. The co-pilot pleaded repeatedly with him to bail out. His reply at this critical juncture was blunt. His words were heard over the interphone, and had a magical effect on the crew. They stuck to their guns. The B-17 kept on.

Near the initial point, at 11:50, one hour and a half after the first of at least 200 individual fighter attacks, the pressure eased off, although hostiles were still in the vicinity. A curious sensation came over me. I was still alive. It was possible to think of the target. Of North Africa. Of returning to England. Almost idly, I watched a crippled B-17 pull over to the curb, drop its wheels and open its bomb bay, jettisoning its bombs. Three Me-109s circled it closely, but held their fire while the crew bailed out. I remembered now that a little while back, I had seen other Hun fighters hold their fire, even when being shot at by a B-17 from which the crew were bailing. But I doubt if sportsmanship had anything to do with it. They hoped to get a B-17 down fairly intact.

And then our weary, battered column, short 24 bombers, but still holding the close formation that had brought the remainder through by sheer discipline and gunnery, turned into the target. I knew that our bombardiers were grim as death while they synchronized their sights on the great Me-109 shops, lying below us in a curve of the winding blue Danube, close to the outskirts of Regensburg. Our B-17 gave a slight lift, and a red light went out on the instrument panel. Our bombs were away. We turned from the target toward the snow-capped Alps. I looked back and saw a beautiful sight – a rectangle pillar of smoke rising from the Me-109 plant. Only one burst was over and into the town. Even from their height, I could see that we smeared the objective. The price? Cheap. Two-hundred airmen.

A few more fighters pecked at us on the way to the Alps, and a couple of smoking B-17s glided down toward the safety of Switzerland, about 20 miles distant. A town in the Brenner Pass tossed up a lone burst of futile flak. Flak? There had been lots of flak in the past two hours, but only now did I recall having seen it – a sort of side issue to the fighters. Col. LeMay, who had taken excellent care of us all the way, circled the air division over a large lake to give the cripples – some flying on three engines, and many trailing smoke – a chance to rejoin the family. We approached the Mediterranean in a gradual descent, conserving fuel. Out over the water, we flew at low altitude, unmolested by fighters from Sardinia or Corsica, waiting through the long, hot afternoon hours for the first sight of the North African coastline. The prospect of ditching, out of gasoline, and the sight of other B-17s falling into the drink, seemed trivial matters after the vicious nightmare of the long trial across southern Germany. We had walked through a high valley of the shadow of death, not expecting to see another sunset, and now I could fear no evil.

With red lights on all of our fuel tanks, we landed at our designated base in the desert, after 11 hours in the air. I slept on the ground near the wing, and, waking occasionally, stared up at the stars. My radio headset was back in the ship. And yet, I could hear the deep chords of great music.

AUGUST 24, 1943

 Mission #20.

Target: airfield and TW-200 (Kuriers) at Bordeaux, France. Bomb load: ten 500-pounders. Bombing altitude: 21,000 feet. Left Telergma, Algeria (North Africa) at 7:00 a.m. and rendezvoused with three other groups over the field. About 80 planes cut over the Mediterranean Sea along coast of Spain, and hit the coast of France at 10:30 a.m. and hit target at 12:15 p.m. Direct hits were scored. About 15 enemy fighters were sighted and intercepted us. No 17s were lost. Arrived at camp around 6:30 p.m. Greeted by Brig. Gen. Anderson as we landed.

> **Resume of Mission #20:**
> First Wing: Villacoublay, France
> Target: airfield and depot
> Seven groups: 110 B-17s dispatched; no planes lost
> E/A claims: one destroyed and one damaged
> Casualties: ten wounded
> Bombs on target: 1,029 500-pounders (demolition)
> Escort: ten squadrons P-47s
>
> Mission II: Diversion: North Sea and Channel
> Three groups: 36 planes – no results
>
> Mission III:
> Fourth wing: Ventoux - Fauville, France
> Targets: airfields
> Seven groups: 42 B-17s dispatched; one B-17 lost
> E/A claims: two damaged
> Casualties: one killed – nine wounded
> Bombs on first target: 280 120-pounders; second: 216 120-pounders
> Escort: 13 squadrons Spitfires
>
> Fourth wing: Bordeaux, France
> Target: Bordeaux - Merignac airfield
> Seven groups: 85 planes (B-17s); three lost
> E/A claims: 3 – 3 – 10
> Casualties: 30 missing
> Bombs on target: 567 500-pounders
> Note: shuttle 17s from Africa
> — *Sgt. Joseph Kotlarz, gunner*

 Twentieth Mission – flew 12 hours – Bordeaux, France.

Got up at 0430. Take-off 0600. Circle field about a dozen times until all the groups got up. We flew at 6,000 feet for several hours. We saw several of the Spanish islands east of Spain. When we hit the French coast, we were flying at 21,000 feet, our bombing altitude. We saw the Pyrenees Mountains for quite some time. They are really rugged-looking mountains. Capt. Ford turned back a few minutes before we saw the French coast. The flak was very light a few minutes after we were in France. It was very cold up there. We were wearing the English flying suit minus its heating element. Ice formed on the leading edge of the wings. Halfway in France, several fighters came up. They did not come in very close – staying out about 2,000 yards waiting for cripples, but no one dropped out of formation while over France. We dropped ten 500-pounds x 2 on a four-engine FW airbase, doing a darn good job of ruining it and the planes. The flak wasn't too heavy over the target. The fighters followed us out to about 50 miles over the ocean. Then they turned back into France. Just as we left the coast of England, we started down from altitude. One Fort flew to England with his Number 3 engine smoking all the way home. The first flak burst we saw, it must have gotten an oil line in that engine. We were all very happy to see England again after spending one week in North Africa. Lt. Neie and Asper were so tired, they let White and Nelson fly home after the fighters left us. They did a darn good job of formation flying.

We landed at 1800 – 12 hours of tough flying. Col. Old, our group C.O., and Gen. Anderson met us as we came out of the plane and gave us the old line of how glad they were to see us, and so forth. After they left, we got all our equipment and put it in a truck and put it away in our lockers. Had a sandwich (Spam) and tomato juice.

In the interrogation room, the crews that flew their two burros back had them here, showing them to everybody there. The burros had oxygen masks made for them in Africa and came through the trip in grand shape. Give them a little sugar and they will follow you all over the place. I believe they will like their new home.

After being interrogated, we took a cold shower and we were really dirty and dusty. In our barracks were three new men. They moved in while we were in Africa. Made our beds. It will be a pleasure to sleep on something soft, even if it is an army cot. Sleeping on the ground gets mighty tiresome.

I fired about 150 rounds on this mission.
— *Sgt. Leo Lakey, gunner*

✠ Mission #20 – Briefed last night for target at Bordeaux, France – FW-200 (bombers) airdrome. Take-off was at 7:00 a.m. and held rendezvous over field. Cut across Mediterranean, passed two Spanish islands, headed to France, cut inland along Pyrenees Mountain range to Bordeaux. Encountered light, inaccurate flak over southern France, and heavy, accurate flak over Bordeaux. Hit target at 12:00 noon and headed out over the Atlantic. Vapor trails were beautiful and were certainly an aid to spotting fighters. We saw about 25 fighters and were attacked several times, but easily fought them off. Arrived home at 6:00 p.m. What a welcome sight! We were a dirty, tired, bedraggled bunch of GIs when we reached here. Debriefed and had a shower and chow.
— *Sgt. Dick Haseltine, radio operator*

AUGUST 25, 1943

✠ A 48-hour pass and we went to London for quite a time. Except an argument with a hotel manager who tried to overcharge us for damage on a burned curtain, which caught fire by a lighted cigarette we forgot to pick up when we laid it down. He tried

to charge us two pounds, and we gave him one pound and left him to argue it out with himself. He really was raising hell as we drove off in a taxicab.
— *Lt. Ruben Neie, pilot*

AUGUST 25, 1943

✠ Woke up early by Sgt. Blake (CI) and told we may get a pass, so we all got set. Also today, we were asked what we wanted to do after our missions were completed. I mentioned that I wanted to go back to the states and OCS. What happens remains to be seen. Left on the 11:07 train for Cambridge, England.

Slept at the Bull Hotel (American Red Cross Club).
— *Sgt. Joseph Kotlarz, gunner*

AUGUST 26, 1943

✠ Rainy this a.m., so I stayed around the Red Cross building.

Met a WAAF (England Army Air Force Auxiliary).

> 2007805
> ACW Douglas
> c/o Mrs. Hilton
> 13 Oxford Street
> Wolverton
> Bucks

— *Sgt. Joseph Kotlarz, gunner*

AUGUST 27, 1943

✠ Took the 10:07 a.m. train back to camp and met a couple of American WAACs en route.

> **Address:**
> PFC Margaret Epp
> 170 Post Headquarters
> APO 635
> U.S. Army

Three of our fellows who bailed out over France got back here. One has been with me since gunner school (Niles Landensegger). He was shot in the leg and was in a hospital 54 days. It took them three months and four days to get back to England. They were not captured. Sure glad to see them. They get to go back to the States.
— *Sgt. Joseph Kotlarz, gunner*

AUGUST 28, 1943

✠ Rainy today, so nothing doing here.
— *Sgt. Joseph Kotlarz, gunner*

✠ Big Officers' Dance in our club, and what a time!
— *Lt. Ruben Neie, pilot*

AUGUST 29, 1943

✠ Slept late and loafed around.
— *Sgt. Joseph Kotlarz, gunner*

AUGUST 30, 1943

✠ Test-hopped Shelton's ship for him because he was on pass. I took M/Sgt. Harter up as my co-pilot, since Asper in hospital with a bad throat. I will have to fly tonight from 11 to one to get acquainted with night flying tactics and lighting systems.
— *Lt. Ruben Neie, pilot*

✠ Nothing doing here today. Was supposed to be a mission, but it was scrubbed. Sent Bernice a letter to find out just what the score was in regards to our romance.
— *Sgt. Joseph Kotlarz, gunner*

AUGUST 31, 1943

✠ Payday: 25 pounds, 10 shillings, six pence, with $164.00 allotment, $6.70 insurance and $21.00 board. The new boys went on a raid today, but the target was closed in. They all struggled back for no reason at all. Poor leadership.

Lt. Haltum returned from France where he was shot down over three months ago. He brought back six of his men with him.
— *Lt. Ruben Neie, pilot*

✠ A mission to France today, but we were not scheduled. The crews that went out on the mission could not find the target on account of bad visibility.
— *Sgt. Joseph Kotlarz, gunner*

SEPTEMBER 1, 1943

✠ World War II, fourth year.
— *Sgt. Joseph Kotlarz, gunner*

SEPTEMBER 2, 1943

✠ The group had a mission today, but we were not scheduled. It's definite now that all we have to do is 25 missions. Sure glad of that.
— *Sgt. Joseph Kotlarz, gunner*

SEPTEMBER 3, 1943

✠ Mission #21.

Woke up at 1:45 a.m. and briefed for mission to Merlin, France. Target: airfield and assembly and repair shops for pursuits. Bombing altitude: 23,000 feet (temperature: 20 degrees). Bomb load: three tons. Had P-47 escort up until I.P. encountered. No anti-aircraft all the way. Saw Paris (Eiffel Tower) about 20 miles away. Two groups hit the target. Results were poor. No enemy fighters encountered. Take-off was 6:00 a.m. Came back at 10:48 a.m. Had 12 squadrons of P-47s on the way back, too. Meulan Les Mureaux.

Went to confession and communion this evening on the base (mass for combat crews). Sgt. White was AWOL and did not go with us today. Nelson operated the top turret.

> **Resume of Mission #21:**
> First wing: Remilly-sur-Siene, France
> Target: Air Corps Rpr. Depot
> Nine groups: 168 B-17s; four lost
> E/A claims: 11 – 1 – 1
> Casualties: two wounded and 40 missing
> Bombs on target: 1,177 500-pounders
> Bombs on secondary: 325 500-pounders
> Bombs on last resort: 138 500-pounders.
>
> Mission II:
> Meulan-les-Mureaux, France
> Target: aircraft factory
> Three groups: 65 B-17s; no opposition; no losses
>
> Mission III:
> Paris, France
> Target: Caudron-Renault Works
> Three groups: 65 planes (B-17s); five lost
> E/A claims: 15 – 4 – 8
> Casualties: four wounded – 40 missing
> 240 500-pounders on target; 204 500-pounders on secondary
> (unidentified airfield).

— *Sgt. Joseph Kotlarz, gunner*

✠ Airport in Paris, France – target was an assembly plant and repair shops for FW-190s. My 21st mission and my first real milk run. No enemy fighters and just a little flak, which was very inaccurate. Lt. Lewis, a new pilot in 413th squadron, went as my co-pilot, since Lt. Asper was in the hospital with a bad throat. He is reported to be doing fine and will be out in a few days.

— Lt. Ruben Neie, pilot

✠ 20-first Mission – flew 4-1/2 hours – Meulan les Mureaux on the Seine, about 25 miles northwest of Paris, France.

Got up 0200. Breakfast 0230. Briefed 0300. Clean gun. Put on GI-heated suit under English flying suits. A Lt. Lewis went along as co-pilot, a very good flyer. He flew in Lt. Asper's place, who is in the hospital with a slight touch of malaria he got in Africa.

Goldberg flew as our right waist-gunner. White went to town and failed to return in time. Maj. Hand will do a little fanny-chewing when he gets back. Nelson took the top turret.

It was very cold. We hit altitude about one hour after taking off. We reached our bombing altitude over England at 23,000 feet. Test-fired over the Channel. All guns okay. P-47 escort met us over the coast of France and stayed with us until 15 minutes before hitting the target. They flew so high, they left vapor trails behind them. We met no fighters during the entire mission. My heated suit worked swell. The only flak we saw was over Paris, and we made a sharp bank to the right and avoided the flak shot up at us. We dropped 12 500-pounders on a big airfield several miles out of Paris. The Eiffel Tower was very plain to see. The bombs hit on both sides of the river, sending high columns of fire and smoke. Three groups hit this target. No flak or fighters on the way home. P-47s met us on the way back.

We landed at 1045. Had a Spam sandwich. Interrogated, cleaned gun. Finished painting my bike to get here.

— Sgt. Leo Lakey, gunner

✠ Mission #21 – Up at 1:45 and briefed for a target to Meulan les Mureaux, France to bomb an airfield and assembly and repair shop. A short mail run – P-47 escort both in and out. No flak to speak of and no fighters encountered. Bombing results were poor. Saw Paris about 20 miles away. Returned at 10:45 a.m. – four-hour mission, different than the longer missions we've been accustomed to. Eddie was AWOL, so Nelson operated upper turret, and Goldberg went as waist-gunner.

— Sgt. Dick Haseltine, radio operator

SEPTEMBER 4, 1943

✠ Scrubbed.

— Sgt. Leo Lakey, gunner

✠ Stood by for mission, but it was canceled. Lost lots of sleep, but wasn't long in making up for it.

— Sgt. Dick Haseltine, radio operator

✠ Got up at 1:00 this morning for an early briefing on Paris, France. But, just as we were about to give it the gun, the mission was scrubbed for military reasons we knew not. This afternoon, I taxied *Kipling's Error* for two hours so Lt. Mitchell could swing a new D.R. compass.

Received letters from Dad, Oliver and Aunt Zella.
— *Lt. Ruben Neie, pilot*

SEPTEMBER 4, 1943

✠ Got up at 0130. Breakfast 0200. Briefed 0245. Clean gun. Clear and cold. Our target was in Paris, France, a big motor works.

Put on my heated suit under the English flying suit just before take-off time, or, rather, time to warm up the engines. Lt. Turner gave us our escape kits with a bar of Tootsie Rolls and a package of good old American spearmint gum. Lt. Turner is taking Asper's place, as Asper is still in the hospital. We taxied up to the take-off runway, ran up all of our engines. They were okay. A few seconds later, two red flares were shot off, calling off the mission. Scrubbed. So, we taxied back to our area, hung around for almost 13 hours, then all went back to bed, slightly peeved off. Take-off time was 0600.
— *Sgt. Leo Lakey, gunner*

SEPTEMBER 5, 1943

✠ Woke up at 1:30 a.m. and briefed for mission to Paris, France. Target was supposed to be a truck manufacturing company. Mission was canceled approximately at take-off time of 5:50 a.m. Unsettled weather. Just lost lots of sleep, but made up for it. Went to mass on base.

On yesterday's mission, Sgt. Goldberg substituted in the absence of Sgt. White (Sgt. Goldberg – Lt. Jergers' crew).
— *Sgt. Joseph Kotlarz, gunner*

SEPTEMBER 6, 1943

✠ Strasbourg, France, and my 22nd mission. The cloud cover was so thick, we could not see over primary target, but we knocked hell out of the secondary. P-47s took us almost in, but had to turn around because of gas shortage. So, we went on in alone. The flak was good, and got five ships in the group just behind us. We only got two flak holes. About 11:15, 50 German fighters attacked us, and the fight lasted until 12:30. Our group lost no ships, but the wing lost 32 B-17s. Lt. Mitchell got one. I saw it blow up and go down.

We had a new crew flying in the high squad and evidently didn't know much about aerial gunnery, because they hit my plane nine times with .50 calibers. Eight shots just missed my head by about six inches, and the ninth one just missed S/Sgt. White, going into our bomb bay and cutting my control cables, radio wires and oxygen lines at 13,000 feet. I have never felt so helpless in my life. I turned the wheel and pulled and pushed on the stick, but nothing happened. I knew at once my cables were cut, so I tried to call my crew on the radio and tell them to prepare to bail out. (This happened between Germany and Paris, France.) But the intercom was also shot out. So the next thing for me to do was to turn on my A.F.C.E. It took hold immediately and straightened my ship out, but it was climbing too fast. So I cut it off again to set it. By this time, my co-pilot (T/O Cullender) found out that his controls were still okay. But he could not tell me, because he had his oxygen mask on and our radio was out. So, he just started beating me on the head – while I was working like hell to get my A.F.C.E. set up – to let me know he could fly from his side. By the time we got the ship under control, the battle ended, and that was also a relief. Our oxygen was also gone, so I went down to the nose and told the navigator our story, and for him to take us home. So, we let down to an altitude where we could breathe, and went in on home.

Just as we circled our home base, Number 1 engine went out. But my co-pilot did a swell job landing on three engines. I would like to give that boy hell that shot at us, but I am satisfied we are alive.
— **Lt. Ruben Neie, pilot**

✠ We had three guns up in the nose. We had one straight ahead that I used, and then they had two – one on either side for the bombardier or navigator, whichever came in handy – that would be used. So we had three .50-calibers up in the nose, and I guess I must have been leaning down on that machine gun.

Well, you know, you claim a kill. I never did – I don't think I ever claimed one. I don't remember that I did.

But I remember once the Group C.O. was in one time. He was a-groaning and a-moaning because his group wasn't getting enough planes – you know, enough credits for kills. He let out an oath: "I'll be so, so glad when we get some new crews, so we can start getting some more kills!" Goodness, the crew – the first few times they went out – they were knocking the German Air Force out of the sky. Burning some lead up.

I guess it was the top turret-gunner who said he saw me hit one. It was coming in so fast and I was far away. He went right over us, and I guess the ball turret-gunner reported that he saw him blow up as he went across us. You know, I never knew.
— **Lt. Lloyd Mitchell, navigator**

✠ Twenty-second Mission – flew 8 hours – Stuttgart, Germany and Strasbourg, France.

Got up at 0130. Had fresh eggs and one orange. Briefed 0230. Clean gun. Flight Officer Joe Cullender flew as our co-pilot. Lt. Asper still in the hospital. Very chilly, so we put on our heated suits several hours before take-off. Take-off time was 0600. We flew in the lead element, Number 3 position – the first time we ever were anywhere near the lead. Our squadron led the entire four wings. We circled over England for one and a half hours, climbing up to 19,000 feet. We stayed at that altitude until 45 minutes from the target where we climbed up to 23,000 feet.

As we hit the French coast, our P-47 escort picked us up and stayed with us for about 45 minutes, turning back a few miles past Paris, France. The clouds were getting thicker, the farther we went toward Germany.

We hit a few flak areas, but not enough to damage anything. Saw several bombed airfields in the vicinity of Paris. Took several pictures of them with the GI camera.

All our guns were test-fired over the Channel and again over Germany. All were okay. Near our I.P., we started to climb again. When we reached 23,000, we leveled off. The closer we got to our first target, the cloudier it got. We did not drop our bombs on the first target because it was covered over by clouds, although we saw about a third of the city.

Our second target was only a few miles away and, this time, luck was with us. We found several holes in the clouds there, when we dropped our ten 500-pounders on a big motor factory and repair depot in Strasbourg. A little flak was thrown up at us here also, but no damage was done to any of the planes.

The target was hit squarely, time and time again. About 150 Forts dropped their bombs on this target. A few minutes after leaving the target, I saw huge fires burning, then huge columns of black smoke coming up in big wide areas. Took several pictures of it with the GI camera. And still no fighters.

But after flying for about 45 minutes more, we finally were hit by about 75 enemy fighters. They stayed with us for a little over an hour. They were mostly Me-109s and Es. A few FW-190s and Me-200s and Me-110s. They did their attacking from the nose of the formation, and they really did attack, coming in four to 12 at a time, hitting us, then hitting the low group after taking a crack at us. Very few tail attacks were made. They just circled around the two formations and came in at the nose again. They kept this up the entire time they were up there fighting.

Saw three 17s go down, and four enemy fighters. One bailed out of the fighters, and three out of the Forts. More might have gotten out of the Forts because they flew under us after being hit.

While all this was going on, several .50 caliber slugs from another Fort came through our ship, hitting only a foot behind Lt. Neie's head, cutting off his oxygen supply, knocking out his interphone and, worst of all, cutting Lt. Neie's control cables in half. He lost control of the ship for a few seconds when Flight Officer Joe Cullender realized he had the controls all by himself. He did a darn good job of flying us back home. We fought for 15 minutes without the use of the interphone. A strange feeling up there with enemy fighters around, and not being able to call them out. We realized something was wrong, so we doubled our lookout for enemy planes.

About 30 minutes from the French coast, they left us, their gas supply was gone, and so was their ammunition. 20 minutes from the coast, our Spitfire escort picked us up – a very warm welcome when we saw them. We saw two Forts turn back after flying several miles out to sea. They must have been German-manned because they had no group or squadron markings. Also, they were too far away to read the numbers on the tail, and also out of range to shoot at.

After we were halfway out over the Channel, we had to signal to the rest of our group that we weren't able to fly in formation and had to get to our field as soon as possible. We really came down from altitude in one big hurry and made a beeline for our field. The radio was out, so Lt. Mitchell, our navigator, had to work by himself, plotting a course for home. Mitch did a perfect job of it. We got home ten minutes before the rest of the group. Flight Officer Cullender, flying co-pilot, circled the field once, then the second time around, the Number 1 engine was ready to blow a cylinder. So it was feathered. Number 2 wasn't running as it should.

Our landing was very good. The meat wagon met us as we got out of the ship. But he had no business, as no one was hurt on this trip. The reason the meat wagon was there – and a big crowd – was because we did not radio in asking for the wind direction and did not identify ourselves to the ground crews. That means one thing: trouble. Our plane was badly hit, and luck was with us that we weren't hit.

We landed at 1400. Looking the plane over, we found that Numbers 1 and 2 engines have to be changed. One hole in the left wing. One hole above the pilot's head. Several holes in the bomb bay, cutting control wires and cables. Our ship will be out for about two weeks undergoing repairs and engine changes.

After being interrogated, we headed for our barracks, too tired to eat or clean our guns. Turned in my laundry. Was issued a Colt automatic .65, number 945647.

Got a hunk of flak from Number 1 engine. Ugly-looking stuff. Fired 300 rounds.
— *Sgt. Leo Lakey, gunner*

SEPTEMBER 6, 1943

✠ Mission #22.

Woke up at 1:30 a.m. Had eggs for breakfast and oranges for dessert. Briefed at 2:30 a.m. for bombing mission to Stuttgart, Germany. Target: spark plug, carburetor and generator factory – a very important target. Bomb load: ten 500-pounders. Altitude: 23,000 feet. Take-off was at 5:40 a.m. The 9th led the Air Division, composed of the 401st, 402nd and the 403rd Wings. Passed through France, then Germany. Stuttgart was closed in, so we bombed the secondary target, Strasbourg, France – just as important a target. As we left Germany and entered France, we were intercepted by some Me-109s, FW-190s and Me-210s (about 60). Sure had some combat time. Saw three 17s go down. Our plane, *Kipling's Error III,* was hit quite a few times. Control cables were hit. The plane will be out for about a week. Came in at 2:00 p.m. About 18 groups of 21 planes each took part in this raid.
— *Sgt. Joseph Kotlarz, gunner*

✠ Mission #22 – They interrupted a beautiful dream I was having at 1:30 this morning, and told us to step on it. Briefing was at 2:30. Sleepily rode through the pitch black darkness to chow, and then on to the briefing room. There's always the question: "Where?" And there is always a tension at the briefings. Officer steps up to the large map and looks for the pinpoint that will be our target. If his finger lands on France, a short way from the coast, a feeling of relief surges over the room. But this time, his finger moved, wandering around, and finally stopped deep in the heart of Germany, and an involuntary chill that comes to the bravest before a hard fight hit me amidships, because I realized the target was only a few miles away from Regensburg, and I remembered the terrific fight we had getting our bombers through once before. The briefing went on, and though each knew the risk, they were all laughing and joking as we left for our ships. A spark plug, carburetor and generator factory – a very important target in Stuttgart, Germany was our goal.

Take-off was at 5:40 and at precisely that time, we left the ramp with ten 500-pound bombs in *Kipling's Error's* belly. The mist that day in all of the little valleys made England look like a mysterious land as we circled to form the formation. Our group led the parade, and we headed out from England over the Channel. We droned on over France and into Germany. Stuttgart was closed in by clouds, so we went to Strasbourg, an equally impressive target.

Turned after dropping our bombs, and then the fighters attacked us. About 60 FWs and Me-109s came in, one after the other. Every gun was going at full blast. Sounded like a crackling fire. Fighters at 11 o'clock now. Another at 1 o'clock low, coming under Steve. "Watch him, Joe." We saw three 17s go down. One I saw fell straight down, spinning slowly. No chutes appeared.

Appearance of our escort – met us over France and drove the enemy away. Our control cables were shot away and quite a few other hits were scored. Co-pilot brought ship in, as his cables were intact. Communication wing was severed. Another miraculous escape of our B-17. *Kipling's Error* will be out of commission for a while.

Over the Channel, we were out of oxygen, so we fired a flare for fighter cover, and left the formation for a lower altitude. Had to feather Number 1 engine over England, and finally landed with three engines. That's what I call "coming in on a wing and a prayer."
— **Sgt. Dick Haseltine, radio operator**

I frequently heard the story of Lt. Neie's injury and the lost throat microphone. I remain amazed at the courage and discipline the crew demonstrated by refusing to "hit the silk" without an order. Obviously, at any moment, the ship could go into a spin, and any opportunity for escape would be lost.
— **James Brooks Mitchell, son of Lt. Lloyd Mitchell, navigator**

SEPTEMBER 6, 1943

This gunner shot down the German pilot and wounded Neie. We were coming back across Occupied France and we were under fighter attack, flying Tail-End Charlie, and that was bad. Your Tail-End Charlie meant that your squadron was flying the lowest. They had positions that each group or squadron would fly in. We were flying at the low point and at the back point, and that was Tail-End Charlie. They arranged it so that you didn't have to fly it too often, because none of the pilots liked it because it was the worst spot – the fighter planes would pick on you.

So, evidently, in our group we had some green gunners. As you would lose air crews, replacement crews would come in. One of our own squad's gunners – probably a ball-turret gunner – kept his finger on the trigger too long and shot the heck out of us – just shot the daylights out of us. We had 50 or so bullet holes in our plane. Well, they shot through the control valve – shot out the pilot's controls. The old 17 had dual controls; the co-pilot and the pilot had separate controls. It shot out the pilot's controls. The plane lurched and fell over and started to go down. The bombardier and I already knew that the plane had been hit – we were losing altitude and the plane was at an odd angle, and we were going into a spin – and we were waiting.

We had our hands on the trap door there and our parachutes all ready, and we were just ready to go. You had to wait until the plane commander said, "Go!" If you went out on your own, you were a deserter. So, we were all just waiting to hear the word "go" because we knew we'd been hit, and the plane was starting down, and we wanted to get out before the spin got too tight.

Well, Rube was screaming, "Go! Go! Leave the plane! Get out!" to the whole crew. The only thing was, his throat mike had dropped off – he wore a throat mike, and none of us could hear him, so we stayed. Well, the co-pilot, in the meantime, had a hard time getting Rube's attention to show him that he still had control. He had a steel helmet and tried to get Rube's attention. He had a steel helmet there, and he started beating Rube on the head with his helmet – "Look at me!" Rube was intent on putting the plane on automatic to give us a level platform to leave from – he was trying to straighten the plane out. Well, finally Rube wondered, 'What in the heck is banging my head?' And he looked up and the co-pilot said, "I got it, Rube! I got it!" Rube had no controls and we still had one set of controls, but if old Rube hadn't lost his throat mike, we would have been gone – we'd have been out over France.

We limped home then. We dropped down to low altitude and flew across France, and flew across the Channel, and flew into home. But our plane was shot up pretty badly.
— Lt. Lloyd Mitchell, navigator

SEPTEMBER 7, 1943

✠ It was my 23rd mission, a target in France that was under construction that no one knew just what the Germans were building. So we loaded up two 2,000-pound bombs apiece and blew the 12-foot concrete walls to hell and back. The mission was a milk run, except for some damn good flak. We had Spitfires cover all the way in and out. We crossed the English Channel at its narrowest point (22 miles wide). It looked like one mile, from 23,000 feet.

The fight was good, but, again, just before we got home, Number 4 engine quit. So we came in, again, on three engines. It is beginning to look as it I am feathering an engine every time just to have an excuse to come in and land first.
— Lt. Ruben Neie, pilot

✠ Mission #23.

Woke up at 2:00 a.m. and briefed for bombing mission to Walten, France. Bomb load: two 2,000-pounders. Bombing altitude: 23,000 feet. Target was not far from Dunkerque. Had Spitfire escort all the way. Flak (anti-aircraft) was really heavy. Take-off was at 6:10 a.m., and came back to base at 9:38 a.m. No enemy aircraft intercepted. This was our crew's closest run and shortest hop. One casualty, not serious, from 337th Squadron. (This target was identified as installations near St. Omer, France.)
— Sgt. Joseph Kotlarz, gunner

Lt. Neie
Wounded

Texas Flier, Wounded, Is Back in Action Next Day

Special to The Star-Telegram

CRANFILLS GAP, Sept. 4.—Lt. Reuben W. Neie was wounded in

LIEUTENANT NEIE.

action over German-occupied Europe on his twenty-sixth birthday, was awarded the Purple Heart and returned to duty the next day, according to information received by his parents.

He is the eldest son of Mr. and Mrs. Otto C. Neie, who live nine miles west of Cranfills Gap in Hamilton County.

Pilot of the Flying Fortress "Kipling Error III," he was wounded when a 20 mm. shell exploded in his cockpit, but X-ray examination showed his injuries were not serious.

His tail gunner shot down the German pilot who wounded Neie.

His parents also have learned that last month he made a safe emergency landing in England after his gasoline tanks were shot full of holes. His engineer, Sgt. Lowell Nelson, transferred the gasoline to a tank which was intact, but Neie was unable to bring his Fortress back to its home base, landing at another field in England.

He enlisted in the Army Air Forces in October, 1941. He received his wings and commission at Victorville, Cal., in May, 1942, and went to England last March.

A graduate of North Texas State Teachers College, he is a former teacher at Lamesa High School.

The flageolet, a wind instrument of the flute family, is usually made from ivory.

SEPTEMBER 7, 1943

23rd Mission – flew 3-3/4 hours – Walten, near St. Omer, France.

Got up at 0130. Breakfast 0200. Had fresh eggs and one orange. Briefed 0300. Our ship, *Kipling's Error III,* is still out of commission after yesterday's raid in Germany. We are flying in Capt. Ford's ship, *Ol' Puss.* Cleaned our guns, put our flying clothes on because it was cold. Take-off time was 0615. Lt. Asper is back as our co-pilot. He got out of the hospital yesterday noon. We flew around England, picking up our 23,000 feet, our bombing altitude. The weather was slightly cloudy.

We flew as Tail-End Charlie again, low group, and last group to go over the target. We dropped our two 2,000-pounders on some installations in Walten, very near to St. Omer, France. Going in to the target and coming back out, we flew very close to Dunkerque. We saw it very plainly from our position. Flak was very heavy over the target. We did not pick up any holes in the ship, but flak came very close to us several times.

Spitfires escorted us over and kept us covered at all times during our entire mission, from the time we hit the Channel the first time going into the target. They left us a few minutes after we left the French coast going home. They flew above us and round us. No enemy fighters were seen. Several of the Spitfires above us made big V's with their vapor trails that they were leaving behind them. Several more played Tic-Tac-Toe. They made a pretty design while cutting up like they did.

Just when we hit the English coast, our Number 4 engine went haywire. Lt. Neie feathered it very shortly afterward and came in on three good engines. We landed at 1000. Had some tomato juice, were interrogated, had our dinner, then back to the barracks to get some sleep.

Several boys in the 339th were hit by flak. I don't think it was very serious.

— *Sgt. Leo Lakey, gunner*

SEPTEMBER 7, 1943

Mission #23 – A short mission today, of the milk-run variety. Seems that the Germans are building some heavy concrete installation on the coast of France. No one knows what they are, but after we marked them a week ago, they've brought in about 40 guns to protect it. So, it must be important. We took off at 6:10 – had fighter escorts over and back. Very heavy flak, but we made it safely back by 9:45 a.m. Only one casualty from 337th squadron – nothing serious.

— *Sgt. Dick Haseltine, radio operator*

SEPTEMBER 8, 1943

Received my second Oak Leaf Cluster presented by Col. Old and Col. LeMay. The rest of the crew also received theirs, also. Rube (Lt. Neie) got his Purple Heart.

— *Sgt. Joseph Kotlarz, gunner*

SEPTEMBER 8, 1943

✠ No mission today, so we had a formation presenting medals to our boys. I got two clusters and my Purple Heart. The other boys all got clusters. S/Sgt. C.E. White got his D.F.C. for two fighters and 15 missions, but he has seven fighters and 23 missions. Awards really come in slow.

— Lt. Ruben Neie, pilot

✠ Decorated again today. All the crew received clusters, and Rube got his Purple Heart. Eddie received his Distinguished Flying Cross. When Rube got his, he forgot how to about-face. Joe forgot to salute, and Steve saluted after he had turned to rejoin formation. What a crew!!!

— Sgt. Dick Haseltine, radio operator

SEPTEMBER 9, 1943

✠ Almost a mission – flew 3 hours – Over Channel, saw Belgium coast.

Our crew did not make the morning mission. Nelson was the only one to make it. He flew with Lt. Talbot's crew as right waist-gunner. They bombed a factory in Paris, dropping 14 500-pounders.

Briefing for the second mission was at 1300. Clean gun. Check new plane.

Put on heated suit before take-off. Maj. Hand took a picture of our crew before take-off. Lt. Wilcox was our co-pilot. Lt. Asper is still in the hospital. This was Lt. Wilcox's first mission since July 28, 1943 when he had to make a water-landing in the North Sea. Two of his engines were on fire, and, losing altitude fast, five of the crew did not get out.

Take-off was at 1605. We climbed to altitude over England. We flew over the field at 24,000 feet. We flew Capt. Flagg's old ship. The weather was cloudy, and when we got out over the Channel, we saw a big cloud front over Belgium, so the entire formation made a 360-degree turn over the Channel, hoping to find a hole in the clouds, but no soap. We landed at 1905. Pilot and navigator were the only ones interrogated. Had several baloney sandwiches. Oil gun. Saw USO show in mess hall, Adolph Menjou. Saw hundreds of boats, big and small, wandering around the Channel.

— Sgt. Leo Lakey, gunner

✠ Group went out on a mission to Paris, France this morning, but we were not scheduled.

Briefed for mission to Cambria, Belgium. Had 24 fragmentation bombs. Target: airfield. Just as we left the coast, had weather set in, and we were ordered back. Take-off was 3:55 p.m., and we got back in at 7:15 p.m. Were supposed to have P-47 escort. Lt. Wilcox as co-pilot.

— Sgt. Joseph Kotlarz, gunner

✠ Two missions today, but I did not get to count either one. We were not on the first one, and the second, we all had to turn around 20 minutes before we reached the target because of bad weather. We were to hit an airfield in France, which would have been a nice milk run. On the morning mission, they hit Paris and lost one ship. Also, one ship hit a tree on take-off and made a crash-landing. No one was hurt, but washed the ship out.
— *Lt. Ruben Neie, pilot*

September 10, 1943

✠ Got in a new member in our barracks. He has completed 25 mission and has an Air Medal and three clusters and the D.F.C. All his combat operational hours guaranteed to 142 hours. We have 23 missions and already have 169 hours, and still two missions to go.
— *Sgt. Joseph Kotlarz, gunner*

✠ Bad weather and no mission. We played "42" and "Chickens" all day. Received package from home – one pipe, popcorn, and one pair of pants.

Diltz was made major yesterday.
— *Lt. Ruben Neie, pilot*

September 11, 1943

✠ Went to Banham, New Buchanham and ended up at Old Buchanham's at a dance.
— *Sgt. Joseph Kotlarz, gunner*

September 12, 1943

✠ Went to mass on the base this morning, but not communion, on account of breaking my fast. Went to Old Buchanham tonight.
— *Sgt. Joseph Kotlarz, gunner*

September 13, 1943

✠ Sent Bernice a letter by Special Delivery Air Mail in regards to the V-mail letter I received from home yesterday (regarding running around with other men, smoking, etc.).
— *Sgt. Joseph Kotlarz, gunner*

September 14, 1943

✠   **Addresses:**
Ruben W. Neie, 0-725519
Cranfills Gap, Texas

Manuel Mendolson
5604 Beacon Street
Pittsburgh, Pennsylvania

Lloyd B. Mitchell
Route 1
Hollis, Oklahoma
— *Sgt. Joseph Kotlarz, gunner*

SEPTEMBER 15, 1943

✠ Dry run – flew 2-1/2 hours – saw Channel.

Briefed at 1300. Clean gun. Flying in ship 227. Capt. Flagg's old ship. Put on heated clothes before take-off. Lt. Asper back with us. Take-off was at 1615. We were Number 2 in the tail-end position of the high squadron. 30 minutes after taking off, Number 1 engine started throwing oil all over the wing. At first, we thought the cap had come loose. Lt. Neie decided to fly it as long as the oil pressure stayed normal. We flew to 19,000 feet. There, it got worse. So they feathered the prop, pulled out of formation, and made a beeline for our home field. All of us were very highly peeved off. But it's just one of those things. No one was to blame for the engine going wacky. The oil regulator just went haywire. It took only a few minutes after we landed to fix it. If we had gone another 15 minutes without feathering the prop, the engine would have burnt up, in which case the pilot and engineer would have been called on the carpet to explain why it burnt up. This way, no one was hurt but our feelings, because we couldn't finish the mission.

We were on oxygen for about one hour. It wasn't too cold. The mission was to Paris, France, hitting a major plant. We landed at 1845. Took our guns to armament. Put away our clothes, and now waiting for the rest of the crews to get in.

Two ships from the 339th and one from the 338th went down in France. Flak was very heavy over Paris.
— *Sgt. Leo Lakey, gunner*

✠ My second time on my 24th raid. This time to Paris, France, but hard luck came my way. I aborted one hour before we hit the enemy because of a bad oil regulator in Number 1 engine. We got to 19,000 feet, but had to feather Number 1 because the oil got to 120 degrees and was all boiling out of the overflow. Knowing it would be curtains to try to go on three engines, we turned around and came home. This was our second abortion out of 24 missions. But maybe it was supposed to be that way, because we lost three ships and crews over Paris by flak. Fighters also gave battle, but none of our ships was lost because of them.
— *Lt. Ruben Neie, pilot*

✠ Went on a mission this afternoon, but had to abort on account of bad oil regulator. Target was a factory for parts for Me-109s. Bomb load: 12 500-pounders. Bombing altitude: 23,000 feet. As usual, we were Number 5 position in the high element until we had our abortion.

In this mission, two fellows from the 337th Squadron were supposed to finish up (25 missions). They went up with another crew, whose plane blew up in a million pieces near Paris, France. Such is fate, going to their deaths on their 25th mission.
— *Sgt. Joseph Kotlarz, gunner*

September 16, 1943

✠ 24th Mission – flew 11 hours – LaRochelle, France.

Briefed 1000. Clean gun. Plane not ready to fly at 1100. Needs gas and oxygen. We got it loaded a little before 1200. Put on heated clothes; also took up several Spam sandwiches because we didn't have any dinner.

Take-off was at 1200. The weather was cloudy. We were to have flown in the Number 2 position on the lead ship, but we took off about last, so we had to fly Number 3 in the high lead element.

The weather over England was cloudy and a slight rain was falling. We flew about 1,000 to 3,000 feet above the ocean for several hours. We hit our bombing altitude about 30 minutes before going over the French coastline. Our first target, Bordeaux, was covered over by a solid cloud formation, so the leader took us over LaPallice. Just before we hit the French coast, three Me-109s attacked us. They stayed with us for about ten minutes. Joe Kotlarz, our tail-gunner, claimed one hit. I saw it tailing smoke before it passed out of my sight range.

Just before we dropped our bombs – ten 500-pounders from 23,000 feet – several more fighters picked on us. They stayed with us until a few minutes after leaving the target area. The flak over the target was moderate, but heavy in spots. I saw one of our ships go down from the group ahead of us. Eight boys hit the silk. I believe they landed on land near the target. I also saw the target while the bombs were exploding on it. From my position, the target was well hit. It wasn't very big to begin with. Sub pens and big slipways. A big ship was sailing in between the island and mainland. When we went out over it, it was untouched, but there were several more groups behind us yet to drop their bombs. So it might have been hit. The weather over this target was very clear.

About 1900, we flew over an old-time sailboat. It was a fairly large one. Probably some French man out there fishing. Some of the new gunners in the ships behind us fired quite a few rounds into this boat. We were almost tempted to fire at these new gunners for strafing his boat. They must have done some damage because I saw one big sail crumple up. Also saw quite a few shells hit near its water line. We never shoot at a boat of this kind because they usually pick up men in the sea who have been shot down and had to ditch. When we landed and found the guilty men, we really laid down the law to them. It was a new crew, not many missions to their records.

After this little incident, we felt rather hungry. All of us missed breakfast and only had several Spam sandwiches for dinner before taking off. They were still a little frozen, but they went down okay. Oh, yes – they gave us an extra bar of candy due to this being a long mission.

It wasn't very long after we ate our sandwiches that six two-engine fighters hit us. They were Me-110s, long-range fighter or medium bomber. Whichever the situation called for this time, they came out as fighters. They must carry .37mm because they stay way off in the distance and peck away at us. But these six were rather a little too brave for their own good. They only made one pass at us and at a great distance. One of them pulled away, his engine smoking. A few seconds later on, he went back home. The other ones were going to try their luck on the three groups behind us. Several sat way up there in the sky, out of range, while two of them came in from the rear. But the boys in these groups were on the ball and threw up so much lead that the second ship turned away. The first one must have been hit because he seemed as if he didn't want to pull away, but kept boring in. The result, from where I was at, there must have been about 50 guns firing at him all the while, which lasted several seconds. The sky was full of tracers, and this Me-110 was in among this hail of lead. As he was about their level, he burst into flame and made one fast dive into the water. He hit with a big splash and was a solid mass of flame for several seconds. No one got out alive from that flaming plane. After seeing what happened to those two planes, the rest high-tailed it back toward France.

It wasn't very long after that it started to get dark, and also we were flying into a cloud formation. Somehow, in the fog, Lt. Asper lost the formation, so we had to go home by ourselves without any G equipment. With Lt. Mitchell's good navigation and Dick's good radio work, we managed to get home.

As we hit the English coastline, we could see searchlights underneath the thick cloud layer, trying to pick us up. There were quite a few other ships that stayed home, so, every now and then, we were picked up by these searchlights. The farther we went inland, the thinner the clouds got, until they gave out altogether. So, every time we were picked up by a searchlight or two, we would flash back the signal of the day. It must be quite a sight to see a Fortress several thousand feet above the ground with a bunch of searchlights on it, burning the night time.

We had to circle the field several times before landing. Other Forts landed before we did. The runways were lit up. It's strange to see lights at night over here, because everything is blacked out. But on a mission of this sort, they had to turn on the field lights.

We landed at 2300. Slight rain after we undressed. Had some hot coffee and more Spam sandwiches. Were interrogated. Saw Gen. Anderson give out a few medals. It was well past midnight, so we didn't even oil our guns, as we were all dog-tired. Got our bikes and headed for the barracks.

Lt. Mendolson and Steve Malinowski are two happy boys because this was their last combat mission over here. Rest of the crew has one more to make. Lt. Mendolson, our bombardier, wore a tan tie on every one of his missions. So, in the briefing room, I took out my knife and cut it up into ten pieces – one for each man on the crew. Sgt. Steve Malinowski, our assistant radio man and ball-turret sharpshooter, didn't have anything special he carried on all of his missions, so we just congratulated him along with Mendy on finishing their 25 missions. Now all we have to do is sweat out one more round trip to hell – then we can have some peace.

I fired 140 rounds.

— *Sgt. Leo Lakey, gunner*

SEPTEMBER 16, 1943

✠ Mission #24.

Woke up at 8:00 a.m. and briefed at 10:00 a.m. for mission to Bordeaux, France. Target: two aircraft centers. Bomb load: ten 500-pounders. Take-off was at 11:00 a.m. and came in at 11:00 p.m. Trip was entirely over water, except over target area. As we opened our bomb bay doors, three fighters attacked us from the tail (six 'clock). I dropped one, and the pilot was seen bailing out. We were attacked once or twice more by ten or 12 more fighters. Two 17s were seen going down over LaPallice, France. Eight were seen bailing out. We were attacked again over sea by Brest, France by ten Me-110s. No 17s were lost here, but three Me-110s were seen shot to pieces and going down.

First time we started night operations and it really seemed odd to have anti-aircraft searchlights all over the sky, searching for us. Our co-pilot jazzed up by leaving the formation, and we sure had a tough time finding the hose without proper equipment. We finally made camp and saw Capt. Flagg, Lt. Barrett, Capt. Mulligan, Capt. Hamilton, Sgt. Morgan, Sgt. Christensen, Sgt. Salinsky, Sgt. Schmitt and Sgt. Wagner get the Silver Star for gallantry in action for one of the previous raids.

Went to communion this morning before the mission.

    Resume of Mission #24:
    Fourth wing: Bordeaux, France
    Seven groups: 71 B-17s dispatched; four lost
    58 B-17s, LaPallice, France
    Target: sub pens and installations
    13 B-17s, LaRochelle, France
    Target: airfield
    E/A claims: 10 – 1 – 4
    Casualties: 13 – 8 – 30
    Bombs on targets: LaPallice: 114 tons; LaRochelle: 37 tons

    Mission II:
    Wing: Nantes, France
    Target: naval installations
    Groups: 147 B-17s dispatched
    E/A claims: 22 – 2 – 5
    Casualties: 0 – 9 – 60
    Bombs on target: 384 tons

    Wing: Cognac-Chateau, Bernard, France
    Target: unknown
    Three groups: 45 B-17s dispatched
    27 E/A destroyed
    12 B-17s lost
    10 personnel killed
    Bombs on target: 63 tons
— *Sgt. Joseph Kotlarz, gunner*

SEPTEMBER 16, 1943

✠ Mission #24 – Up at 0800 and went on a flight with *Kipling's Error* to check it out. Landed, and were told that we were going on a mission. Briefed at 1000 for mission to Bordeaux, France. Target: two aircraft centers. Bomb load: ten 500-pounders. It was an over-water trip. Broke out of the clouds over the Atlantic and proceeded over water to a point opposite Bordeaux. Made a left turn and started our bomb run. Clouds closed the target in, so we proceeded on to LaPallice. As we opened the bomb bays, three fighters attacked us at the tail. Joe and Eddie and I opened fire on them until Eddie's automatic stopped his shooting, as it was too close to the tail. I shot bullets that were just missing our target, but the fighter got us behind the vertical fin and I had to stop shooting. So it was up to Joe, and he downed him in flames – no one bailed out.

Dropped our bombs, fought off two more attacks by ten to 15 Me-109s.

All was quiet for a while, and we headed out over the Atlantic. There we were attacked again by ten 109s. It was just dusk, and our tracers cut a flaming path through the sky. I saw one fighter attack the group behind us and his gun opened up at him, so we formed the point of a cone of red hot lead. He fell into the sea and burned on the water and swept on. Lost two of ours.

Darkness settled just as we entered cloudy areas about halfway to England, and Asper got panicked at flying in the dark with other ships, and, before Rube could stop him, banked sharply upwards and, by the time we straightened out, we lost formation, so it was left to Mitch and me to get us to England. Decided to go above the low clouds and I started getting fixes. Crossed English coast, and I got QDMs that took us to the base. Landed at 11:00 p.m. First time we'd flown in England after dark – a novel experience to be caught in those British searchlights. Debriefed, and went to bed. Capt. Flagg's crew received Silver Star – good job!
— Sgt. Dick Haseltine, radio operator

✠ Number "24 C," as we referred to it, because it is our third attempt. This time, LaRochelle, France Airport. I was not supposed to go, but since we now have a short-age of crews, I was asked to go. We took off at 11:20 after waiting on gas for a long time. I had Number 2 position today, but since we took off too late, I ended up in Number 3 in the high squad, which was a good position. Clouds were low and thick, so we buzzed England and most of the water, finally breaking through and finding the target okay. Just as we opened our bomb bay doors, S/Sgt. Kotlarz, tail-gunner, called out, "Fighters at six o'clock, level and coming in." "I got him," was next. The others yellow and turning around.

We were attacked several times, but not a scratch. The flak was better than good. Those boys are heck out on that stuff. I saw one BMF hit by flak go into a five-turn spin and pull out okay. One chute came out, and then a fighter slipped up and shot a wing off. So, the ship started spinning and burning and pieces falling off. It hit the water and no more chutes were seen.

Just before dark, six twin-engine fighters hit, and three went down. I have never seen so many tracers going out at once in all my life. I didn't blame the other three to high-tail it home. This took place just west of Brest, France.

By now it was dark, and a large cloud front was in our way. And just as I expected, it was 168 B-17s lost from their formation. I called my navigator and told him we would be on instruments the rest of the way, and it was up to him to get us home, and I would try to keep from running into any of the other planes. I didn't have to tell my crew to keep their eyes open for other airplanes. They called them out from all directions. I had nine good sets of eyes besides my own, looking like hell. My first orders from Mitch were, "Climb." I was on instruments and couldn't see five feet from my plane. But, finally, we broke out of the clouds and found ourselves in a black night. But we could see navigation lights of other ships, which my crew never let me get close to. Even if I saw it, they yelled their heads off if I didn't turn from it. In the air, we say, "It is not us that runs into someone. It is the other so-and-so who will hit you." So, we watched and finally settled down, and flew in on our radio compass. It was Mitch's only means of navigation, since we had no G or Pundant's Charts.

But we got home okay and landed at 11:00. 11 hours and 40 minutes is a long time in one seat, even if it is in the air.

This was Lt. Mendolson's (my bombardier) and S/Sgt. Malinowski's (my ball-turret man's) 25th mission, and they really sweated it out. This was one of our roughest missions. The boys cut Lt. Mendolson's "combat tie," as he called it – because he only wore it on raids – into ten pieces, and we all got a piece of it. By the time we ate and had a few beers on Mendolson, it was 1 o'clock, and we retired.

— Lt. Ruben Neie, pilot

SEPTEMBER 17, 1943

 Scrubbed.

Still a little tired when we got up. Got up at 0700. Breakfast 0800. Went down to Squadron Operations and filled out my gunnery report for yesterday's mission. After that, I went to the armament shack and cleaned my gun. Just as I got there, the rest of the boys came in from briefing to clean their guns before taking them out to their ships. Found out from the rest of the boys that we weren't scheduled to fly this mission.

This one was to have been in Stuttgart, Germany. About 1245, the entire mission was scrubbed because of bad weather. So, back to the barracks with everyone. They had 20 500-pounds in each plane. Our ship, *Kipling's Error,* is almost ready to fly. Only a few more minor adjustments before test-hopping.

— Sgt. Leo Lakey, gunner

Just to be awakened at 7:00 in the morning to go on our 25th raid. This was also a rough one as planned, but luck hit and the mission was scrubbed. So, we are praying for an easy one tomorrow.

— Lt. Ruben Neie, pilot

SEPTEMBER 18, 1943

✠ Nope. No mission today, but my crew was sent on a 48-hour pass. Naturally, we went to London. This time almost a very quiet time. Went to see three good shows, the best being "Keeping Watch on the Rhine." Beyond all doubts, it was the best show I have ever seen. Lt. Mendolson was sent to Wing for duty, but made out like he knew nothing, but wanted to go home. So, in the end, he got orders to return to the U.S. So he met us in London tonight and, naturally, we celebrated his good luck.
— *Lt. Ruben Neie, pilot*

SEPTEMBER 19, 1943

✠ Went to mass on the base. After meeting quite a few combat crews on pass, I've found out there are quite a few casualties from freezing. Some never got back on combat crews. So far, I've heard of two radio operators freezing to death.

On mission #24, a ship from 339th Squadron was struggling behind the formation near Brest, France, when suddenly we were attacked by ten Me-110s, which concentrated on this struggler. A .20mm blowing up the ball-turret operator's ankle, and another the waist-gunner's foot, on their 25th mission. So, again, fate takes a hand.
— *Sgt. Joseph Kotlarz, gunner*

✠ Came back from pass, and Joe told me – from talking with other crews – of two radio operators who have froze to death. All in all, many casualties from freezing. Really is cold here.
— *Sgt. Dick Haseltine, radio operator*

SEPTEMBER 20, 1943

✠   **Addresses:**
    Miss Edna J. Ranson
    c/o Quidenham Hall
    Quidenham
    Norfolk

    Home:
    62 Schreiber Road
    Ipswich
    Suffolk

Went on a 48-hour pass to Norwich. Just looking around and having a good time. Slept at the Bethel Red Cross Dormitory.
— *Sgt. Joseph Kotlarz, gunner*

SEPTEMBER 21, 1943

✠ Lt. Wilcox's crew went down in the sea on their last raid. Four officers and one EM bailed out and safely made it to shore in the dinghy. When told to prepare for a water landing, the radio operator died of fright, according to one enlisted man who made it to safety. Plane stayed up for 30 seconds – not long enough for all to get out. Some of our men just arrived from France, where they had bailed out and were taken care of by the French Underground. They used to stand on a balcony in Paris drinking wine and watch us bomb LeBourget.

— Sgt. Dick Haseltine, radio operator

 Lt. Wilcox, who had to bail out, or, rather, make a water landing in the North Sea, said only four officers and the engineer made it out safe in the dinghy. Their plane went down in 30 seconds after the water landing. The engineer said the radio operator died of fright after being told to get ready for a water landing.

— Sgt. Joseph Kotlarz, gunner

Scrubbed.

Our crew was not scheduled for this mission. Nelson was the only member of our crew scheduled to fly with Lt. Tanner.

Heard Capt. Ford's crew get up at 0100. They had breakfast later on. Briefing was at 0200. The weather was rather clear and very chilly. Same thing like our brisk autumn days.

Take-off was at 0600. They had 12 500-pounders in each plane. Mission was to Paris, after more factories. They got up to where they were just putting on their oxygen masks when they were called back and told the mission was scrubbed.

They came in the barracks, moaning something awful, because the mission was scrubbed. Their beefing woke us up. I got up and they went to sleep. Another nice, chilly day out. Our ship, *Kipling's Error,* is ready to be test-hopped.

— Sgt. Leo Lakey, gunner

SEPTEMBER 22, 1943

Addresses:
Miss Joan Hewlett
32 Mar 1 Prt Lane
Lakeham
and
42 Council House
Bromwell (between Wymondhmanam and Attenborough)

Roger H. Bancher
3rd Bomb. Div.
APO 634
U.S. Army

Elvedon Hall – Hut #8

— Sgt. Joseph Kotlarz, gunner

SEPTEMBER 23, 1943

✠ 25th Mission – flew six hours – Kurling Bastund, France (near Lorient).

Got up at 0100. Breakfast 0130. Had fresh eggs for breakfast. Briefing was 0200. It was very cold and clear. Clean gun for the last time. Also, checking ammunition.

We had an hour to spare before taking off, so this being our last mission – all except Asper and Nelson (Asper has four more to make, and Nelson has one more) – we got a bunch of flares and two extra flare guns to shoot off while buzzing the field after completing our mission. Lt. Neie brought out his English flying suit and we stuffed it with two blankets. Half of our ammo box filled the rest of it with empty brass casings and some other junk. We fixed it up so that a parachute was tied to it. Lt. Spencer from the 339th was flying in Lt. Mendolson's place. Mendy finished several days ago. This was Lt. Spencer's last mission also. Joe Tony flew in Steve Malinowski's place. Steve finished several days ago with Mendy.

Take-off time was 0515. It was still dark. We flew around England for one hour before putting on our oxygen masks. It was very cold up there. Our heated suits came in very handy. We flew at 26,000 feet over the target.

Our P-47 escort picked us up over the French coast going into the target, and stayed with us all the way back. Saw several fighters.

Parachute would open about 15 to 25 feet below the plane. We were only 300 feet above the ground at one time. The rope broke and the chute did not open. Our stuffed dummy landed in a field one mile from the field. It did not hit anyone. It was a good thing that it didn't, because it was rather heavy.

The reason we threw out this stuffed dummy was that our pilot, as well as the rest of us, for the past ten days or so kept on telling everyone that on our last mission, one of us would bail out over the field. After buzzing the field and throwing out the dummy, we came in to make a landing. About a mile from the field, we started shooting our flares. The only time any flares are shot off near the field is when someone is hurt, and then only red ones, and some of the mixed ones. It looked like the Fourth of July, shooting off all those flares. As we got out of the plane, our ground crew and loads of buddies, as well as some of the operations officers, came to congratulate us on completing our 25th mission. Now we can live like regular soldiers again.

Put all our equipment away. Were interrogated. Had a Spam sandwich. Went back to the barracks. After dinner, Joe and I went out and filled out our gunnery report. Also signed a few papers stating we were through as combat men.

After that, we took some pictures of ourselves in our flying clothes near our plane, *Kipling's Error.*

After taking more pictures, we went through an English airplane called *A Short Sterling.* It's a big, monstrous plane. Also took several pictures of it with Joe and myself by the tail.

After taking a shower, we are ready to go to bed. Oh, yes – maybe a little supper would help out a little.

— Sgt. Leo Lakey, gunner

✠ Mission #25 — Woke up at 1:00 a.m. and briefed for a mission to Kurling-Bastund, France. Target: airfield and installations. Bomb load: ten 500-pounders. Bombing altitude: 24,000 feet. Take-off was 5:10 a.m. and landed 10:45. Had P-47 escort from the coast of France into the target, and all the way back. Only saw and attacked by enemy fighters (three Me-109s) once. Anti-aircraft fire was very little. Saw one 17 go down at the coast of Lorient. Eight men parachuted in the Atlantic and, the last I saw of the 17, it was still soaring and going.

It was the finish for me, Leo Lakey, Dick Haseltine, Eddie White, Lt. Neie and Lt. Mitchell. Sure had a lot of fun as we came in, shooting flares and hedge-hopping all over the field. Even dropped a dummy with a chute on his back from our plane. It was a red-letter day for all of us.

In all of my combat missions, I used up 8,660 rounds of .50 caliber ammunition.

Turned in all my flying equipment to Tech Supply. Don't know what will happen to us.

Bill Kelly came in to visit us today. He lost the small finger (first joint) and severely impaired middle and right fingers of right hand. He will get an MD in another two weeks and return to the old U.S.

> **Resume of Mission #25:**
> First Air Task Force: Nantes, France
> Six groups: 117 planes; 132 tons bombs
>
> Second Air Task Force: Vannes
> Three groups: 67 planes; 165 tons bombs
>
> Third Air Task Force: Kerlin-Bastard [Kurling-Bastund], France
> Three groups: 63 planes; 159 tons bombs.

— *Sgt. Joseph Kotlarz, gunner*

✠ Mission #25 – Came back from 48-hour pass at 2:30 a.m. and found crew ready to go on mission to France. Took off at 5:10. Had escort all the way. Sweated out the flak, but made it okay. Before landing, we thoroughly buzzed the field and could see the ground crew jumping up and down and cheering. As we made our landing approach, we shot flare after flare – red, green, yellow – all colors, like a Fourth of July celebration! Certainly a red-letter day for us all! Went to Norwich and got Rube's gift (the scarf).

— *Sgt. Dick Haseltine, radio operator*

✠ Finally a chance to go on our 25th big one! This time, Kurling Bastund Airfield, France, and what six hours of real hell! With myself, there were only three old crews on the mission. The other 17 were new, and the formation was almost as lousy as dangerous. It takes lots of time to fly good wing formation.

I was leading the second element of the squadron, and had a chance to lead the whole group over the target, but Capt. Ford decided not to abort after losing one engine. We got back safe after losing only one crew and ship, which happened to be Lt. Wilcox. It was his second mission since he ditched and spent 48 hours in a dinghy in the North Sea. He went with me as co-pilot on the one just before this one, and he was as nervous and flak-happy as a nerve-wracked kitten. He was not ready to go on a mission, but he just got in the wrong place at the right time for a German fighter. He was a very good man and we are praying that he is a prisoner of war and on his way home. We saw eight chutes open, which means the pilot and co-pilot went down with the ship.

Before we took off, we stuffed a flying suit as a dummy, tied a parachute to him, and when we returned, we threw "Oscar," as we called him, out. The parachute failed to open as we planned for the spectators. But we did fool the MPs. They posted a guard around it for two hours until I told them what it was. They thought it was a German explosive booby-trap.

We buzzed the tower three times, running all spectators off and scaring them like hell, and as we came in for our last landing in the ETO [European Theater Operations], every man on the crew shot flares as fast as they could (each flare cost 40 cents). When we finally landed our ship, it was crowded with men and officers to congratulate us on successfully completing 25 dangerous combat missions over enemy territory. We shook each other's hands and started sweating our orders to see if we go home or remain in the ETO.

— Lt. Ruben Neie, pilot

SEPTEMBER 23, 1943

✠ We finished our 25th mission sometime about the middle of September. We had a real good squadron commander. His name was [Maj.] Stanley Hand, but I wouldn't have dared to call him anything but "Major"! Stanley did everything he could to nurse his flight crews through 25. He was a good fellow. He really did love his crews. The squadron commander had about 12 air crews and would fly about nine. Most of the raids would be flown by nine crews from the squadron, and Hand had a policy. For the first 20 missions, it was kind of catch-as-catch-can. There was no consideration about it being a tough raid or an easy raid. You just went your turn, the first 20. You just took the missions. Hand was the one who would select which one of his air crews, or how many of his air crews, would go out on a given mission. And until you got 20, why, he just put you in when it come your turn.

And then he made a practice of – after you got your 20 missions done, and this was something that was, I am sure, not practiced in every squadron – Stanley wouldn't put you out on the long, tough ones. Some of the missions weren't too tough. Some of the missions were a lot harder than others – you would have a lot more opposition. If you had a real long mission, going deep into Germany, Stanley would hold you back. And then, when one came along, going into Occupied France, why, you would take that one. The Germans had sub pens on the French coast. Going into Occupied France wasn't as bad as flying over Germany. He would hand-pick the raid that he selected you to go on. He was trying to nurse as many of his crews through to 25 as he could, and I thought that was really a humane act on his part. So, you could imagine how his air crews really loved him for that.

Not too many years ago, they had a reunion in Tulsa, and I went up there because I knew Rube was going to be there. I introduced myself to Hand and told him who I was, and whose crew I was on, and his comment – this is 40, 50 years after – his comment was, "Well, Mitchell, do you realize I only lost one of my original crews?" And that was right. He lost a lot of crews – replacement crews – but only one of his original crews didn't get through, which is really some record when you consider that, overall, only 34% of the bomber crews made it through their 25 missions – only 34%.

There were a lot of tough raids. We were, our squadron, was very fortunate. I don't know how it happened.

I was reading something interesting in the book, *Citizen Soldiers*. See, when we were over there in '43, we had P-47 escorts, and they were very short-range. They could only go 250 miles, then they had to go home because of their limited fuel. The Germans would hold off until they left, and then they'd hit you. Then, sometime after that, they started outfitting P-51 Mustangs with wing tanks, and they could go a lot further than the 47s. An interesting statistic in *Citizen Soldiers* said that, initially, only 34% of the bombers – when the P-47s were escorting – made it through, but after they got P-51 protection, 61% got through. I thought that was a fantastic statistic, you know.

But then, later on during the war, I read that the 96th took a heavy, heavy beating. I was reading somewhere that there were 45 heavy bombardment groups, and out of the 45, we took the second heaviest loss – our group did. We were fortunate.

— *Lt. Lloyd Mitchell, navigator*

The following diary entries and memoirs by the crew of Kipling's Error III are dated after they completed their 25th mission together on September 23, 1943.

SEPTEMBER 24, 1943

✠ We turned in all our equipment and cleared the post today, but we did not get our orders. But we were told that Lt. Mitchell and myself are going home! Anyhow, we took a drink on it. I will pack tonight. Lt. Asper lacks four more missions. So, today, he was given a new crew and I gave him my old ship, *Kipling's Error III*.

— *Lt. Ruben Neie, pilot*

SEPTEMBER 25, 1943

✠ Just checking around on all equipment, etc., today.

As a parting gift, the crew pitched in and got our pilot, Rube, a silk scarf with the insignia *Kipling's Error* on it, and the signature of each crew member on it. It sure was a perfect gift for a perfect pilot and a thoughtful, deserving fellow.

— *Sgt. Joseph Kotlarz, gunner*

✠ Not a thing to do all day but wait on orders and, finally, late this afternoon, they came through. We could hardly wait to see what they said. Happy? Hell, yes! Just as we prayed for.

— *Lt. Ruben Neie, pilot*

SEPTEMBER 26, 1943

✠ Presented scarf to Rube. He certainly was pleased. Made a little informal speech about thanking him for being plain Rube and not "Lt. Neie" to us. About how some said we were lucky, but we knew it was because we had a pilot who was always on the ball, every second of every flight. He couldn't get over the embroidered work. We were satisfied that we gave the perfect gift to the perfect pilot.

Sent cable to Mom and Jinny.
— *Sgt. Dick Haseltine, radio operator*

✠ As I said, we finished up in September 1943, and then it wasn't too long – I don't know, a week or two, maybe less – until the pilot and I caught a C-54 (that was a big transport plane), and it had some empty space, going back to New York. So Rube and I went back to New York then.
— *Lt. Lloyd Mitchell, navigator*

✠ Eight o'clock and a truck met us to take us to the train, which would take us 15 hours to reach the 12th RCD. So, we talked with Lt. R.P. Mayhand, in station, to fly us down instead of riding the train. He was more than glad to do it for us. But what do you suppose happened? The British almost shot us out of the air with flak, because we were over a restricted area. But they missed, and we made the 15-hour train trip in two hours in a B-17G.

The first person we bumped into was our bombardier, Lt. Mendolson, who finished up a week ahead of us. He is now waiting on a ride home, the same as we are. It is getting cold as hell here now, and I am damn glad that we are getting out of here!
— *Lt. Ruben Neie, pilot*

✠ My missions are all over with, so I had to turn in my flying equipment in order to get my clearance papers signed. Joe, Dick and White left by train this morning. It was tough to say "So long" after what we all went through, but this is the Army. Lt. Neie and Lt. Mitchell left by plane. It was tough saying "So long" to these two also. A very good pilot. Brought us back several times. We don't know how, but he did. Mitch is a very good navigator. He really did a good job, always. Someday, we hope to meet back in the States.
— *Sgt. Leo Lakey, gunner*

✠ Getting ready to leave on a transfer to another group.

Left Snetterton Heath (Eccles Road) for Bovington. Arrived in London 1:30 p.m. and waited for train connection at 6:45 p.m. Stayed at the Liberty American Red Cross until we left. Arrived at Hemel Hempstead Railroad Station at 8:00 p.m., and assigned to quarters and told to report to base headquarters at 8:00 a.m., Monday (tomorrow).

No stores here and the barracks are really cold. Looks as if we will be instructors here, so tomorrow should tell the story.
— *Sgt. Joseph Kotlarz, gunner*

INDIVIDUAL RECORD OF COMBAT MISSIONS
COMPLETED

NAME....... Lloyd B. Mitchell........RANK... 1/Lt.......SERIAL NO.. O-662075.

QUALIFICATION.........................CREW POSITION...... Navigator...........

Combat Mission Record

MISSION NO.	DATE	TARGET	LENGTH OF MISSION	ENEMY AIRCRAFT LOSSES	REMARKS
1	15/5	Emden Germany	6:15		
2	17/5	Lorient France	5:55		
3	21/5	Emden Germany	6:15		
4	29/5	Rennes France	5:25		
5	11/6	Wilhelmshaven Ger.	6:00		
6	22/6	Huls Germany	4:30		
7	29/6	Le Mans France	5:15		
8	4/7	La. Pallice France	11:00		
9	14/7	Le Bourget France	6:00		
10	17/7	Hamburg Germany	6:15		
11	24/7	Bergen Norway	8:10		
12	25/7	Kiel Germany	8:00		
13	26/7	Hanover Germany	7:20		
14	28/7	Oescherleben Ger.	6:00		
15	29/7	Warnemunde Germany	8:00		
16	12/8	Bonn Germany	5:30		
17	15/8	Lille France	5:00		
18	16/8	Abbeville France	3:45		1/Lt W. P. Baker, Pilot
19	17/8	Regensburg Germany	11:30		
20	24/8	Bordeaux France	12:00		
21	3/9	Meulans	5:00		
22	6/9	Strasbourg Germany	8:00		
23	7/9	Wattens France	4:15		
24	16/9	La Rochelle France	12:00		
25	23/9	Lorient France	6:00		

All flights with 1/Lt R. W. Nele, Pilot except
as noted

CERTIFIED CORRECT

Theo R. Diltz
THEO R. DILTZ,
Major, Air Corps. Operations
Officer.

CITATIONS

DATE	NAME OF AWARD	DATE	NAME OF AWARD
11/6	Air Medal		
17/7	Oak Leaf Cluster		
29/7	Oak Leaf Cluster		
24/8	Oak Leaf Cluster		
23/9	Oak Leaf Cluster		
23/9	D. F. C.		

HEADQUARTERS
NINETY-SIXTH BOMBARDMENT GROUP (H), ARMY AIR FORCES
Office of the Group Commander

A.P.O. 634,
New York, N.Y.,
24 September 1943.

SUBJECT: Letter of Recommendation.

TO   : Whom It May Concern.

1. This is to certify that 1st Lt. Lloyd B. Mitchell, O-662075, has completed an operational tour of combat duty with this command and has completed twenty-five (25) high altitude bombardment missions over enemy and enemy-occupied territory.

2. During this tour of duty, for his courage, coolness and skill and his devotion to duty he has been awarded the Air Medal with Three Oak Leaf Clusters.

3. The manner of his performance of his duties has been rated as excellent in his assigned task as Navigator.

4. He has conducted himself, in the face of the greatest danger to his life, in a manner reflecting the highest credit upon himself and the Armed Forces of the United States.

JAMES L. TRAVIS,
Lt. Colonel, Air Corps,
Commanding.

**Air Medal
Recommendation**

SEPTEMBER 27, 1943

✠ All my bags are packed, ready to leave. Straightened out a few things with the First Sergeant. Left by jeep about 0930 after seeing most of the old crews.

It was about noon when I pulled into my new base. Gave up all my records to the Base Adjunct in Base Headquarters. Was assigned to Squad 548, Barracks 93. Several crews that have between ten and 15 missions living in it. A bunch of nice guys.

Will report to Group Armament tomorrow to see what's cooking.
— *Sgt. Leo Lakey, gunner*

✠ Reported to Base Headquarters and told that we would be transferred to Cheddington. Told there would be nothing doing for us. Eddie, Dick and I went to Watford. Watford is a typical, modernistic American-type town. Sure had a lot of fun with Eddie.
— *Sgt. Joseph Kotlarz, gunner*

✠ Second day here and nothing to do. Just wait on a ride to U.S., and that is a hard job. We did go out and shoot skeet this afternoon, but spent most of our time laying on our bunks and playing a little shilling-limit poker. I should write a letter or two.

Last night, I dreamt of a battle that was much tougher than any I have been on. Maybe I will quit that soon.

— Lt. Ruben Neie, pilot

SEPTEMBER 28, 1943

✠ It looks as if nothing will happen today in the line of a chance for a ride to the U.S. So, we all went to a nearby town and really had a farewell party. We got back at seven in the morning and had orders to leave by nine, so we just made it!

— Lt. Ruben Neie, pilot

Distinguished Flying Cross

✠ Left for Cheddington Air Base and arrived there 12:00 noon. Told we were slated to be instructors, but we would keep getting flying pay, etc. All in all, the setup seems okay. I just hope it works.

> **My new address:**
> S/Sgt. Joseph F. Kotlarz
> 2904 Rpl. and Ing. Sq. (B)(P)
> 2901 C.C.R.C. GP (Bomb) (Prov)
> A.P.O. 634 c/o P.M.N.V.N.Y.

— Sgt. Joseph Kotlarz, gunner

SEPTEMBER 29, 1943

✠ Reported to Base School and told I would be an instructor on the Malfunction Range. Dick Haseltine on radio, and Eddie White on turrets.

The new base is okay. Neat, clean barracks with lots of windows and grass around the site. The grub isn't bad. And the fellows are really grand. The following groups are represented here: the 96th, 305th, 36th, 92nd, 91st, 94th, 351st and 95th, and all are 25-mission men.

— Sgt. Joseph Kotlarz, gunner

SEPTEMBER 30, 1943

✠ Up till the time we went on our 25th mission, our group lost 16 B-17s from the time we started operations on May 14, 1943.

In some of these raids, fellows have died due to lack of oxygen and due to freezing. Also one known case of a fellow dying of fright. Went to Aylesburg tonight on a "Liberty Run."

— Sgt. Joseph Kotlarz, gunner

DFC for twenty-five missions

GENERAL ORDERS)   R E S T R I C T E D   Hq VIII BOMBER COMMAND,
                    :   APO 634,
No.   158)   E X T R A C T   24 September 1943.

Under the provisions of Army Regulations 600-45, 8 August 1932, as amended, and pursuant to authority contained in Section I, Circular 36, Hq ETOUSA, 5 April 1943, and ltr Hq Eighth Air Force, 20 September 1943, Subject "Awards and Decorations", the DISTINGUISHED FLYING CROSS is awarded to the following-named **Officer**, for extraordinary achievement, as set forth in citation. This individual has previously earned the Air Medal and three Oak Leaf Clusters for wear therewith.

*   *   *

LLOYD B. MITCHELL, O-662075, 1st Lieutenant, 96th Bombardment Group (H), Army Air Forces, United States Army. For extraordinary achievement while serving as navigator of a B-17 airplane on twenty-five bombardment missions over enemy occupied Continental Europe. Displaying great courage and skill, Lieutenant Mitchell has materially aided in the success of each of the twenty-five missions. The courage, coolness and skill displayed by Lieutenant Mitchell on all these occasions reflects the highest credit upon himself and the Armed Forces of the United States. Home address: Hollis, Oklahoma.

*   *   *

By command of Brigadier General F. L. ANDERSON:

                                              JOHN A. SAMFORD,
OFFICIAL: Colonel, GSC,
                                              Chief of Staff.
EDWARD E. TORO
Colonel, AGD,
Adjutant General.   R E S T R I C T E D

DFC
Recommendation

SEPTEMBER 29-OCTOBER 5, 1943

✠ On our way to point of departure (Prestwick, Scotland). Got there safe and slept one good night, and on the 30th, we were on our way to the U.S.A. on a C-54 by way of Iceland, which is a very cold and damp country, and Newfoundland. We only landed long enough at these places for gas and eats, and on October 1st, we were on U.S. soil at Presque Isle, Maine. That was a good feeling! The first thing we did was fill up on ice cream. Then, of course, we had to get orders to go home. By 5:00 that afternoon, we had orders for 20 days' delay en route and six days' travel time for home. The weather was closing in and planes were not going any further.

In Boston, I bought a ticket to Chicago and ran short of money. So, I wired my bank for $200.00 and, lo and behold! It was waiting for me in Chicago when I arrived! The trip was long (15 hours), but not bad, because I was on my way home. Got to St. Louis, changed trains in a hurry, and forgot my $37.00 raincoat. But I couldn't worry about that now; home was next.

Arrived in Fort Worth October 4th at 1300 hours. Only 100 miles from home, but since I was tired and no train till midnight, I got a room and took a good night's sleep. Also bought a new cap, socks, handkerchief and shirts, equaling $32.45, while in Fort Worth.

Mission's End

Then, finally, on October 5th, boarded a train at 9:00 in Fort Worth, and arrived in Meridian at 11:00. There was Mother, Dad and Oliver waiting for me. The best sight I have seen in a long time. Went home, ate dinner, and made Oliver's house. And went to see Granddad and Grandmother tonight. My folks are all happy and proud of me. But they can't be any luckier and happier than this "Happy Warrior."

— *Lt. Ruben Neie, pilot*

Kotlarz at the Ready

The remaining dated diary entries (not included here) are by Sgt. Joseph Kotlarz and Sgt. Leo Lakey, recorded after most of the crew of Kipling's Error had gone their separate ways, some of them returning to the States. They conclude in December of 1943.

LT. LLOYD MITCHELL, NAVIGATOR, DISCUSSES FEAR:

Were we ever scared? Oh, yeah! Always. Always scared. There was a book about the old boy that flew the *Enola Gay*. He was the pilot. He first flew 25 missions in England, and then he started training to drop the atomic bomb, and he said he was never scared. I think he was lying. I never talked to a guy yet who wasn't scared witless, you know. You wanted to quit – really, you know. If there was an honorable way to quit, you'd quit.

I think I said this before – it went the same with the infantry people as it did with the Air Force. The big reason that you didn't quit was a camaraderie and a love for your crew. You didn't want to – you wouldn't dare let your crew down, and that was why, when they formed the crews – when they initially formed the crews – they kept them together through the training period in the States, and then we flew as a crew, flew the combat missions. There was only one combat mission that I wasn't with my crew, and the reason I wasn't with them that time is I had ear problems – I was in the hospital with my ears.

But there was such a cohesion, and you had such an admiration and love for your crew. Oddly enough, in Stephen Ambrose's book – that was the thing, he mentioned the same thing about the infantry squadron. It was their loyalty to their crew that kept them fighting.

LT. LLOYD MITCHELL, NAVIGATOR, RECALLS HIS CREW MEMBERS:

Freddie Breeson was with the ground crew. They had two planes [to maintain] and those guys – I mean, they really loved their crews. They would work all night to get your plane in shape, and there really developed a camaraderie between the ground crew and the flight crew. I've seen – coming home from raids – when a plane didn't come home, and I'd seen them just beat their heads against the concrete because their crew didn't come home. You developed that kind of camaraderie.

There was something ironical about Freddie. None of us really got hurt. Rube had that superficial wound. But Freddie was out on the flight line one time, and there was a dumb gunner testing his machine gun, and offed one, and if he didn't hit Freddie and

**Ground Crew
l-r Doffi,
Kisor, Howard
"Freddy" Breson,
Byciewiez, Shell**

knock a leg off. Freddie lost a leg on the ground from a machine-gunner – one of his own machine-gunners.

Ed White was the assistant engineer. He was a really peaceful fellow. Rube really depended on him, more than he did [engineer Lowell] Nelson. Wasn't anything wrong with Nelson, but Rube depended on White more to help him. They would help him wash the engines and everything. They were trained for that. White was also the top turret-gunner and the top turret – that was the best gunning on the plane. Most of our planes then just had a ring sight, and he had – I don't know the name of the sight – but he had an automatic. He had some help in sighting the planes, and he was credited with a lot more kills than any of the rest of us because of the good guns he had up there.

The four officers were Neie, Mendolson, me and Olie Asper. Manuel [Mendolson] – we just called him "Manny" [or "Mendy"]. I don't even know what Olie's [full] name was. He was a Norwegian from the northwest, and we just called him "Olie."

Then there was [Leo] Lakey; he was the waist-gunner. And [Steve] Malinowski, he was a waist-gunner. Ed White was top turret and assistant engineer. And there was Lowell Nelson who was an engineer. [Dick] Haseltine was the radio operator. [Joe] Kotlarz was a waist-gunner. Now, Steve Malinowski was the ball turret – second guy. Ball turret had to be kind of a small fellow. Malinowski was skinny and thin – small. In the '80s, we had a reunion in Las Vegas. I bet he weighed 300 pounds – he was huge! You wouldn't believe it! So, that's the non-commissioned officers.

I can't vouch to the veracity of this, but I heard it. After doing 25 missions, I heard that the three Polish guys went back for another tour,* which would have been Malinowski, Kotlarz and Lakey. Now, whether that's true… Those fellows were all from the North, and they were of Polish blood, probably second-, third-, fourth-generation. But they had a personal vendetta against the Germans for the way the Germans were treating

the Poles. For me, I didn't have that. But that's what I call a personal vendetta, and they were good warriors. I mean, they were good men – those Polish guys were.
— **Lt. Lloyd Mitchell, navigator**

＊ *According to the remaining diary entries, Sgt. Leo Lakey was reassigned to Air Sea Base Rescue Patrol stationed in England while awaiting orders to return stateside.*

Sgt. Joseph Kotlarz spent Christmas on the high seas heading back to the U.S. on H.M.S. Aquitania.

HOMEWARD BOUND

The following are excerpts from tape-recorded interviews with Lloyd Brooks Mitchell by his granddaughter, Amanda Mitchell, and his son, James Brooks Mitchell. They describe the early years of Lloyd's life, including his family's ancestry. (Some of the content has been slightly expanded or compressed strictly for purposes of clarity.)

HOMECOMING – MEETING BROOKS

As I said, we finished up in September of 1943, and then it wasn't long – I don't know, a week or two, maybe less – until the pilot and I caught a C-54 (that was a big transport plane), and it had some empty space, going back to New York. So Rube and I went back to New York then.

I remember, we got to one of the air bases there in New York, and there was a B-24. It was going to Omaha. They were just the stateside crew that was flying the B-24 around to get hours, and they had one vacancy on the plane and one parachute. So me and another old boy – I don't remember his name – but we tossed a coin to see which one of us got to ride that B-24 over Omaha, Nebraska, and, sure enough, I got it! So I rode the thing to Omaha and I called Mable from there and told her where I was at – to look for me, that it wouldn't be long because I'd be home. So the B-24 pilot – he was a nice guy – he didn't intend to go to Tulsa; he was going somewhere else, and I told him I was just coming back from England and trying to get home, and he said, "Oh, shoot! We are just flying around getting flying hours." He said, "I'll fly you down to Tulsa."

So we stayed in Omaha, and I remember I couldn't get over the lights. In England, why, at night, everything was blacked out. I mean, it was totally blacked out in England. And the lights in Omaha were so bright, and that night when I talked to Mable, I was telling her how bright the lights were.

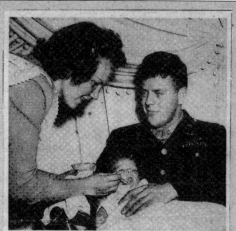

—Tribune Staff Photo.

FATHER MEETS SON—Lt. Lloyd Mitchell left the British Isles, where he has been stationed for five months with the air force, Friday and Sunday he was in Tulsa, in time to help his young son, whom he had not seen, observe his second (month) birthday. Today, he was still taking instructions from his pretty, blonde wife as to how to hold the young man.

Navigator Arrives Home for Son's Second (Month) Birthday

Ever since the day they were married, First Lt. Lloyd Mitchell and his wife have talked about the child they would have some day, about who he—of course, it would be a boy—would look like and what they would name him.

"You get the medal for your first five raids, and then a cluster for each five thereafter until you've piled up 25. That's when the DFC comes."

Lieutenant Mitchell's Fortress bears the unusual name, "Kipling's Error." "Well," he explains shyly, "the pilot was German, the co-pilot was Norwegian, we had three gunners who were Polish, and I, well, I'm just plain American. Anyway, we remembered Kipling's poem about 'East is east and west is west and never the twain shall meet,' and we decided that was one time he was wrong."

Until you point out the numeral "III" that follows the plane's name, indicating that two others of the same name have gone before it, he doesn't admit to any danger on the raids.

"Oh," he says, with a quick glance at his wife, "the pilot got the only Purple Heart on the whole crew. He did have' rather a narrow escape one time, when a 20 mm. shell missed his head by six inches and exploded when it hit the armor plate behind him.

"We did have two ships pretty badly shot up, but none of us were hurt. They just won't let you fly in a ship where anything at all might go wrong."

A native Tennessean, Lieutenant Mitchell has lived in Oklahoma since 1927 and attended the University of Oklahoma before he entered the air force. Now that he's back in the states, he'll be an instructor for a time, probably in Oklahoma or Texas, and when the war is over, he's going to A. and M. college, Stillwater, to complete his last year of college.

"I was studying to be a chemist," he says, "and I think I'll go on with it. Looks like that'll be a coming thing after the war and I'll want to be in something where I can make money. After all," and he looked significantly toward the 'droom, "I'm a father now."

So, when the baby was born two months ago today, what happened?

"I had been sent to North Africa," grins the boyish-looking lieutenant, "and for 20 days I didn't know a thing except he was a boy and weighed eight pounds!"

Lieutenant Mitchell, a navigator on a B-17 Flying Fortress, arrived home Sunday after five months overseas and 25 missions over continental Europe.

Long before he left American ll April 18, Lieutenant Mitchell ew he was to become a father n ' he and his pretty, blond wife d decided upon the name: "James oks if he were a boy and—oh, it just couldn't have been a

"Talk about fathers walking hospital corridors," grins the lieutenant. "I paced the soil of England and North Africa for five months."

Lieutenant Mitchell was based in England during his five months overseas and took part in the shuttle raid to North Africa and back.

"We bombed Hamburg going over and Boulogne coming back," he says matter-of-factly. And in the same calm tone of voice, he tells you how he "happened" to have the air medal with three oak leaf clusters and the Distinguished Flying Cross.

Navigator Arrives Home

So, the next day, sure enough, we flew to Tulsa. And I remember locating from the air – I knew where we lived, where Mable lived. There were some real good friends of ours named Brown – Kate and Ernest Brown – and they had a little one-bedroom apartment behind their house. So they had rented it to Mable and me, and Mable and Brooks. Brooks was two months old – this was October of '43 – they lived there.

Well, I had the pilot circle that a couple of times at a kind of low altitude to let her know it was me and to come out to the airport to pick me up. So, we landed at the airport there in Tulsa, and Mable was there, and you could imagine what a glad reunion that was. She had left the baby with Kate Brown, and I remember when we drove home, why, she said, "Oh, Lloyd – come look what we got!" And he was the cutest little old thing you ever saw.

Pueblo, the Pacific, Baby Bottles and Whiskey

Getting home, why, I had a week or two leave, and then the Air Force shipped me to Tucson, Arizona, to Davis Munthon Air Base, and I was navigation instructor there. And – lo and behold – I wasn't there two or three months, and I got orders to go to Pueblo, Colorado, to join a bomb group that was going to the Pacific and, man, was I ever shook up! You know, I thought, "I am home for good!" And here they are, just after two or three months, shipping me off again! I was so mad, and I applied for leave and I didn't even wait to get my leave approved. Mable and Brooks were with me. So, we just went home to Tulsa for a couple of weeks. I thought, "Well, they will probably count me AWOL and punish me."

But after two weeks, I went on back to Pueblo, Colorado. Well, wouldn't you know – that group had found another navigator, and they had taken off and gone on, and there I was, left at Pueblo, Colorado – and that was the best time I had in the Air Force! I was the head navigation ground instructor. Pueblo was what they called a three-phase training base, and new crews that had just formed would come in and would get experience in navigation and bombing, and that type of thing. And so, I was one of the staff there on the base. And I got to stay there a whole year and, boy, that was good duty.

I remember one incident, after I had come back from England, and Mable and I were traveling to Tulsa. I was headed for Pueblo to the base, but we were going to Tulsa to spend a little while. So we had to change trains, I remember, so we got off the train and got our suitcases and started out. Pretty soon, here come an old boy just screaming, "Stop! Stop!" So we turned around and asked him what he wanted. It turned out that we both had two suitcases that looked just alike. Well, Mable had packed baby bottles and diapers and things like that in our suitcase for Brooks. This other old boy had a lot of whiskey that he had packed in his. So we accidentally switched suitcases. He got the baby bottles and the diapers, and we got the whiskey! When he found out, he was kind of alarmed about it. We, too. We much rather would have had the baby bottles than had the whiskey. It was kind of funny.

Well, after a year was up, or before, about the time when a year was up, they needed lead navigators for B-29 groups, and they started putting the heat on me: "Mitchell, we are going to put you on a B-29 to be the lead navigator." Well, that didn't suit me at all! I thought, "My goodness! Here I've suffered through one combat tour, and why should I go through another one, when hundreds of air crews in the United States haven't been into one yet?" So I started casting around to see what I could kill time doing. Well, they were also training navigator bombardiers as pilots – B-29 pilots is what we were being trained for. So I put in my application to go back through pilot training school and, luckily, I was accepted.

Well, I went back to Kelly Field a little while for processing and paperwork and all of that, and then they shipped us to Chickasha, Oklahoma, for primary flight training. It seemed like it took about two-and-a-half, three months for primary. Mable and I rented a nice little home there in Chickasha. That was a good experience, going through that. And then I went to basic flight training at Sherman Dennison, Texas. There was an air base just west of Sherman, and Mable went back to Tulsa for this. She was pregnant with Martha. Martha was due in a couple of months, so she went back. We kept our little apartment at the Brown's there, and I was flying AT-6s for basic.

Mable would follow me from base to base. Whenever it appeared – you could never know for sure – but whenever it appeared that I might be at a certain base, say, for six weeks or two months, why, Mable would get the baby – Brooks was little then – he was born in August of 1943 – and she would get on a train and she would come up. Sometimes, if we were going to be there for a short while, she would get a room in a motel. But if it appeared like I was going to be there for any length of time, why, we'd try to find a place to rent.

One of the things I remember so well is that members of the church were so good and treated us so nice that the guys were all jealous of me. We'd move, and Mable and I would be one of the first couples to find a place to live. A lot of times, we'd go to a church and we'd get acquainted and asked if they knew of a place to live, and they'd either own or rent property, or knew somebody who owned or rented property. So we were kind of fortunate in that regard. But that was kind of tough on her – having to drag the baby around.

I remember one incident. I had been up for a visit with Mable over the weekend and hadn't slept much. I guess – I don't know – I guess I hadn't slept but a couple of hours in the last twenty-four, so I was just dead on my feet. Well, I went over to an auxiliary base there for the AT-6s, and I was shooting landings, and I remember I was coming in for a landing and the tower started screaming at me, "Go around! Go around!" And I gunned it and didn't touch ground. Took off again. And the guy started screaming at me, "You were coming in with your wheels up! You didn't have your wheels down!" What do you mean? So I went around and sought another landing or two, and then come back in the second time. "Go around!" And I didn't have my wheels down again! Well, the next day, you can imagine, the C.O. – I had a notice: "The C.O. wants to see you." So I went into the old colonel's office. I tried to explain to him that my wife was very close to having a baby, and I was just dog-tired. I hadn't had any sleep for so long. I should have told him I shouldn't have been flying – I shouldn't let him put me in a plane. So he understood and he didn't wash me out, and he didn't penalize me.

MARTHA, ENID AND EYEGLASSES

I remember it was while I was there, flying AT-6s, that Martha came. She was born in Tulsa. I can remember, somehow or other, that we thought we were having twins. We thought Mable was having twins, and I remember, as I rode the bus from Sherman to Tulsa, I thought, "Well, you are going to have little twins this time." And it wasn't. It was Martha. Mable, you can imagine – she was tickled to death! Her first child had been a boy, and she wanted a girl in the worst way! She vowed and declared, "Now, if this is boy, then we'll have another child, and it will be a girl." Well, it turned out to be a girl, and Mable was overjoyed.

Then, when I completed my basic training at Sherman, I was sent to Enid to fly B-25 bombers. That was what you call the advanced flying school. We got an upstairs apartment in Enid. It was a rat-trap, and I remember our landlady – she was an old witch. She would come into our place and prowl around and look around. I remember we'd dust flour out in the hallway so we could see her tracks if she came in! This was the summertime. It was July and August of '45, and it was so hot, and the upstairs apartment was just terribly, terribly hot. But, just the fact that we could all be together, why, we would put up with anything.

They would give you eye tests occasionally then. After getting in, they would give you tests from eye charts, and I sort of sweet-talked and bribed the sergeants. Generally, it was the sergeant letting you read the chart, and that worked until Enid when I had a tough, hard-boiled doctor. He gave me a test on an eye chart, and I flunked it. I remember him saying to me, "Son, there are two things gonna happen. You are going to quit flying until you get glasses." So, I thought, "Well, no. I don't want to quit flying because I am killing time here. Instead of having to go back overseas, I am killing some good time. So I'll choose getting the glasses."

He fitted me up with glasses. But I didn't realize what was happening – it threw my depth perception off. I remember going out for a check-ride with a check-instructor, and he had me shooting landings. And I had my blamed glasses on, and I was bringing that old B-25 in to land. It's got a tricycle landing gear, and you've got to land on your two main wheels, and then when your two main wheels hit, you pull the stick back into your belly, and then as the plane loses speed, the nose wheel drops. Well, this time, I couldn't tell where the ground was, and I landed that thing on all three wheels at the same time – a terrible jolt, a jar. And the check-instructor started screaming at me, wondering how in the world I had got this far. He was a lieutenant, and I was a captain. So I just looked over at him and grinned and said, "Ah, I think I know what happened." I pulled my glasses off and put them in my pocket, and took it around again and just breezed in – did that three or four times. So I satisfied him that I knew how to land one of those B-25s.

END OF THE WAR AND DOWN ON THE GROUND

So I almost didn't quite complete my advanced flying training. I had a number of first-pilot hours in the twenty-five [combat missions] – quite a lot of hours for first-pilot in the twenty-five. It seemed to me like we lacked about two weeks of completing our flying training, and then, of course, we heard they dropped the atomic bomb. This was in September of '45. Well, we couldn't believe it. We thought that this was just another bit of propaganda. Of course, we kept reading it through the papers and hearing it on the radio that it wouldn't be long until the war was over and Japan was going to surrender, but we absolutely couldn't believe it. But that's the way it happened. After they dropped the second atomic bomb, Japan surrendered, and the war was over.

I did not put another step into another airplane after that flight. It seemed to me like some guys got the bug, and flying was living to them. They didn't think they were living unless they were flying. Not me. I had too many close encounters with death, and I wanted to be a husband to my wife and a father to my children. I was so pleased – I've never been as happy about anything as when the war was over, and I didn't have to crawl back into those old tin birds again.

Immediately after the war was over, I high-tailed it down to Stillwater, which is just a short distance from Enid, and Mable and I found a little two-bedroom home right on the railroad tracks. We didn't mind that. We rented until I could complete my schooling. I remember it was a little frame two-bedroom. It had a nice garden out back, and we gardened. The railroad was right by the garden there. I went to school in September of '45 – I didn't get completely out of the Air Force. I was decommissioned at Fort Smith, Arkansas – a big base down there – in October. So, I really didn't get started back to Stillwater until October of '45. But, of course, they were being very generous with the veterans, and they [the school] were very glad to accept me, even though I was two or three weeks late.

Mable and I stayed in Stillwater then until '48. I got my bachelor's degree in January of '47. Then I decided I would stay on at Stillwater and get a master's degree in agronomy, or soils. Agronomy is a combination of field crops and soils, and I was majoring in soils.

But then, come the late fall of '47 – early part of '48 – we had a chance to go over to Guthrie and teach veterans. They had a program going that the veterans could enroll in, and they paid them and they could take so many hours – they had to come to school so many times a week. Then the instructor would go out on the farm with them and help them and teach them how to do things on the farm. So that was three hundred dollars a month. Boy – that was big money!

Going to school in Stillwater, I got ninety dollars a month. And so, you didn't have much money left over by the time you paid your room and by the time you paid your tuition. I worked at everything possible while I was up there. I worked in a soils lab, and I'd go out and hunt up jobs washing windows, cleaning houses, doing things like that. I remember the day I was supposed to graduate in January of '47, I made an appointment with a woman to come over and clean all of her windows. And Mable had to remind me that was graduation day, so I called her up and went out and cleaned her windows another day.

But it wasn't easy getting through – it was hard work. I remember one summer, one semester I took twenty-two hours. I had to get special permission to do that. But I got special permission and took twenty-two hours one semester so I could graduate.

Anyhow, we went to Guthrie and stayed a few months. Then I got a job at the Bureau of Indian Affairs as a soil conservationist, and that was a neat job. Despite having two children and working at different hours, I did rather well in school. I was selected Alpha Zeta, which is an honorary agricultural fraternity. Also, I was Phi Kappa Phi, which is the upper ten percent of the graduates. So, I worked hard, as most of the veterans did. They were older then, and a lot of us had families, so we weren't fooling around. We got busy – we wanted to get out of there and get a job.

In 1948, we moved to Shawnee, and I was a soils conservationist. The reason we went over there was because they had a nice home to offer us, and it was furnished. The houses that we had lived in through the war and immediately after the war… we were overjoyed to have a nice home to live in. So we went over there and worked through '48 and through '49 – not quite through '49.

In the fall of '49, we got an offer to go to Washington on a training program. It was a real good offer. The Department of the Interior was starting this training program to take young men and train them to be administrators in the various bureaus of the department.

I remember just before, in '49, Mable was expecting Sarah. We'd go to the doctor and I was real hesitant about her going with me, but Sarah had just arrived. Her birthday is August 1 of '49, and I think she was about a month old – just about a month old when we went to Washington. We had a little old Ford coupe, and it was a small thing and an undependable car, and we had a lot of trouble with it. I remember we couldn't afford nice motels. We'd stay wherever we could, and we let Sarah stay in the drawer. We'd open the drawer of the dresser, and she'd sleep in the drawer.

There were only three of us selected over the entire United States. There were two Indian boys and myself. One of the Indian boys was Ernest Bowman – he was a Navajo, and Jose Zuni – he was Isletta, a Pueblo Indian. The three of us then went to Washington in the fall of 1949, and we stayed there for about six months, and it was good training. We got to kick around and work in different offices, and work in different bureaus of the Interior Department. Then we went for field training – six months for field training. Mable and I went to Oregon – Portland, Oregon, and we spent about six months field training there. Then I was assigned permanent duty in Aberdeen [South Dakota].

Aberdeen

I completed the rather intensive training in Washington, D.C. My boss, Evan Flory – he was the head of the Soil Conservation Department in the Bureau – he gave me a double promotion. Now, that was something that was unheard of. I am sure it happened before, but I didn't know of it happening. I was a Grade 9, and he jumped me to a Grade 11 and, man, that was some jump in salary. So, I jumped at the chance, and he sent me to the Aberdeen area office as the area soil scientist. Now I had my training in soils. I had two degrees in soils – a master's – but I never did any soils mapping, and I was kind of nervous about being thrown out [into the field] like that, but it worked out. I found a guy that was a rather experienced soils mapper, and he showed me some of the tricks of mapping soils, and I appreciated that.

So Mable and I spent five years in Aberdeen. We got up there on the Fourth of July, 1950. I remember Sarah was quite small – just a few months old at that time – and we rented a house, some little old house that we could find and rented it. One thing I remember – this was in August – we got up there in July, then in August, we had a nice garden. Somebody that had rented the house in front of us [before us] had some real nice tomatoes, and they were big, old luscious green tomatoes, and I was real happy. I felt, "Boy, here we just fell into something. We are going to get a tomato crop." And, wouldn't you know – on the twentieth night of August come a killing frost! Those blame tomatoes all got killed!

Well, from that little house, we rented another house on the other part of town. It was a bigger house, and it was a frame house – a nice house. But it had an old coal-fired furnace and hard to build a fire in, and you'd freeze to death until you got the thing going.

And then when you got the furnace going, it would burn you out of the house, it was so hot. That was a real stinker – that old coal-fired furnace. And I was having to travel quite a little bit. The Aberdeen area office had jurisdiction over North Dakota, South Dakota and Nebraska. And poor Mable – she was left with the children, one of them a baby, and two small children. She had an awful time – when I had to leave – with that blame coal-fired furnace.

ROSEBUD SIOUX RESERVATION AND ONE DEEP SNOW

It must have been about '51, I guess it was, that they sent me down to the Rosebud Sioux Reservation to live down there for about a year. They had some special work they wanted me to do. So Mable and I moved down to the Rosebud. We first lived in an Indian boarding school. It was three or four miles away from White River, South Dakota, and there was a teacher and his wife who lived there. Mable and I and the three children lived there, and that was kind of an experience, too, because it was isolated. I remember the only electricity we had was our own generators in the basement, and we had to get those blame generators started to have lights and to have power. Half the time, they wouldn't work, and that was a real traumatic thing. Kids loved it. Brooks and Martha loved it. The White River ran right behind the boarding school, and they had a big time playing in the river in the summertime.

Then we moved from there. We were still on the Rosebud. We moved up the White River into a nurse's home. The home must have been built for a nurse's home for the Bureau, and it was vacant. That was a lot better. We had a good time there at White River.

I remember one incident – Mable tells about it, and it was kind of traumatic for her. It was in October – late October – and it came a terrible snowstorm, just a terrible snowstorm. I was in Aberdeen, which was a couple of hundred miles from there, and I started home and I couldn't get home. I was riding the bus and I couldn't get home because of the snow, and we had to stay overnight. Mable was left with the children in a deep, deep snowstorm. Luckily, the house was heated with propane gas, and she had gas. She tells about the kids trying to get home from school, and Brooks made it home, and Martha didn't make it home, and she was scared to death. It's just a short distance from the town, but she didn't know what to do, how to find Martha. Well, it happened that one of the storekeepers saw Martha struggling to get home, and he stopped her and kept her, and then got in touch with Mable and told her that he had Martha, and not to worry. But that was pretty scary times there.

WARNER AND ANOTHER DEEP SNOW

We stayed on Rosebud for about a year, and then we moved back up to Aberdeen, and instead of moving into Aberdeen, we moved into Warner, which was a little town about nine miles south of Aberdeen. We moved into a rather nice home. It was a two-level home with a basement, and that was the home we finally bought. We lived in there a little while, and we managed to buy it on a sale contract from the owner. That was a good experience there, living in Warner.

We moved up there in late '51. In early '52, Mable was expecting David, and that was a terrible winter. The drifts were ten, fifteen foot high in places. That was a terrible winter.

Warner was primarily Lutheran people, and they were a little bit stand-offish when we first moved in. We were foreigners. But with Mable's personality, it didn't take long for them to move up to us, and we had really nice neighbors. They were very, very helpful, and they were very generous, and we really appreciated that little town of Warner.

So we didn't know it, but the neighbors were planning on how they were going to get Mable to the hospital. There were several of them that were going to get together by tractors or whatever to take her to the hospital. The hospital was in Aberdeen, and it was about nine miles away. But, sure enough, we did manage. When the time came, we got Mable to the hospital and didn't have to resort to getting all of the neighbors to helping us. David was born then. It was kind of funny. Mable went in, and they were trying to find the doctor, and they couldn't locate the doctor. Well, the baby came, and a nurse was there to assist Mable in having David, so it turned out okay. But then she saw – a month or two later – she saw the nurse on the street, and the nurse remembered her very well. She said, "You know, I wasn't going to tell you, but your baby was the first one I ever helped deliver." That kind of startled Mable then.

I had to travel quite a lot for my work. Working with the Aberdeen area office, they had jurisdiction over the reservations in Nebraska, South Dakota and North Dakota. We covered quite a large area, and so, particularly in the spring, summer and fall, I imagine I'd be gone probably seventy-five percent of the time, and it was really tough on Mable. She liked the area and all that, but she did not like me being away from home so much, and her with all the children.

In the wintertime, I was home most of the time, but the wintertime was bad. It was bad news for me, because my job was mapping soils, and in soils mapping, you have to dig into the soil with an auger, and the ground was frozen, and so that just knocked you in the head. Oftentimes, I did not have nearly enough to do in the office, and I got awfully restless. The weather was delightful, except in the winters – and they were very cold. Oftentimes, the snow would start in October and it wouldn't be over until, I imagine, probably March. We had snow in March. And then the rest of the year was just delightful. The growing season was kind of short. We'd raise turnips and potatoes and carrots and beans. I remember one time I planted okra and tried to raise okra. That was no-go. Okra is a hot-weather crop, and it didn't do any good at all.

APPRAISING ANADARKO

All in all, it was a good experience for us. I tried to get out of there before I was able to because of the winters. In '55, I had a chance to go to Anadarko. They were starting a real estate appraisal program in Anadarko, which was new to the Bureau. I had a good friend who transferred down there as the Anadarko area officer, and so he brought me to Anadarko to work in appraisals. I was the first appraiser in. And then the program started ballooning, and I probably had eight or ten appraisers under me there for the last few years. We covered the whole western half of the state of Oklahoma and also had one reservation in Kansas, and we did all of the appraisal work.

Appraising for the Bureau of Indian Affairs was a good job. It was a lot of variety. At that point in time, a lot of the Indians were selling their allotments. We had to do appraisals for the allotments, and rights of way, gift deeds, partition months – and so it provided me a good deal of variety of appraisal work. There was a little bit of commercial – not too much. Mostly, it was farm, ranch, raw land, some residential. But all in all, it was a very good job. For a while there, I had a really good boss, Glenn Waller, and I really appreciated him.

We weren't there long until we bought an old house – 610 West Boulevard, I believe it was. It was an old house. It had been kept well, but it was small – probably eleven hundred square feet, and it just had one bathroom. We made a three-bedroom out of it – it wasn't intended to be that way, but we made a three-bedroom out of it.

It was hot in the summer and cold in the winter. It didn't have any wall insulation. What it was, it was the lathe tacked onto the two-by-fours, and then chicken wire. And when the wind blew, why, it came right through all the electrical outlets. So it was kind of a cold house. We had a floor furnace, and that wasn't too satisfactory. It provided heat for a very local area, and the kids got their feet burnt on it once in a while – it would get pretty hot. And then, in the summertime, we had what we called a water cooler for air-conditioning. It was just a box, and it had a pad there, and the water would drip into the pad, and the wind would blow through the pad into the house. I remember when we first moved there, we turned that water cooler on and closed all of the windows and doors. Well, that was the wrong thing to do, because with a water cooler, you need to leave everything open, and we likely smothered. But after a while, we learned how to do it.

The kids remember that house probably the best as their home. David was three years old when we moved there, and Sarah was six, and Martha was ten, and Brooks was 12 – I believe that's right – when we moved there. So Brooks got to go through part of junior high and all of high school. And Martha – let's see… She was ten years old, so she would have been in about the third or fourth grade, and she went through all of elementary school there, and then went through high school there. And David – he started the school there, and he was in the tenth grade when we moved to Albuquerque in 1967.

The kids all seemed to like it. Anadarko was a pretty good town to raise a family in. It had a large population of Indian kids, Indian people, and quite a large black population. So there were a lot of Indian children, black children and white children going to school there. But it was kind of a segregated town. It was a shame the way the black people were treated. There was a street that ran through town, and it was widely understood that the black people did not move to the other side of the street. They were restricted by a street on the west, and vacant land on the north, and a vacant lot on the east. When we first moved there, they had an elementary school of all black children, but, gratefully, they changed that, and the black children started going to school with the white children then.

KIWANIS COACHING

I remember one incident. I belong to the Kiwanis Club, and I was president of the chapter that year, and there was a big question as to whether to open the swimming pool or not to black children. They just had one swimming pool in the park, and the Kiwanis owned the swimming pool. So I remember very well that it was a real close vote. We were voting on whether or not to allow black children to use the swimming pool. The vote was tied. And as president, I was able to vote, and voted yes. And so we did open the swimming pool in the park to the black children.

I coached Little League for several years while I was there. I wanted David to be able to play PeeWee Baseball, and to get him to do it, I had to agree to coach. Well, I didn't know anything about coaching. I had played baseball in high school, but I started coaching, and it was a lot of fun. The little black boys liked to be on my team. I don't know how it happened, but it happened that way. Every year, I'd wind up with about half of the team of little black boys and half of them little white boys, and they just had a ball together! They didn't make any race distinction, of course, at that age.

Oftentimes, I would do pretty good with my baseball team with those little black boys playing. I remember one little black boy particularly. His name was Booty. I don't remember what his last name was, but Booty was a tough little rascal. He was about nine or ten, and Booty was kind of the manager of the black boys on the team. And when Booty felt good and was playing good, I had a ball club. But when Booty was moody – and he oftentimes was kind of moody – and when he was kind of messing around, why, that just seemed to permeate all of the other kids. And my club wasn't so good when Booty was moody. Booty could fly. He was a runner, and so I was always thrilled to see Booty get on base, because I knew I could get that run in with Booty on base.

Had another little black player I remember particularly. His name was Davelle, and Davelle was half-brother to Booty. He was a little kid, and his helmet came down clean over his ears, and he batted left-handed.

THE MITCHELL FAMILY
MARK

We'll start with the youngest: Mark. Mark was born in 1957, and he is five years younger than David. We were almost forty years old when Mark came, and we wondered how it would work out with the other four children, and us at that age, but it worked out real good. We called Mark our "little fall child," and we had more time to spend with Mark, the last one. We had a little more financial means. We weren't as strapped for money always as when we were with the other children. And so, Mark was an easy kid to raise. He was even-tempered. He was popular with other children – he made friends easily. He cared more about sports than he did about schoolwork, so we had to stay on his back a little bit on school work. But he generally made it okay.

I remember he was developing a liking for sports early. We had this old house there at 610 West Boulevard, and it was built in 1905, as I remember. So, one time, Mable and I decided we were going to re-paper the thing, and it was a chore. We had to take off four or five layers of paper to get down to the plaster, and then we had to re-plaster. But we got the job done – papered it – and we were so proud of it.

Well, then the living room – on one wall, there was a hole about four inches in diameter that had been the flue where the old coal stove set one time, and the flue pipe went up through that hole and out and, of course, we papered that over. Well, Mark was sitting – he must have been about three or four – and he was sitting in the middle of the floor with either a tennis ball or a baseball, and he drew back and threw that thing, and threw it right through that flue hole and made a big old mess in our wallpaper! It tickled me because he was such a little guy and he could throw like that! Mable wasn't as tickled as I was.

I remember he got a little bigger, and every spring, why, he and I would start playing catch. And one time, I was letting him bat and I was throwing to him, and he hit one straight back at me and hit my hand, and knocked my little finger clean out of joint! That thing was just right angles, and he just jumped up and down and went into the house, yelling to his mama, "Mama! Mama! I broke Daddy's finger! I broke Daddy's finger!"

When Mark got to be about eight, he started playing PeeWee Baseball, and I was coaching. I wanted to make a pitcher out of him and succeeded. He was a good little pitcher. Then when he got to be about eight or nine, in springtime, he and I would get out and play catch, and he could throw pretty hard for a kid that age. I remember my legs were just black and blue, from my ankles to my knees, where he had bounced one in on me and I'd miss it. I just kept bruised legs the whole spring long.

I remember one team we had about three good pitchers – Mark, the Pinter kid and the Delworth kid – I remember were my pitchers. I went to District that year and didn't win, but we played a good game. That was a whole lot of fun.

DAVID

David – he was a high-energy kid, always looking around: "What can I get into? What can I do next?" I remember one incident – one July 4th, I believe it was – he went out and was popping firecrackers where he wasn't supposed to be, and a policeman collared him and brought him home. I remember the scared look on his face when the policeman knocked on the door there with David in tow.

One time – I didn't know this until much later – one time, he told me he was out with one of his buddies shooting a .22 rifle, and he shot an insulator out somewhere, and knocked the light out in the town. Of course, I didn't know about it at the time. That's what happened.

David, too – he loved sports. He loved baseball; he loved basketball. He was on my team. I remember one funny incident – we'd gone to District, and he was playing. He was about eight or nine, playing second base, and he either tripped or got knocked down, and here come a runner from first, going to second, and David was laying on his back, reached up, and tagged him out. I thought that was kind of funny.

I remember one incident – one of David's little buddies – his name was Wilkerson. I can't remember his first name. They were about eight or nine. We were out practicing one day, and I looked over, and there was little Wilkerson – he was playing first base – taking a pee right there on first base! And I went over: "What do you mean, out here taking a pee?" "Well," he said, "Mr. Mitchell, I was afraid if I left first base, you wouldn't let me play it again."

David was a good student. I never had to get on him about his grades. He always liked school. There was one year when David was in the eighth grade, I remember. Mable, by this time, had gone over to OCW in Chickasha and had got her degree, and she was teaching eighth-grade science. And that was the year David was in the eighth grade, and Mable and I talked about how it would work out with him being in her class, and if that would be a bother to her. But it didn't. He was just the model child that year in the eighth. He didn't give his mother a bit of trouble.

MABLE WAS A GOOD TEACHER

Mable taught eighth-grade science there for – I don't know – three or four years, and she really liked it. It was kind of – to me – it was a little funny. She was supposed to teach science, and she taught science, but she taught everything else. She taught home economics to the kids because she was a home economics major, as well as an elementary teacher. And I remember, she taught fry bread. She learned how to make Indian fry bread and taught fry bread to the kids. She had all kinds of things in her classroom. Her room was a marvel – snakes and frogs and everything else.

One funny incident happened one time. There was colored water – the kids somehow or another had colored water in the beaker – and they were heating the beaker and forgot to turn the flame off like they were supposed to, and the blame thing blew up and splattered that colored water over several people, and it looked like blood. And other teachers come running into the room when they heard the noise, and there was those kids and Mable all covered with that colored water. They thought they had all been killed!

But she had a real good time teaching eighth grade there, and she was a good teacher. She had to go to OCW – it seemed to me, at least a couple of years to finish up – and that was when Mark was about four or five when she did that. Oftentimes, she would take Mark over to Chickasha with her, and they had a place where they took children. It was kind of a training experience for the girls that were going to school there, and they all wanted to pick Mark, Mable said. He was a cute little old blond-headed, curly-headed kid, and when the girls were picking out their children to work with, why, Mark was one of their very favorites that they all wanted.

That was a real joy when Mable graduated. She graduated, as I remember, about the same year as Brooks did from OSU. Then we had a good friend, Jim Smalling, who was superintendent of schools there. So Jim hired her as a teacher. It was kind of hard to get hired there as a teacher in Anadarko. There were more people wanting a job than there were jobs.

SARAH

Sarah – I called her "my little hard-luck kid." It seemed like anything bad that happened to one of the kids, it happened to Sarah. Up in South Dakota, she was playing with a girl, and the girl seemed to accidentally hit her in the face with a baseball bat. Then she had a real bad astigmatism, and we didn't know it until she was about five-, six-years-old, and we got her glasses in Aberdeen. I remember Mable asking the eye doctor, "Well, am I going to have trouble keeping glasses on her?" He said, "Mrs. Mitchell, this kid will enjoy these glasses so much, and they'll improve her eyesight so much, that there will not be any difficulty there." And there wasn't. Sarah was so proud. She went out one night and said, "Mama! Mama! I can see the stars!" And she thought her distant vision was a marvel. We would drive to church down in Huron, which was eighty-one miles away, on Sunday morning, and there was a train that ran between Huron and Aberdeen, and she said, "Mama, see that choo-choo?" But none of us could see the train except Sarah, and she could really see it! Up close, of course, her eyesight wasn't good at all. She couldn't see. The glasses really did improve it.

I remember she broke her wrist one time when she was a teenage kid. Seemed to me like she was about the only child that had a broken bone while they were growing up.

That scared us because it was broken at the point of growth, and the doctor told us that it might not go ahead and grow properly, but it did. He did a good job of setting it.

Sarah was a real good student at school. We didn't have to get onto her about her homework. She loved band. She played flute and piccolo in the band, and she was a drum majorette, and I think she was the band queen one year. She was a good student and she loved school. She graduated at Anadarko before we moved to Albuquerque. When we moved to Albuquerque, I remember we bought a nice home – three-bedroom – and we called one of the bedrooms "Sarah's bedroom," but she never used it. She went to Oklahoma Christian right after graduation, and then she and Jim were married shortly after that.

MARTHA

Martha was also a very good student – just always made top grades. She was a pretty girl, very popular with the other kids, and she was nominated for – and, most of the time, won – every office Anadarko High had. She was football queen and basketball queen and band queen, and all of the other type of queens you can talk about. Sometimes it got a little tense in the household. Martha would get a little tense, a little bit uptight, and it kind of permeated the rest of the household. Martha went through school in three years. Her junior year, she took some courses over at OCW in order to get enough credits to graduate. She just turned seventeen when she went to OC.

One summer, she went down to visit my mother in Arkansas and while she was there, she met a boy. I don't know whether his family was a friend of Grandmother's or… I am not sure how she met him. But, anyhow, she was about sixteen, and the boy asked her for a date to go to a show one night, and Martha said, "Yes." When he came to pick her up, why, Grandma was all dressed up, and she walked out to the car, and Martha thought she was walking out to tell her goodbye, but Grandma just proceeded to get right into the back seat of the car and go with them. She was going to be a chaperone, and that tickled Martha to death!

Another story I remember about Martha – when she was about a sophomore or junior, she was running for basketball queen, and the way they elected basketball queen was the players elected the girl that they wanted to be their queen. So it turned out that Martha and another girl were in a tie, and they were having another vote to see if they could break the tie and select which one was going to be queen. Martha walked into school one day, and there was one of her friends. His name was Donny Kirkendall, and Donny was a black boy who went to church with us. Well, he really did like Martha, and he had one or two of those white boys pinned up against the wall and holding his collar, threatening what he was going to do to him if he changed his vote. "Now, you keep your vote with Martha Mitchell!" He was really threatening this guy with what he was going to do if he changed his vote. So Martha got to be basketball queen that year.

BROOKS

Brooks was kind of a happy-go-lucky kid. He loved hunting and fishing and scouting and things like that, better than he liked sports. He was at kind of a disadvantage. He was in seventh grade when we moved to Anadarko, and the coaches already had their boys picked out that they wanted for the teams, and they devoted all of their time to the guys they picked out, and the other kids just got pushed to one side. So, Brooks didn't really play any sports at Anadarko. His main thing was scouting. He loved scouting. He made good friends in scouting, and some of his friends that he has today – even thirty-five, forty years later – are friends he made there in scouting. Of course, I liked that because most of the kids in scouting were good kids. They weren't the kids that got into trouble all of the time. They were good kids.

Brooks didn't care about his grades. He made average grades, and I remember telling him, "You are not an average kid, Brooks. You've got more than average, and you ought to do better." And he'd say, "Oh, Dad! You know C's are okay." So he wouldn't strive to excel. Of course, in his later life, he woke up and he did much, much better in his later schooling.
— *Lloyd Brooks Mitchell*

NOTE FROM JAMES BROOKS MITCHELL:

Clarence Breedlove was the dean of men at Cameron who helped Lloyd Mitchell with employment so he could attend school after his time in the Civilian Conservation Corps, and the person who got Lloyd interested in chemistry. He was also a colonel and a chemist for the 8th Air Force. He invented a machine that was important for the 8th Air Force. He invented some type of smoke signal machine to make it more obvious to planes behind the lead plane when it dropped its bomb load. The bombardiers couldn't see when the bombs were being dropped by the lead plane, but they could see the smoke when they dropped, so they knew when to drop their own bombs.

Col. Breedlove lived a long and productive life. Believe it or not, he was my chemistry professor at Oklahoma State University in 1961. I was aware that he knew my father, but I had no idea of the close connection between him, the CCC camps, Cameron College, and the 96th bomber group.

PERSONAL LETTERS

Lloyd B. Mitchell
REAL ESTATE APPRAISALS • S.R.A. • A.R.A.

July 15,1993

Dear Brooks:

Perhaps I shouldn't write this letter at this time as I am in
a melancholy mood. I've just completed reading, again, my
1943 diary, chronicling my thoughts and emotions during the
most stressful period of my life. I've hesitated letting
anyone except Mable, read this. I don't know exactly why
except that it reveals more of my inner self than I was willing
to share. You can never know how much your mother and I looked
forward to your coming. At the time of the writing of this
diary, I had despaired of ever getting to see you. My happiness
in October of 1943 at seeing you and Mable is indescribable.
I'll leave it to your discretion as to how many people you
want to share this diary with. It is yours now.
Mable and I have always loved you. We are so very proud
of your accomplishments. Have a happy 50th.

Love,

Dad
Dad

May 1, 1999

Dear Son:

      Enclosed is a complete diary of the combat tour that
I did in World War II. The writer is Leo Lakey. He was a
waist gunner on our plane. He and I did 24, out of a total 25,
missions together. His widow recently mailed it to me. When
you do your thing be sure to give him full credit and please
mention Florence Lakey Huebing, his widow. Leo became a
professional golfer, in Tucson, after the war.

This is a copy so you don't have to send it back.

While in was in Tucson, this year, I typed out a brief account
of John's participation in the war. He is no longer able to
do so. I will set down shortly and force myself to give you
some of my experiences. For some reason it seems hard to do so.

I have recently completed reading " A complete history of the
Second World War" by Martin Gilbert, a british historian. It
is very encompassing, as the name indicates. I would highly
recommend it to anyone who is interested in WW II.

I am also reading the first part of a two part series on
"Adolph Hitler", by Ian Kershaw. It too is a fasinating book.

Nancy and I are planning an automobile trip, the first week in
June. We will plan on stopping by to see you'all on the trip.

Today, Saturday, Nancy and I are going to see a baseball game
between O.S.U. and O.U.   Wish you were here.

                    Love,

                    Dad.

Jan. 14, 2005

Dear Brooks:

I have read your draft , (twice, in fact) I have made a few corrections, all minor.

Words fail me to say how much I appreciate what you have done. You have been too flattering

In some of the comments that you have made, about me, (but I like it)

I like the manner in which you have written it. There is nothing Hollywood about. It. The

Diaries tell the story. They were written at the time that it all happened so 'time' did not have

The opportunity to warp anything.

You are a good son and I am proud of you and what you have done with your life.

dad